# Continent Aflame
## Responses to an Australian Catastrophe

There has never been a more critical time for reflection, collectiveness and positive action at both a local and global scale to protect what is most dear to us all ... We must respect and walk with fire, not think we can just fight with it. Fire and Country have lore and we must learn our place in it.
— Oliver Costello  CEO FIRESTICKS ALLIANCE INDIGENOUS CORPORATION

This collection is written by and for grieving hearts and awakening minds in a time of innocence lost ... With eyes so opened, stronger minds, and more courageous hearts, we can now set a path to healing the rift between ourselves and the rest of Nature.
— Penny D Sackett  FORMER CHIEF SCIENTIST OF AUSTRALIA

I hope that those with eyes to see, ears to hear, welcome the authors of these contributions, and give heed to their analysis. We all depend on that.
— Thomas Keneally  AUTHOR (FROM HIS FOREWORD)

CONTINENT AFLAME
Responses to an Australian Catastrophe.
A Palaver Book. Copyright © 2020
The editors, authors and artists.
All rights reserved. No part of this book may be reproduced, stored in a retrieval system, or transmitted by any means, electronic, mechanical, photocopying, recording, or otherwise, without written permission from the publisher, author, or artist, except in the case of brief quotations embodied in critical articles or reviews.
ISBN 978-0-6488551-0-1

First Palaver edition published November 2020
Typefaces: Tiempos (Kris Sowersby/Klim)
Neue Haas Unica (Toshi Omigari/Monotype)
Design/typesetting: Ian Robertson
Printing: IngramSpark

For additional information, bulk or educational purchases, and other resources, please contact Ethica Projects, Pty. Ltd c/o Paul Komesaroff
paul.komesaroff@monash.edu

www.palaver.com
Palaver is an imprint of Ethica Projects, Pty Ltd.
10 Barnato Grove Armadale Victoria 3143 Australia

# Continent Aflame

## Responses to an Australian Catastrophe

EDITORS
Pat Anderson  Sally Gardner  Paul James  Paul Komesaroff

PALAVER 2020

# Contents

| | | |
|---|---|---|
| Thomas Keneally | 7 | **Foreword** |
| Pat Anderson | 11 | **Introduction** |
| Sally Gardner | | |
| Paul James | | |
| Paul Komesaroff | | |

## Orientations
'Alarm. Shower. Breakfast.' ... Hugo Muecke

| | | |
|---|---|---|
| Tom Griffiths | 18 | **It is the Season of Reckoning** |
| Bruce Pascoe | 22 | **Now is the Time** |
| Pat Anderson | 25 | **Our Beautiful Country is Burning** |
| David Bowman | 28 | **Recognising the Ancient Skill of Cultural Burning** |
| Greg Lehman | | |
| Alexis Wright | 32 | **Learning from the Stories in our Ancient Library** |
| Will Steffen | 36 | **The Science Behind Australia's Catastrophic Bushfires** |

## Communities
'It was a quiet and still evening' ... Hugo Muecke

| | | |
|---|---|---|
| Vanessa Cavanagh | 44 | **Grandmother Trees, Aboriginal Women and Fire** |
| Helen Szoke | 49 | **We Face a Tipping Point** |
| Maithri Goonetilleke | 53 | **An Unequal Flame** |
| Catherine Larkins | 56 | **Fire Place** |
| Arnold Zable | 60 | **Where is the Light? Black Saturday Speaks to Black Summer** |
| Lionel Bopage | 64 | **Bushfires in the Land of My Birth and in the Country I have Chosen** |

## Mortalities
'It started with rain' ... Hugo Muecke

| | | |
|---|---|---|
| Kieran Donaghue | 70 | **Water, Fire, and Ashes** |
| Lorraine Shannon | 73 | **Signs, but No Wonder** |
| Miranda Nation | 77 | **Her Date of Birth, 20 November 2019** |

## Elements
'An uncontained oil-fire on water' ... Susan Norrie

| | | |
|---|---|---|
| Susan Norrie | 84 | **Undertow** |
| Paul James | 85 | **Some Say the World Will End in Fire** |
| Sally Gardner | 91 | **Is Fire a Feminist Issue?** |
| Kate Judith | 95 | **Errinundra Shimmer** |

## Realities

'Glassy eyes' ... Hugo Muecke

| | | |
|---|---|---|
| Raimond Gaita | 100 | **Creatures of the Earth** |
| Philipa Rothfield | 104 | **The Taste of Reality** |
| Freya Mathews | 107 | **Koala Makes Us Australian** |
| Stephen Muecke | 111 | **It's the Greenies' Fault** |
| Phillip Darby | 113 | **Perspectives on Fire and Food from the Stanley Plateau** |
| Anne Elvey | 118 | **The Sense is Porous to the Thing** |

## Traumas

'The burnt leaves on the trees' ... Hugo Muecke

| | | |
|---|---|---|
| Bhiamie Williamson<br>Jessica Weir<br>Vanessa Cavanagh | 122 | **Aboriginal People Find Strength Despite Perpetual Grief** |
| Jane Fisher | 126 | **Moving Beyond Powerlessness During the Fires and COVID-19** |
| Paul Valent | 130 | **A Fire Symphony of Traumatic Stress** |
| Rimona Kedem | 134 | **Fire** |
| James Collett | 135 | **Responding Psychologically and Culturally to the Catastrophe** |
| Stephen Duckett<br>Will Mackey<br>Anika Stobart | 139 | **These Fires Have Consequences for Our Health** |
| Guy Rundle | 144 | **Who by Fire?** |

## Retro(pro)spectives

'No birds and black trees' ... Hugo Muecke

| | | |
|---|---|---|
| George Browning | 150 | **How Good are the Fires!** |
| Bill Gammage | 152 | **An Ally Forsaken** |
| Helen Caldicott | 154 | **Reflections on Opportunities Lost** |
| Paul Carter | 157 | **Oracle of Fire** |

## Changes

Undated Untitled ... Hugo Muecke

| | | |
|---|---|---|
| Ross Gittins | 164 | **We Can't Stop Climate Change by Refusing to Change** |
| Mark Beeson | 166 | **Talking About a Climate Revolution?** |
| Ross Garnaut | 170 | **Crossing the Bridge to a Safer Climate** |
| Philip Freier | 174 | **Cosmic Calling with Christ** |
| John Funder | 176 | **Can a Phoenix Rise Out of the Ashes?** |
| Paul Komesaroff<br>Ian Kerridge | 180 | **Ethical Lessons from the Australian Bushfire Disaster** |
| | 184 | **Contributors** |

# Foreword

## Thomas Keneally

In the Australian autumn of 2019 and all through winter a group of retired fire chiefs wanted to meet with Scott Morrison, the Prime Minister, to warn him that Australia had passed, as if through a gate, to a new level of combustibility, and that therefore the fire peril for the coming Southern summer would be unprecedented in terms of length and ferocity. For fear that the group might link this menace with the forbidden term, climate change, the leader Australians now called 'Scotty from marketing' refused to meet them, though in good faith they kept on trying to arrange a session with him all through the winter and into the spring. As they themselves pointed out, he gave considerable time to meet with church leaders who wanted to be exempt from anti-discrimination laws involving the employment of gays and similar 'freedom of religion' matters. The fire chiefs were worried that we share our combustibility with the Pacific Coast of the United States, and that with the overlapping of North American and Australian fire seasons, the hiring of air tankers was going to get more and more difficult. Above all, they were concerned that fires would take on a new scale and would not surrender to normal firefighting. They also felt they had been seeing abnormal fire symptoms since the 1990s.

Once we Australians got over our colonial Eurocentrism and realised that the Australian bush was not going to go to any trouble to imitate European flora, we began to take a perverse pride in the fact that so many of our plants are germinated by fire, and thus are Phoenix plants. We know now that our species has been in Australia so long, for tens of millennia, that indigenous humans learned firestick farming — regenerating the continent with skilfully lit fires, which also had the benefit of flushing out protein-rich marsupials into the open. The reality is that swathes of Australia must burn for its own good. Les Murray, the late great poet, said Australia had only two seasons, drought, of which fires were symptomatic, and flood. Drought was caused in eastern Australia by a current called the El Niño, a Pacific current which derives from the coast of Peru and reduces the effect of the trade winds on Australia.

Drought in Western Australia can similarly be caused by variations in temperatures between two oceanic poles, one near the Persian Gulf, one near Australia — the Indian Ocean dipole. Hence both sides of Australia have had calamitous drought and fires in their time, and especially in this last year. But the drying out to which Australia has been subjected is unprecedented in the record and seems to most people to proclaim climate change. The denialists made a stand by accusing the Greens of preventing back-burning in national parks, and of course the Murdoch press embraced that proposition, and emphasised cases of arson. The fact that there were cases of arson, and always have been in Australia and California, explains a minority of blazes, but does not explain the unprecedented voracity and appetite of the flames in 2019–20. Yet firefighting volunteer and former denying prime minister Tony Abbott said, 'We are in the grip of a climate cult'. And on the right-wing of the coalition party which governs Australia, and which Scott Morrison needs if he is to govern, sturdy climate denial is un-dented by what has happened, and denialists are fatally comfortable with their explanations for what has occurred. Yet climate change had in that fatal summer for the first time in history, and until the onset of COVID–19, replaced the economy as the chief political issue. For the very question of the habitability of Australia now stared us in the face. An outer suburb of Sydney, Penrith, below the Blue Mountains that were burning at the time, achieved on January 4 the highest temperature on earth that day, 48.9 C. Sydney suburbs, as hot as they can be in summer, have never achieved such Saharan heights before.

What have I noticed, living as I do between the Harbour and the Pacific Ocean on the North Head of Sydney? Day after day, beginning as early as August–September 2019, fire smoke rendered going abroad in Sydney an unknown risk about which experts want us to be careful but cannot predict accurately. By the height of the fires, air quality was for days on end eleven times the hazardous level. Particles in the smoke have been four times or more above the safe limit. The water in the smoke condenses on particles and creates a kind of cloud we have seen a lot of, the pyro-cumulonimbus, which blankets the earth but does not bring rain, although it is capable of creating dry lightning. For most of my life, heat waves used always, after a time, to bring a southerly change in the late afternoon or evening. There were always strong winds and a drenching thunderstorm. In the last few years we have had to get used to the southerly buster that brings no rain, the dry southerly that whips up fire.

I am lucky enough to live next to a National Park on top of the headland, and when I first moved here there was what was called a hanging swamp on top of the vast sandstone block of North Head. This was a swamp that in most seasons had water in it, though it would occasionally dry out for short periods. It was the home of a number of species of frogs. It was visited by ducks and other water birds and by a handsome lizard called the water dragon, which enjoyed eating the tiger moths that lived there. That swamp had been dry for two years when the fires came to New South Wales. The significance is that drying-out has happened all along the coast and we have had the extraordinary spectacle of fires burning down to the fringe of beaches, and populations taken off the coast by warship.

The coast is a place of childhood vacations and dreams, with atmospheric paperbark swamps running behind beaches that run for miles. The lagoons and swamps were once too moist to be capable of burning. Fires burning down to the coast is, to use the catchphrase, the new normal. The coast and its valleys and beaches have been places where great numbers of nature lovers and retirees and escapees from the city have chosen to settle. The coast is a dream every city-dweller has entertained. That migration has always been on the cards for all of us. Now an exceptional vulnerability has overtaken regions where people have previously lived securely in the bush. The Keneally's chosen town on immigration, Kempsey New South Wales, has for the first time since settlement been ringed by fire. Its long, exquisite river, the Macleay, has become tainted with so much ash that fish have died. Altogether, coastal swamps and lagoons have dried up and become flammable, and rainforest has become combustible as never in the record.

During the days of smoke on a walk in the bush I encountered one of the species threatened — by the fires and the state of the world — with extinction. It is one of the two survivors from the ancient supercontinent Gondwana Land, the echidna, a spiny anteater that both lays an egg and suckles its young in the comfort of its burrow. I love this creature: she gives off an air, despite her limited movement, of industry, and she was turning over the earth to the depth of her beak in her search for provender. It was touching, of course, to see this most enduring of animals at its ancient earthwork and, to this point, unchallenged by fire here, unlike in other forests. It reminds me too of how much human occupation, a tower of millennia, there has been in Australia, and of the contrast between Indigenous stewardship and the stewardship of us immigrant groups. It has taken us less than two and a half centuries to bring the 50-million years surviving echidna, and the system sustaining it, to crisis.

Amidst the flames, the volunteer bush firefighter was an unassertive creature like the echidna. In a time of bitter politics and economic palaver, they asserted themselves as a miracle of social cohesion and human good will. The volunteers often came from the area in which they were fighting the fire, and helped save houses in many cases where they did not know whether their own house was surviving. They were also of necessity the first comforters of those who survived the loss of their houses. They themselves have lost wages and tested the patience of their employers by needing to take tranches of time off work.

One of the retired fire chiefs who tried to speak to Sco Mo last year was Greg Mullins, a volunteer who recently said, 'Like countless other men and women, I have faced off against 30 metre walls of flame, seen so many homes burn to the ground, tried to console the inconsolable residents, been forced to run for safety and seen native animals bounding out of the burning bush to collapse'. He is angered as politicians describe climate change as, 'perhaps one of the factors'.

The fires have not been a mere straw in the wind. They have been brutally manifest and undeniable in the force of their argument. They have the power to change politics here and in other places, as long as they are read honestly. After our long glorying in minerals, it is promised that if it wishes, Australia can be a leader in the new post-fossil fuel world. It is a destiny our politicians seem unwilling to embrace. But they may have to, in the face of events such as the summer of unprecedented fires.

I hope this book goes some distance to convince them, as experts and scholars come together in its pages to explain the phenomenon to us. I hope that those with eyes to see, ears to hear, welcome the authors of these contributions, and give heed to their analysis. We all depend on that.

———

Manly NSW

# Introduction

Pat Anderson, Sally Gardner, Paul James, Paul Komesaroff

The ferocity and extent of the fires that ravaged the Australian continent in late 2019 and early 2020 have been recognised as involving a qualitative ecological shift. The nature of observed and documented phenomena within these fires and sheer size of areas incinerated have required a recalibration of global pyrological scales. They represent the culmination of a larger process that had been developing slowly over a long period of time. While the fires themselves were experienced by many as unexpected and overwhelming, elements of the larger ecological crisis were already very apparent to many people, including experts and ordinary citizens. Protracted and intense global debate had largely established the basic facts. Global changes in temperature, rainfall, sea levels and wind patterns are gradually making themselves felt, leading to intensifying weather events, droughts, floods and fires.

Well before the Australian summer of 2019–2020, a growing sense of alarm had been taking hold among diverse communities across the world. Extended discussions had taken place about the possibility of disasters to come, the responsibility of the present inhabitants of the earth to future generations, and the prospects for sustainable approaches to power-generation, agriculture, resource-use and waste-disposal. The fires demonstrated that the crisis could come upon us suddenly and with such force that the basic premises of our economy and culture would be completely thrown into question. This was compounded by the second strike of the COVID–19 pandemic, linked to closely related processes of global environmental destruction and climate change, which would in a matter of months transform not just Australia but the entire world order. The word 'catastrophe' used in the title of this anthology is chosen precisely in order to signify an 'event subverting (the) system of things'.[1]

While geographically the two events appeared separately, the lines between them are entangled. Both events have occurred as effects of long-standing processes of environmental destruction and climate change, disruption of the delicate balance involving land, water, sky and species, and erosion of the resilience of micro- and macro-ecological environments. While the fires and COVID–19 are consequences of different variables in this panoply of destruction and disruption — with COVID–19 now linked to increased deforestation, industrial-level farming of animals, temperature fluctuations, and changing relationships between human and non-human animals — both are signs that humans are destroying the basic conditions of ecological flourishing. Both draw attention to the violence inherent in our current predicament, generated as it has been by rampant and unrestrained economic change, the degradation of the political processes, the neoliberalisation of civil society, and the intractable exclusion of alternative cultural pathways.

Hopefully, future generations will look back on 2020 as also involving another turning point. Yes, this is the time when the dangers precipitated by the disruption of the precarious ecological balance so wantonly taken for granted since the European Enlightenment, have been evidenced beyond doubt. However, this is also a moment when, even if we do not yet have all the answers, we can recognise that we have access to the resources for understanding the damage that has been done, the risks that have been created, and the complex dimensions of the tasks that lie ahead. The aim of *Continent Aflame* is to draw together the ideas and the people grappling with these problems and tasks.

*Continent Aflame* makes clear that the years of ferment have already produced within Australian civil society a vast and rich array of resources, spanning many disciplines and multiple cultures, ethical perspectives and intellectual dispositions. These together have the capacity to fertilise the growth of new ideas and to inspire future joint constructive action. These resources draw on Australia's rich and diverse cultural history and on the many fields of theory and cultural creation that have already been brought to bear on the problems we collectively face.

These include Indigenous experience of conservation, which for millennia effectively guarded and preserved the delicate balance of land and life across the entire continent, the work of other tenacious and ecologically committed activists, the vast body of scientific knowledge that has accumulated, the detailed cultural analysis and the philosophical and ethical modes of inquiry and expression that have sprouted and grown despite the hostile conditions. Artists in the literary, visual and performance fields have also played a vital role, often through their prescience over decades, regarding the increasingly drastic effects of the instrumentalisation and massive exploitation of nature.

An early formulation of the project of the book referred to its intention to document an unprecedented national 'trauma'. That was later revised, not because of a dismissal of the importance of the psychological elements of the cultural experience that was so devastating for so many of us, but because of a recognition of the diversity of the responses. Also, as a characterisation of the overall project, 'trauma' alone failed to capture the vigour and optimism inherent in the many hopeful responses of artists, philosophers, scientists, Indigenous thinkers and activists. We canvassed widely for contributors across these fields and were honoured by the energetic and high-level overall response. Given the diversity of responses, we have organised the book contents into eight sections in order to capture shared themes and to allow for a play of ideas, disciplinary approaches, images and affects across the collection as a whole.

The book is both an archive of responses to the fire catastrophe, and something of a landmark in bringing together in conversation Indigenous and non-Indigenous perspectives and responses. This collection is also testament to a long-awaited but now wide recognition of Indigenous land-care and other cultural practices as critical to the health of First Nations people, their traditional lands across the whole continent and all others, plant and animal, who dwell here.

The brutal violence of the bushfires is expressed loudly and clearly through the voices collected here. *Continent Aflame* is one contribution among many to what we hope will be a vigorous and expanding civil society debate, and a rich and flourishing dialogue that can enable us to understand the forces underlying the current predicament and nourish a renewed local and global action.

---

1. *The Concise Oxford Dictionary of Current English. Based on The Oxford English Dictionary and its Supplements.* Sixth Edition edited by J.B. Sykes, Clarendon Press, Oxford, 1976.

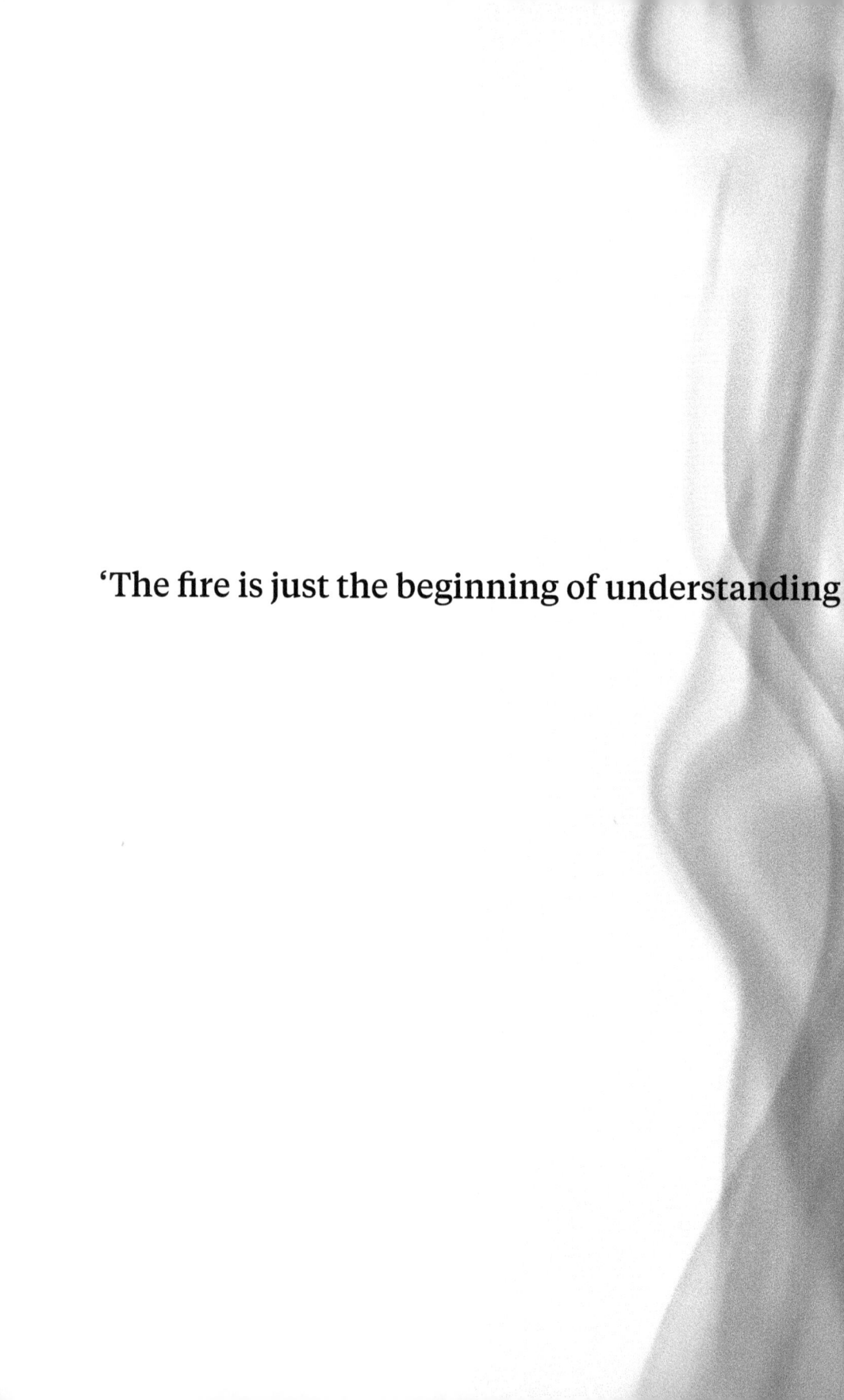

'The fire is just the beginning of understanding

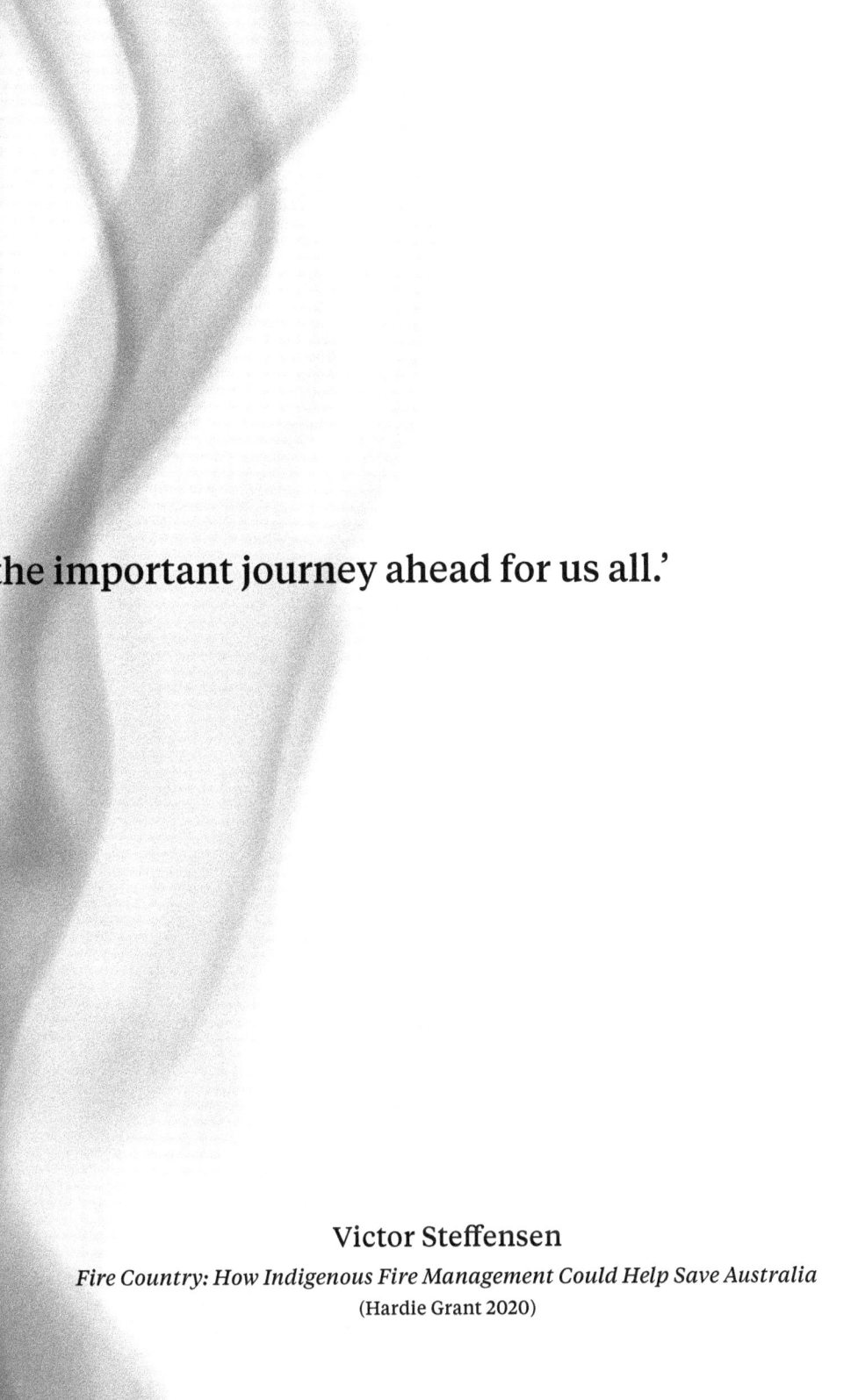

the important journey ahead for us all.'

**Victor Steffensen**
*Fire Country: How Indigenous Fire Management Could Help Save Australia*
(Hardie Grant 2020)

# Orientations

10.02.20
Alarm. Shower. Breakfast.
I picked up the cat, said goodbye and went to the airport to fly to Wagga Wagga to help with the bushfire relief.
I was met at the airport by one of my colleagues who had her akubra hat next to a tall coffee.
Had your coffee yet?
Nah, I'm more of a tea drinker.
Excited for the trip?
I don't know about being excited, I don't know, I don't really know what to expect, you know coming from the city and everything.

Text & Drawing • Hugo Muecke

# It is the Season of Reckoning

Tom Griffiths

What do we call this terrifying summer? The special bushfire edition of ABC's *Four Corners* predictably called it 'Black Summer'.[1] Perhaps the name will stick, for it builds on a vernacular tradition. Firestorms are always given names, generally after the day of the week they struck. There are enough 'Black' days in modern Australian history to fill up a week several times over — Black Sundays, Mondays, Tuesdays, Thursdays, Fridays, Saturdays — and a Red Tuesday too, plus the grim irony of an Ash Wednesday. The blackness of the day evokes mourning and grief, the funereal silence of the forests after a firestorm. Black and still. And when the fires burn for months, a single Black Day morphs into a Black Summer.

But does this name truly capture what is new about this season? The recent fires have left a black legacy, but the terrifying thing about them was that they were relentlessly red. Red and restless. The colour of danger, of ever-lurking flame. Acrid orange smoke and *pyrocumuli* of peril. The threat was always there; it was never over until the season itself turned. The enduring image is of people cowering on beaches in a red-orange glow. It was the Red Summer.

In early January, in an essay for *Inside Story*, I called it 'Savage Summer'; I was writing while the fires were still burning and there was no sign of a black day-after. Stephen J. Pyne, a great wordsmith of fire, reached for another alliteration, calling them the Forever Fires. That name signals the change Pyne perceives in fire behaviour, from occasional visitations to total engulfment, which is the predicament of the Pyrocene, a new Fire Age comparable to past Ice Ages. His term 'Forever Fires' also reminds us, as James Bradley did in the *Guardian*, that 'this is not the new normal. This is just the beginning'. The future will be worse than this, *much* worse, unless we swiftly address the cause.

Whether we call the summer black, red, or savage, we shouldn't forget that the fires started in winter. Even the season was ruptured. Where can language go once a whole summer is declared black and the fires are forever? What will we call the next eruption of fire? Will the black days that fused in a red summer become nameless, seamless years of inferno?

There is something personal about fire, something frighteningly irrational and ultimately beyond our comprehension. It roars out of the bush, out of our nightmares. Not only do we give the great fires names, we also assign them the characteristics of monsters: they have flanks, fingers, and tongues; they're hungry; they know where we are; they lick and they devour. In reports of the fires of 1919, 1926, and 1939, houses were 'swallowed' and people were 'caught between the jaws of the flame'. Fire 'with its appetite whetted … sought more victims, and fiercely attacked', and 'with each change of wind … made a thrust towards the township, threatening to lick up the scattered homes on the fringe'. Bushfire makes its victims feel hunted down and its survivors toyed with. Why did the fire destroy the house next door and leave mine unscathed? A Black Saturday survivor who lost his home confessed, 'I felt as if the fire knew me'. A book about the 2003 Canberra fires took as its title a child's question: *How did the fire know we lived here?*

Fire is the genie of the bush ready to escape, 'the red steer' jumping the fence and running amok, the rampant beast that can savage and kill. Instead of the sprites, elves and wood nymphs that populated the forest folklore of the Northern Hemisphere, Australian colonists found that their bush harboured a rather different creature. As poet Les Murray put it, the 'gum forest's smoky ambience reminds us that the presiding spirit who sleeps at its unreachable heart is not troll or goblin, but an orange-yellow monster who forbids any lasting intrusion there'. People on the New South Wales south coast referred to the Currowan fire which rampaged for seventy-four days as 'the beast'.

During this searing summer, we have seen the best and worst of Australia: the instinctive strength of bush communities and the manipulative malevolence of fossil-fuelled politicians. The clash between the two — symbolised by a prime minister forcing handshakes on survivors — added to the trauma of the fires. As we watched our political establishment double down on denial, we were forced to realise that even the shock of this season may not change our national politics.

Where does this Australian intransigence come from? It is embedded so deeply in our history that we can hardly identify it. It comes from a conquest mentality that was built on denial, the denial of Aboriginal sovereignty and cultural sophistication. It comes from a frontier mining history and an economic dependence on coal. And it comes from enduring puzzlement about the nature of Australia, a nature that British settlers slowly learned was prone to climatic extremes that were natural rather than aberrant. Dealing with the traumas of flood, drought, and fire, and learning to expect and fight them, was part of becoming Australian. Many farmers and bush folk have been slow to accept climate change because they have spent their lives coming to terms with extreme natural variability. Their rural experience makes them sceptical about a different variability, especially when it is global, one-way, and unnatural. It is as if the rules of the game have suddenly changed. Thus, the history of modern Australian settlement sedated the populace against recognising its greatest peril.

But there are signs of hope in the exponential growth of quality Australian writing about fire. Black Friday 1939 produced one outstanding literary statement: Judge Stretton's powerful and poetic Royal Commission report that was included in anthologies of nature writing and became a prescribed text for Matriculation English. Ash Wednesday 1983 found its greatest literary expression in Pyne's *Burning Bush* (1991), which was written in its long afterglow. Black Saturday 2009 produced a crop of fine writing, impressive in its range and cultural depth, notably Adrian Hyland's *Kinglake-350*, Karen Kissane's *Worst of Days*, Robert Kenny's *Gardens of Fire*, Peter Stanley's *Black Saturday at Steels Creek*, Chloe Hooper's *The Arsonist*, and Peg Fraser's *Black Saturday: Not the End of the Story*.

This savage summer has already germinated a very different forest of literary reflections. Writing sprouted immediately from active fire-grounds, and it described something that was neither an 'event' nor just 'Australian': it was a planetary phenomenon. Fire is no longer a local or national story. Australia is the canary in the coal-mine, a belated warning of planetary peril. The world is watching us. We are the burning frontier of a warming world, the perilous cliff-edge of the Sixth Extinction. This may be the first fire season that Australians have tried to calculate the mortality of wildlife.

Fire was not just more extensive, intense, and enduring; it went rogue. Australia burnt from the end of winter to the end of summer, from Queensland to Western Australia, from Kangaroo Island to Tasmania, from the Adelaide Hills to East Gippsland, in the Great Western Woodlands and up and down the eastern seaboard. The season did indeed represent something new or 'unprecedented', to use the word avoided by denialists, who used history lazily to deny that anything extraordinary was happening. But our long history of bushfire is significant precisely because it makes us the prime site for a global eruption. Bushfire is integral to Australian ecology, culture, and identity; it is scripted into the deep biological and human history of a land of drought and flooding rains. But reciting Dorothea Mackellar does not forestall heeding Ross Garnaut (see his essay in this volume). They are not in tension, for one amplifies the other. Of all developed nations, the sunburnt country is the most vulnerable to climate change because of her history of 'flood and fire and famine' and the chemistry of 'her beauty and her terror'.

In a searing piece of reportage from the New South Wales south coast for *The Monthly*, Bronwyn Adcock was witness to 'Australians doing everything they could, even when their government didn't'. If the fires revealed the strength of bush communities and the innate goodness of people *in extremis*, so too did they reveal the absence of federal leadership and the weakness of our parliamentary democracy. As if neglect and omission were not enough, coalition politicians hastily encouraged lies about the causes of the fires, declaring that they were started by arsonists and that greenies prevented hazard-reduction burns. Yet we know that these fires were overwhelmingly started by dry lightning in remote terrain and that hazard-reduction burning — which is far from a panacea — is constrained by a warming climate. The effort to stymie sensible policy reform after the fires has been as pernicious as the failure to plan in advance of them.

The recent fires delivered a liminal moment for the nation, landing us on the beach of a fearsome planetary future. There can be no evacuation. Whatever we call this summer, will we make it a season of reckoning?

---

1. ABC: Australian Broadcasting Commission.

---

An earlier version of this essay was published in the *Australian Book Review*, no. 419, 2020.

---

# Now is the Time

Bruce Pascoe

A few days before the devastating eastern seaboard fires, I stopped to walk through a forestry coup on the far south coast of NSW. I'm in the CFA,[1] but there seemed to be no interest at the time in the threat that such forestry operations posed to our safety. Trees are snipped off at the base like celery sticks, the logs trimmed and then fed through a de-barking machine, with all the waste left on the forest floor — ripe for conflagration.

These trees are grown mostly to convert into pulp before being sailed to Japan for paper processing. Australia sells this premium timber for a song, and then we sail it through the Great Barrier Reef, and it comes back to us through the same seaway as food-wrap. This is completely unsustainable, and the danger to our coastline is immense.

When I moved into this district in the 'seventies I used to do bird surveys for forestry so that we could protect endangered species. Well, that was the theory, but really it was window-dressing to decorate the fact that the bush was being prepared for clear felling at the start of the wood chip industry at Eden.

In those days, prior to this new style of forestry, we would work in the coups making lists and maps of bird distribution and we'd have our lunch with the foresters around a decent camp fire. It was pleasant, it was communal, and there was no cynical talk of greenies; we were all bushmen (there were no women in the industry in those days). Most times there'd be 15 to 20 loggers: some to cut, some to snig, and some to trim and load. There was employment in the bush in those days. Hundreds of families were raised on the back of saw-log production. Real timber for real products. Houses and furniture for Australia.

Now, when you go into those coups, they are silent but for the growl of massive machines. The old camaraderie is gone. We are the enemy of the people. The contractors label anyone they see as greenies, having been fed this mantra by the bosses who need to sell a message to the public. The greenies have stolen our jobs! Those mill towns should know there is more timber being cut now than ever before, but it is the bosses who have stolen the jobs by employing machines.

A few winters back we were arguing for the retention of a bush-block which was haven to Powerful Owls and rare orchids. We were met and massaged by some forestry spin-doctors who had the foresight to include a compliant blackfella. The contract with the clear-feller demanded that if he couldn't get his crew onto a low block because of heavy rain, 'Forestry' had to allow them access to a dry high block. Too bad about owls and orchids. We argued and argued, but there never seemed any intent to protect this patch. They read out their rules and regs: no logging within 50 metres of a watercourse, protection of non-target vegetation, protection of wildlife, and no sluicing of outfall into the river. All of these things were part of the legislation and they promised those rules would be followed, but we were not allowed within 200 metres of the site during the operation.

When I returned after the period as agreed, and with infractions punishable by jail terms, I have never seen such a mess. Tree trunks, limbs, tree ferns and wattles bulldozed into the creek, wheel-ruts two metres deep, and everywhere sub-surface gravels dumped onto the forest floor. There was litter everywhere, some piles three metres high and one hundred metres long, and rivulets of sludge two metres deep sluicing mud and gravel into the Genoa River.

The machinery used these days is so huge that the wheels are higher than a church ceiling, and when pushing over forest giants the wheels spin and act like a mining dredge and bring up gravel from two metres below the surface. It looked like a bomb site. Our protests were sneered at until a local farmer and National Party voter complained about the gravel being dumped on his pastures. Suddenly there was action — not to repair the forest or tighten compliance to the law, but to compensate the farmer! So, on that day of 29 December, just before the 2020 New Year's Eve fires, I stepped out a one-acre block in a forestry coup and counted 300 small silver-top ash trees, the desired species for pulp operation. There was trash on the ground a metre high. It wouldn't burn; it would explode because the crown of every tree touched the ones around it. The bush was a wick for a stick of gelignite.

Old Aboriginal land-care had created a forest where ten or twenty massive trees stood on an acre and their crowns never touched. The branches were so high off the ground that ladder fueling was impossible. Those forests could never create a crown fire. They might burn, but never explode. We need to examine that methodology and its outcomes.

On 1 January, when I returned to that corner, after a slalom of fires on both sides of the highway, the site was unrecognizable. Even the road signs had melted. The whole site looked as if it had been covered in snow. The fire has to be like a furnace to create that appearance: steel poles had become blobs of metal; and signs had disappeared into the atmosphere.

Now is the time for us to talk seriously about our forestry operations. Let's cut the cackle about country jobs and talk openly about what has caused forest unemployment. We need a new and truly sustainable forestry practice with maximum value placed on every log. Perhaps if Australia re-entered the furniture market, as we did in the first two hundred years of the colonial period, our forests could add to our economy as well as help country employment. At the moment we have been seduced by ad campaigns into believing that clear fell pulp operations are sustainable.

Last year I went through a plantation of second-growth blue-gum production in another state. It looked as if a fire had been through it, but a local told me that, after the first growth had been cut, the soil fertility was so low that the rebound of the second crop was below cost value. So, they poisoned it from the air.

Spreading poison from the air is as accurate as throwing a handful of smarties at the garage wall. Some of them end up in the dog bowl and the fish pond. It's poison, Australia; you're chucking it out of a plane to kill an uneconomic tree! If that isn't a prompt for us as a nation to begin genuine discussion of how we use and protect our forests and rivers, I'll go he. This is the perfect opportunity to talk business and economy while remembering that all the trees belong to the commonwealth, and any utility of them must not endanger the lives of those living in the forestry zone.

This project must be sustained over 70 years, not five; we need to think of our forests as our grandchildren's inheritance, not one more trophy to go straight to the pool rooms of a few rich people in other countries.

---

1. Country Fire Authority.

---

# Our Beautiful Country is Burning

Pat Anderson

Early this year, great expanses of our old and fragile home were on fire. Whole towns were destroyed, lives lost, and hundreds of homes incinerated. Countless animals and insects were killed by the flames, and smoke blanketed our cities and suburbs. This is unprecedented in the human habitation of this continent.

For 65,000 years or more, our First Nations cared for and sustainably regulated the diverse natural ecosystems of this place. Looking after Country was our job. We cherished the land, understanding that *our* health relies upon *its* health. However, in less than 250 years of colonisation, our knowledge and practices, developed and refined over millennia, have been marginalised just as we have. Our adaptability, creativity and wisdom have been ignored, sidelined or suppressed, or seen to be of no value. Our ability to care for Country has been profoundly undermined.

Today, the results are all around us. Everywhere we look, we see the damage being done to the living systems that sustain life: by drought and fire exacerbated by the climate emergency; and by those industries that take from the land but give nothing back. We see the increasing numbers of ever-larger, ever-fiercer bushfires. We see the rivers run dry. We see the oceans filled with rubbish and toxins.

We are in a crisis that poses an unparalleled threat to the sustainability of life in this land and the whole planet. This is a threat to the environment, to the economy, to our health, and to our wellbeing. And it is a threat to the human rights of all Australians and our children and grandchildren. For how can any of us enjoy freedom, justice and peace, the foundation of our rights, if our land is burning? In this desperate place we find ourselves, we First Nations have the knowledge that can help heal this country. Our Indigenous knowledges can help halt and turn back the destruction we see. As Murrandoo Yanner, the prominent man and activist from North Queensland, said recently, 'The greatest thing we have to offer today is our humanity, because this is all we ever had'.[1]

The *Uluru Statement from the Heart* makes that offer. It provides a roadmap not just for healing past injustices, but also for creating a future where our knowledge can be reintegrated into the life of the nation and can help heal this continent.

In May 2017, several hundred Aboriginal and Torres Strait Islander delegates met in the heart of this land, to consider proposals for constitutional reform that genuinely recognise our place here as First Peoples. That meeting, however significant, was not the first step: it followed an extensive process of Regional Dialogues around the country held over the year leading up to the Convention at Uluru. These Regional Dialogues were the first time in Australia's history that we as First Nations sat down across the nation in a formal manner to deliberate on constitutional matters. As such, they were a significant — if much belated — response to our exclusion from the process that led to the adoption of the Australian Constitution in 1901. Participants in the Regional Dialogues and those at Uluru showed overwhelming consensus around three proposals.

First, for a constitutionally established representative body that would give First Nations a voice directly to the federal parliament. Second, for the establishment of a Makarrata Commission to supervise the making of treaties with us. And third, a concurrent process of local and regional truth-telling which could form the basis for genuine reconciliation. These three things — Voice, Treaty, Truth — were the key consensus demands that arose from the Dialogues, and were captured in the *Uluru Statement from the Heart*.

As delegates we consciously addressed the *Uluru Statement* to the Australian people. This was based on our faith that ordinary Australians of good will, if they heard our voice, would not turn away from us — just as they did not in the 1967 Referendum when over 90 per cent of Australians voted 'yes' to change the Constitution to ensure that, amongst other things, we were to be counted as Australians for the first time.

And the immediate response from many of those in politics and the media to the *Uluru Statement* showed the wisdom of our delegates in seeking to speak directly to the Australian people. The carefully thought out and extensively debated proposals for truth-telling and treaty-making were attacked by many mainstream commentators as if the history of dispossession didn't happen. And our proposal to establish a Voice to the federal parliament was immediately and wrongly painted as an attempt to establish a third chamber of parliament, and was dismissed out of hand by our then Prime Minister, Mr Turnbull. There seemed to be an underlying assumption that it was an attempt to gain something for ourselves at the expense of non-Indigenous Australians.

However, I believe that the Voice to Parliament is something that could be of great benefit to all Australians.

Of course, it would lead to better, more effective processes to address the intergenerational disadvantage that many of our communities suffer, and it would address the long-standing historical inequity by which we are effectively excluded from many of the forums in which decisions are made about our lives. In these ways, it would be of great symbolic and practical value to all Aboriginal and Torres Strait Islander people. However, in addition, the Voice to Parliament would be a gift of great value to the Australian people as a whole. It would be a place where we bring our stories and our knowledges to the symbolic centre of contemporary government.

This country could really use our knowledge now, particularly when it comes to looking after the environment on which all of our lives and economy are based. Our Indigenous knowledges could help halt and turn back the destruction we see. The bushfires — well, if there's one thing us mob know about, it's fire: how to use it creatively to promote life and productivity; how to manage it; and how to prevent it becoming destructive and harmful. The rivers — we have always known how to manage them, how to take the water we need, but always leave enough for other living creatures. The oceans and the reef — we have thousands of years' experience looking after them sustainably.

I'm not saying we have all the answers, but I can say that as First Nations people, we have accumulated 65,000 years or more of knowledge about how to care for this land, and that the Voice to Parliament, enshrined in the Constitution, would be a permanent place in which to share that knowledge, and use it to help all people now living here, and to help prevent the kind of suffering we are seeing this year. What the *Uluru Statement* asks for is a Voice to Parliament that is enshrined in the Constitution, because this will make it a permanent part of the life of the nation. It would not be subject to the whims of the government of the day and not be able to be dissolved at the stroke of a pen when it becomes inconvenient, as has happened with so many consultative bodies set up in the past. The *Statement* seeks recognition of us as the sovereign First Peoples of this nation. This is our place, and we are not going anywhere.

This is the promise held out by the Uluru delegates, trusting in the decency and sense of justice of the Australian people. It is a gift from Australia's First Peoples to *all* Australians, made in the spirit of justice and reconciliation, a gift that will help heal this land.

---

1. A. Wright, 'Want to Stop Australia's Fires? Listen to Aboriginal People', *The New York Times*, 15 January 2020, https://www.nytimes.com/2020/01/15/opinion/australia-fires-aboriginal-people.html. Viewed 17 January 2020.

---

This is an edited version of a paper presented as part of the 2020 Gandhi Oration at the University of New South Wales on 4 February 2020, and was prepared in collaboration with Edward Tilton.

# Recognising the Ancient Skills of Cultural Burning

David Bowman, Greg Lehman

The bushfire crisis that occurred in southern NSW and eastern Victoria in the summer of 2019–2020 was completely unprecedented. In a few days in early January we saw a sequence of events that were truly extraordinary: clusters of fire thunderstorms. Prior to this time, pyro-cumulonimbus (pyroCb) events were quite rare.[1] There had, for example, only ever been one previous fire thunderstorm in Tasmania that we know of — in 2013.[2] When a pyroCb event occurs the weather, the fire, the atmosphere and the land all become coupled and the situation goes completely out of control — just like in an atomic explosion.

What happened earlier this year was that Australia's total list of known pyroCbs increased by about 40 per cent.[3] According to the 20-year satellite record, the area burned was seven standard deviations larger than in the previous 19 years.[4] This is absolutely extraordinary. If it had been a chance phenomenon its probability would have been less than that of the earth being hit by a one-kilometre-wide asteroid. Probably, what happened has rarely, if ever, occurred in the history of Earth.

The recognition that the climate has changed drastically, and that we are facing a situation of extreme danger that we have never previously encountered, has led to a search for new solutions. In this search one of the key areas that has attracted interest is the way in which Aboriginal people have managed fire over the millennia.

It is now widely understood that Aboriginal people used landscape burning to sustain biodiversity and mitigate large disastrous bushfires. This is acknowledged in the terms of reference of the Australian Government Royal Commission into the Black Summer Bushfires, which include the direction to explore 'any ways in which the traditional land and fire-management practices of Indigenous Australians could improve Australia's resilience to natural disasters'.[5]

There is no doubt that Aboriginal knowledge about fire management is an essential element in solving the bushfire crisis. Aboriginal fire management should be informing and shaping mainstream fire-management practices. The geographic scale and pace of the bushfire threat demands we move quickly. A basic question that needs to be resolved urgently is how we can apply Aboriginal knowledge while recognising and protecting Indigenous intellectual and cultural rights? Without care, Australian society could perpetuate historical injustices by appropriating cultural knowledge without any recognition or compensation.

A practical way to achieve this is some form of explicit federal and state-government funded affirmative action to protect and extend Aboriginal burning cultures. Specifically, such an affirmative action program should provide pathways for Aboriginal people to maintain and renew traditional cultural practices, develop programs and partnerships with non-Indigenous fire managers, or enter mainstream fire-management. In some instances, where the impact of colonisation has been most intense, action is needed to support Aboriginal communities to re-establish relationships with native vegetation or bushland areas following generations of forced removal from their Country.

The challenges are complex. They require responses that address social justice and economic issues, as well as scientific and planning matters. Australians must change their expectations and their understanding of how to manage fire.

## Aboriginal Fire Practices

Prior to 1788, Aboriginal cultures right across Australia and Tasmania used fire to deliberately and skilfully manage the bush. Broadly, traditional Aboriginal fire management was characterised by numerous, frequent fires that created fine-scale mosaics of recently burnt and unburnt patches. Developed over thousands of years, such mosaic burning benefited wildlife and sustained biodiversity as animals and plants adapted to a mosaic of habitats. The breakdown of traditional fire-management has been associated with reduction in biodiversity, tree invasion on grasslands, and an increased frequency of larger more destructive bushfires.

In modern day Australia, there exists a spectrum of Aboriginal fire-practice. In some regions, such as on some clan estates in Arnhem Land, there are unbroken traditions of fire management that trace back to the late mid-Pleistocene some 50,000 years ago. Persistence and accumulation of traditional Aboriginal knowledge of fire and its associated ecologies is the reason that Australia holds international significance for understanding how indigenous people used fire to manage landscapes and sustain biodiversity.

It is too often overlooked that all around the world indigenous cultures that inhabited flammable landscapes, including in Western Europe, used fire to manage landscapes. Dramatic land-use shifts and cultural changes caused by industrialisation, intensive agriculture and colonisation have resulted in a shift toward excluding fire from landscape management, resulting in significant loss of these practices world-wide. In most cases the bulk of this knowledge has faded in public consciousness, with historical records the only source of information about them.

## Towards Cultural Burning Renewal

In many Australian landscapes, particularly in densely settled areas, cultural burning practices have been severely disrupted. Nonetheless, many Aboriginal people are rekindling cultural practices, sometimes in collaboration with non-Indigenous land managers. Cultural burning draws on retained community knowledge of past fire practices, in some cases embracing traditional cultural practices from different regions across Australia. Burning programs can be adapted to the challenges of a rapidly changing world, including the need to manage for capital assets, and new threats like weeds, climate change, forest disturbances from logging and fire, and feral animals.

This process is well described in the book *Fire Country: How Indigenous Fire Management Could Help Save Australia* by Victor Steffensen.[6] Steffensen describes how, as an Aboriginal man born in two cultures, he made a journey of self-discovery in learning about fire management, guided and mentored by two Aboriginal elders. Together, they reintroduce fire into traditional lands on Cape York, practices that had been prohibited following the imposition of European-based systems of land tenure and management. Steffensen then extended his experience to cultural renewal and ecological restoration across many parts of Australia.

Steffensen argues for expanding this approach as being critical to address the bushfire crisis. He writes:

> The bottom line for me is that we need to work towards a whole other division of fire managers on the land, looking after country in all the ways possible, which includes fire as well as other practices. A skilled team of indigenous and non-indigenous people that works in with the entire community, agencies and emergency services to deliver an effective and educational strategy into the future. One that is culturally based and connects to all the benefits for the community.[7]

To realise Victor Steffensen's ideal and 'help save Australia' from future bushfire disasters we need to focus on rapidly building capacity to train and employ Aboriginal fire-practitioners, foster Aboriginal burning programs, and employ Aboriginal people in mainstream fire-management teams. We need to see more Aboriginal people employed and taking leadership in fire management in a broad cross section of agencies, Indigenous and non-Indigenous community groups.

Importantly, some of the outcomes of this empowerment will enable Aboriginal communities to re-establish their own cultural priorities in caring for Country. Where these differ from the Eurocentric values of mainstream Australia, there will be a need to understand and accept the wisdom of those who have been custodians of this flammable landscape for millennia. Such accommodation is the long-overdue and necessary accompaniment to advances in providing land rights and native title in recent decades. It is an essential part of the 'unfinished business' of post-colonial Australia.

Addressing this requires a willingness to shift our paradigms of environmental management and investment. To a significant degree our recent fire crisis is a reminder of the brutal acquisition of land in Australia. The consequences of this are not limited to social injustice that continues to impact on Aboriginal people. By preventing Aboriginal people from continuing fire-management practices that mitigate the risk of massively destructive events like those experienced in 2019 and 2020, Australia ignores the complex inter-dependence that develops between human societies and nature. It's time, instead, to embrace this.

To achieve this goal demands dedicated funding to rebuild the capacity of Aboriginal communities to share the practice of cultural burning through an affirmative action program. Non-Indigenous Australians need to value, and pay for, the ancient skills that have enabled people to co-exist with the flammable bush. Fundamentally we must recognise that Aborigines are 'fire people' who live on 'fire country'. Non-Aboriginal Australians need to learn from them.

---

1. J.J. Sharples, G.J. Cary, P. Fox-Hughes, S. Mooney, J.P. Evans, M.S. Fletcher, M. Fromm, P.F. Grierson, R. McRae and P. Baker, 'Natural hazards in Australia: Extreme Bushfire', *Climatic Change*, vol. 139, no. 1, 2016, pp. 85–99.
2. M.N. Ndalila, J. Williamson, P. Fox-Hughes, J. Sharples, and D.M. Bowman, 'Evolution of a Pyrocumulonimbus Event Associated with an Extreme Wildfire in Tasmania, Australia', *Natural Hazards and Earth System Sciences*, vol. 20, no. 5, 2020, pp.1497–1511.
3. Sharples, et al., op. cit.
4. D.M. Bowman, G. Williamson, M. Yebra, J. Lizundia-Loiola, M. Pettinari, S. Shah, R. Bradstock and E. Chuvieco, 'Wildfires: Australia needs national monitoring agency', *Nature* 584, 2020, 188–191.
5. https://naturaldisaster.royalcommission.gov.au/publications/commonwealth-letters-patent-20-february-2020. Last accessed 5 July 2020.
6. V. Steffensen, *Fire Country: How Indigenous Fire Management Could Help Save Australia*, Hardie Grant, Melbourne, 2020.
7. Ibid, p. 152.

---

An earlier version of this essay was published in *The Conversation*, https://theconversation.com/australia-you-have-unfinished-business-its-time-to-let-our-fire-people-care-for-this-land-135196.

# Learning from the Stories in Our Ancient Library

Alexis Wright

I often speak about our ancient library — the stories of the ancestors kept in the largest library in the world — the land, sea, skies and atmosphere of this country, in all life, and in ourselves. These stories, formed over millennia of our existence on this continent, have guided us as the world's oldest surviving culture through catastrophic changing climate to the present. I also talk about our need for a self-governing literature, and changing the literary landscape with our own unique perspective. This is the perspective that belongs here, and is the legacy passed down to us through countless generations so that we can know who we are in this place.

Storying our world through traditional practices ensures that we will always have responsibility for caring for our country. This responsibility is about keeping and respecting ancient knowledge systems tied to land through sacred storytelling practices; and the practice of storying extends into our everyday life. We live and work in our collective world of story-making, story-telling, and story-keeping practices that are recognizable in core principles guiding our sovereignty of mind, and sovereignty of imagination.

One core principle is that we have survived the whiteman's world. Another, is that this always was and will always be Aboriginal land. In the Gulf of Carpentaria, one of our land council's core principles is to excite young people to continue living on their land, and be good custodians for a sustainable future. A principle in land management is to fight fire with fire. Our great song man Archie Roach nicely describes another principle: *when one shines, we all shine*. We collectively feel great pride when our people demonstrate the enormous wisdom of our culture, or when we win back our stolen land, or when we prevent destruction of our sacred places, or when our people show enormous resilience on an everyday basis, and just as much as when we shine as leaders, as leading scholars and practitioners, or as leading sportspeople.

Many more Australians understand from the 2020 summer of infernos that we are at the very front-line of climate change. We expect far more people, country and animals will be affected by future apocalyptic climate change events. We are a shell-shocked nation. But if Australia is on the front-line, in front are many Aboriginal communities in Central and Northern Australia living on their homelands in even more extreme conditions in extended and hotter summers of unbroken heatwaves, where in the Centre, temperatures exceeding 50 degrees Celsius may be the new normal before long.

I have seen many years of our crucial work with governments bear little fruit, and we expend a lot of energy trying to change national policy narratives, so I am not confident of quick government responses to this global warming emergency. ABC journalist Chris Ulhmann in borrowing a line from a past Labor leader said recently, 'we have got the national politics we deserve because, we are us'.[1] We are who we are. We still vote for governments continuing the legacies of previous governments ... *for doing a hellish thing*, to kill the thing *that made the breeze blow*, which of course is a line from a famous old English poem written by Samuel Taylor Coleridge 220 years ago called *The Rime of the Ancient Mariner*. The Mariner is condemned to carry the albatross he killed around his neck forever more, like the Australian Prime Minister, the scapegoat in our political times, condemned for the billion native animals and billions of trees destroyed in the pyre of this year's infernos. The new stories of this hell are of the world committing suicide or omnicide, when you kill everything — the greatest of all crimes as Danielle Celermajer explained in a recent opinion piece for the ABC *Religion and Ethics* program.[2] We look around and there is nobody on the job. If this is an emergency, where are the law-makers and enforcers of new international laws against omnicide and ecocide? Where is the responsibility for enforcing the law storying for the survival of the planet?

The second thing I have often spoken about is that literature across the world needs to be braver, and be willing to take more risks to work with our times. Australian educators need to be a force for greater critical and comparative studies of Australian literature aimed at creating better understanding and knowledge of the complex global issues impacting this part of the world right now, and into the future. We need to learn how to imagine and tell our own stories stronger: *I bid thee say — What manner of man art thou?* We need to write the overwhelming stories of our times stronger: *who loveth well both man and bird and beast ... who loveth best all things great and small.*

I believe that the imaginative literary mind is as boundless as it is borderless and bountiful in its wayfinding, powerfully creating anew the already imagined with the unimagined, or unimaginable. Possibly George Orwell had similarly thought something like this when he explained that the imagination was like certain wild animals that do not breed in captivity. Writers who denied this fact, he said, were in effect demanding their own destruction.[3] The dreamlike state of imagining is continuously curious while it shifts, reshapes its positioning and influences. But imagination is never alone. There is a fight going on all day long in the mind of the writer about how to counterbalance the fanciful world of the imagination. The moral compass governs, asserts its sovereignty, and wants you to reinstate some sense of restraint to flights of fancy. It wants you to be mindful of the reality of what writing ought to be, and to take notice of real or perceived restrictions, responsibilities, expectations that call into question, to take another deeper look about what is going on in your world. It needs you to reign in, or realign the imagination, to decrease its force in these continuous arguments and counter-arguments to control the process and risk-taking through each long literary journey.

When I began my writing life, I had already learnt from elders in Central and Northern Australia who had always claimed that *we have always governed ourselves*. These senior custodians of great wisdom and deep knowledge of country, teach their young people to think afar, to broaden our horizons, to bring back ideas, visions, imagination, to increase our knowledge so that we can better fight the battles of how to control our future. I learnt as a young woman that they expected us to search the world for ideas about how to achieve solutions to questions about our rights as Indigenous peoples. These master story-makers, storytellers, story-keepers and experts of story-practice, had actually taught me the joy of reading and writing even though the books they read were the epic stories held in vast areas of land and desert country, and where they travelled through stories networking seemingly unremarkable landscapes, but they always intimately knew where they were in their country through story.

What has become clearer to me the more I write, is that I have been trying to build a self-governing literary landscape through what I have learnt from our ancient library, of being continuously shaped by its stories, of always governing ourselves through our own Constitution of Sacred Laws for this country. I can see that one of my personal challenges has always been to develop a literature more suited to the powerful ancient cultural landscape of this country.

In both my fiction and non-fiction work, the balance I am trying to create is how this country thinks — both Aboriginal and non-Aboriginal, and the land itself — and how the world thinks. What we share in common? What we care for? What animals are universally cared about? I explore all literature, both the local and global.

In writing *Carpentaria*, I wanted to create a work of authenticity to honour my traditional homeland. In the writing, I understood more fully how the powerful spirits of our ancestral homeland are imbued in the soul of our people who are country itself, and where true sovereign governance lay, with the ancestors. We are governed by the stories of the ancestral spirits of place in our traditional country. Their strength is in our sovereignty of the mind as a powerful force that feels like a flash light, a beacon swarming with moths. I had this understanding through years of working on our land rights and self-government campaigns. Our old people often told us: *We govern ourselves. Our laws never change. White man's law changes all the time. It is a weaker law.* Their deep cultural knowledge guided my understanding of being comfortable with the gravity of responsibility and the depth of relationships to our traditional country, loved as family, and in our deep understanding that country is always alive and forever powerful, and if its deep laws are broken, it can and will turn against us, and this is how we had learnt to survive millennia of changing climate. *Carpentaria* is a novel where stories of all times are intertwined like a spinning helix of stories, where all times are important, alive, and no time resolved.

The research I undertook of the world's swan species, poetry, and old epics was unrestrained and ceaseless to write a future climate-changed world in *The Swan Book* published in 2013. The research began ten years earlier in 2002–3 on wide-ranging issues of global warming in a time when there was very little literary fiction about climate change. I wanted to explore how far we would go as Aboriginal people to survive backward government policies by anticipating a climate-changed Australia of a hundred years' time as predicted by science.

I believe the pursuit of knowledge without restraint is necessary to be in the world, to freely explore other realities, to try to respond to our times. I have always understood this from the grounding in cosmopolitan thinking of our elders who taught us to seek widely to find consensus. As a child, I had seen how my wonderful storytelling grandmother embraced the world. She helped me to be literate to a much older literature for thinking about, and imagining this country. Her perspective and worldview were both huge and cosmopolitan in teaching the benefits of having eyes wide open and having an openness to the world, and of being attuned to a spiritual understanding of the environment through self-knowledge. She saw the world anew and marvellous on a constant basis and helped me to build an internal world of visualization and exploration, and perhaps the endurance for holding onto a vision, and perhaps this is the great gift of cultural teachers which helped me to create *The Swan Book*.

My new novel *Praiseworthy* explores strength of character for surviving catastrophic, apocalyptic times of the future. The work of a novelist requires great passion for exploring ideas and imagining worlds that grow enormous in the mind. This idea of imagining and re-imagining will be the great challenge of the future. Recently my Gangalidda countryman Murrandoo Yanner, a man made for these times, said *the way forward is back, and the greatest thing we have to offer today is our humanity because this is all we ever had.*

---

1. Chris Ulhmann, 'In Despair, I Wondered How Politics Got so Bad — Then I Looked at Twitter', *The Age*, 18 February, 2020.
2. Danielle Celermajer, 'Omnicide: Who is Responsible for the Gravest of all Crimes?' ABC *Religion & Ethics*, 3 January, 2020. https://www.abc.net.au/religion/danielle-celermajer-omnicide-gravest-of-all-crimes/11838534.
3. George Orwell, 'The Prevention of Literature, 1946', in *George Orwell Essays*, Penguin, 1994, p.340.

# The Science Behind Australia's Catastrophic Bushfires

Will Steffen

The bushfires in Australia across 2019 and 2020 were unprecedented in many ways, but probably most striking was the massive area burnt across an extended period. Across New South Wales and Victoria, the states most affected by the fires, about 5.8 million hectares of eucalypt-dominated temperate forests burned, often for weeks, in intense, rapidly spreading and hard-to-control fires.[1] The constituent fires were also notable for their huge size individually — for example, the Gospers Mountain fire near Sydney burned over 500,000 hectares — and for their massive impacts on World Heritage forests (Figure 1).

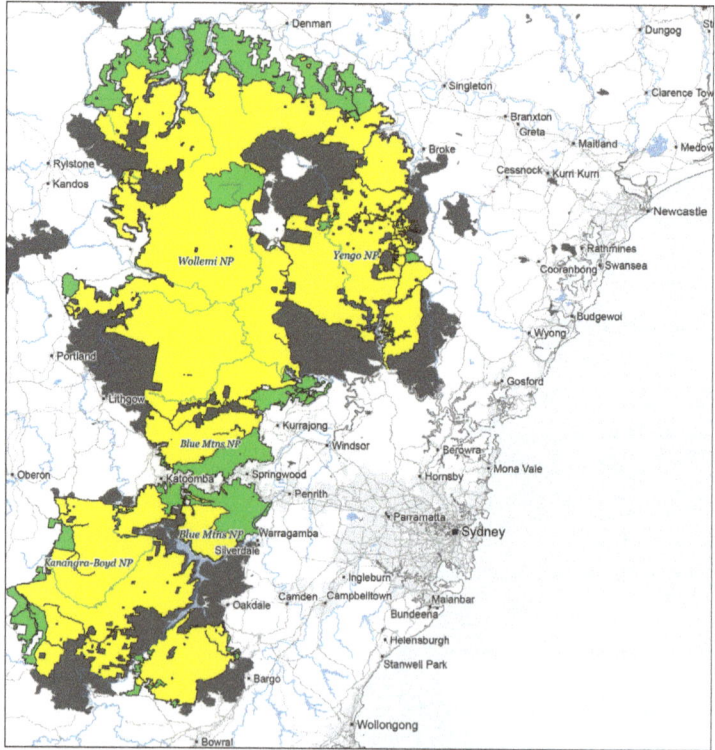

**Figure 1.**
Area burned in the Blue Mountains World Heritage Area. Yellow shows world heritage areas burned, green shows world heritage areas unburned, and grey shows burned areas that are not world heritage. Source: Department of Agriculture, Water and the Environment (2020).

The area burnt in total was unprecedented, not only for Australia but globally. Although eucalypt forests are well-known for being fire-prone and bushfires are not uncommon, the area burned in eastern Australian eucalypt forests are typically only 2 per cent or less, even in extreme fire seasons.[2] This fraction of average area burnt annually is similar to that of temperate broad-leaf forests on other continents, where the fraction is well below 5 per cent (apart from Africa and Asia, where the burn area can reach 8–9 per cent on average). However, the 2019–2020 eastern Australian fires consumed about 21 per cent of the total forested area, an expanse far beyond anything previously experienced in Australia and, indeed, in the rest of the world.

Scientific indicators used to assess dangerous fire weather also reinforced the unprecedented nature of the fires. The Forest Fire Danger Index (FFDI) which is a composite indicator of bushfire weather that incorporates temperature, humidity, wind speed and antecedent conditions such as longer-term rainfall, reached record-high levels in 2019.[3] As early as September 2019, well before the normal start of the bushfire season, catastrophic fire danger conditions (FFDI above 100) were recorded at several locations in New South Wales.[4]

The interval between major fires in the temperate forests of eastern Australia has been shortening.[5] The gap between the 1939 fires, thought at that time to be the worst possible fires, and the Ash Wednesday fires (1983) was 44 years. But the gap shortened considerably between those fires and the Black Saturday and Canberra/alpine fires of the 2000s — down to about 23 years. The recent 2019–2020 megafires have now come only 10 to 15 years later than the previous ones.

## The Short and Long-Term Climate Drivers

Australia experienced exceptional heat in 2019, with the annual average temperature for the country 1.52°C above the 1961–1990 baseline. 2019 was the hottest year on record. Perhaps more importantly, the average maximum temperature for Australia was 2.09°C above the baseline, breaking 2°C for the first time, and a full 0.5°C higher than the previous record.[6]

The year 2019 was also the driest year on record for Australia, with rainfall across the continent a staggering 40 per cent below the long-term average. In some locations in southern Queensland and northern New South Wales, rainfall for the January–October period was 70–80 per cent below average, setting up the forests to burn.[7] Figure 2 (overleaf) shows the two-year deficit in rainfall across Australia, with most of the forested area along the east coast from southern Queensland to eastern Victoria experiencing its driest ever two-year period.[8]

The weather conditions leading up to the 2019–2020 megafires represent an intersection of longer-term trends of increased extreme heat and less

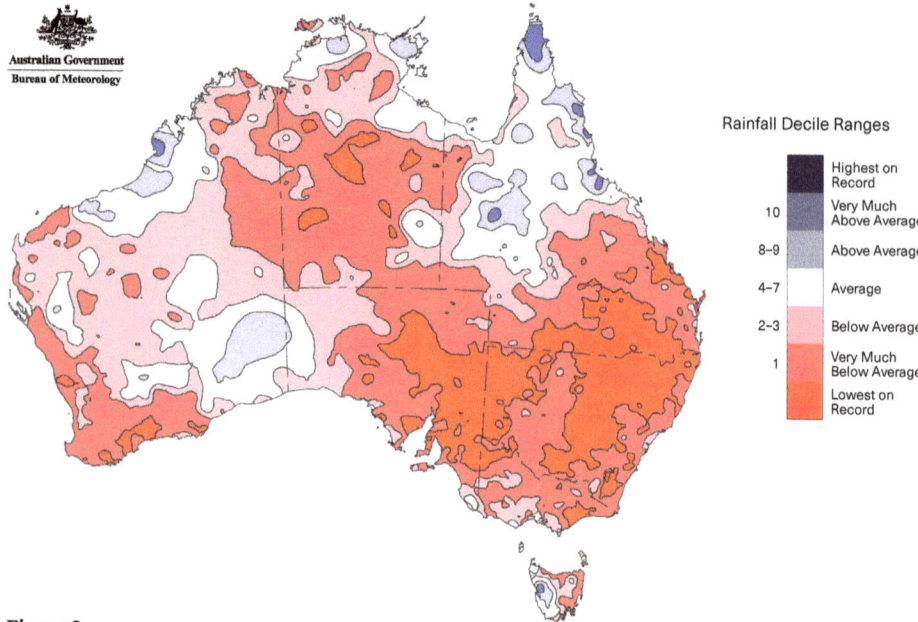

**Figure 2.**
Australian rainfall deciles from 1 January 2018 to 31 December 2019. Source: Bureau of Meteorology, http://www.bom.gov.au/climate/current/month/aus/archive/201912.summary.shtml.

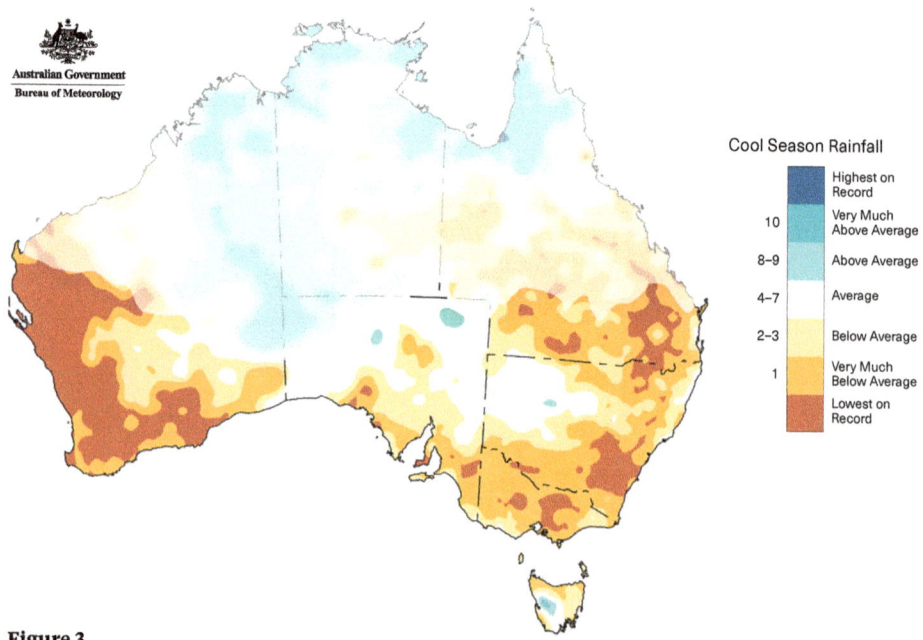

**Figure 3.**
Cool season (April–October) rainfall has been below average across southeast and southwest Australia in the past 20 years compared to the entire rainfall record from 1900. Source: CSIRO and Bureau of Meteorology, Melbourne, 'State of the Climate 2018', http://www.bom.gov.au/state-of-the-climate/australias-changing-climate.shtml

cool-season rainfall in the southeast of Australia. Shorter-term modes of natural variability also played an important role in the fires. In particular, the extreme dry conditions of the last few years have been linked to the absence of a negative phase of the Indian Ocean dipole (IOD) and a La Niña phase of the El Niño–Southern Oscillation (ENSO), both of which normally bring rain to Australia. Understanding how these shorter-term modes of variability are being influenced by a heating climate is a critical research challenge.[9]

## The Role of Climate Change

Long-term climate trends are well understood. The ongoing rise in temperature, which has contributed to the observed strong increase in the Forest Fire Danger Index, is caused by the increasing concentration of greenhouse gases in the atmosphere, the most important of which is carbon dioxide emitted by the burning of fossil fuels such as coal, oil and gas. Global average surface temperature has risen by a little over 1° Celsius compared to the pre-industrial period, with somewhat larger rises in Australian temperatures averaged over the continent, compared to the pre-industrial period. The record high temperatures of 2019, which were a major contributing factor to the conditions conducive for megafires, were thus the latest in a multi-decadal trend of rising temperatures, driven by climate change.[10]

The extraordinarily dry conditions over the past two years are associated with a longer-term trend of decreasing rainfall, particularly in cool season rainfall over the southeast of the continent over the past two to three decades. A decrease of about 15 per cent in late autumn and early winter rainfall, compared to the long-term average, has been observed across southeast Australia since the mid-1990s (Figure 3). A similar, but more pronounced, trend has been observed in southwest Western Australia.[11] These observed trends have been linked to the poleward shift in storm tracks, positive trends in the Southern Annular Mode, an increase in atmospheric pressure in the sub-tropics and the expansion of the Hadley Cell. All of these changes in atmospheric circulation are, in turn, linked to climate change.[12]

Recent research has also suggested a link between climate change and the unusual strength of the positive phase Indian Ocean dipole in 2019, which was a major factor in the exceptionally dry conditions last year.[13] Paleo studies show that over the past 800 years, there have been ten exceptionally strong Indian Ocean dipoles, and four of the ten have occurred in the last 60 years. Furthermore, climate change is very likely a key factor in the recent increase in strong Indian Ocean dipoles, and is thus increasing the odds that we'll experience more of them in the future.[14]

In summary, there is strong evidence that climate change has played a key role in the size, intensity and destructiveness of the 2019–2020 eastern Australian bushfires. Although we await formal, model-based attribution studies of the likelihood of such extensive fires occurring without climate change, the observational and paleo evidence coupled with the fundamental physics of climate change and bushfire dynamics strongly suggest that fires of the magnitude and ferocity of the ones we have just experienced would have been virtually impossible without climate change.

Finally, there is a direct link between the Australian fossil-fuel industry and climate change, and thus also to the bushfires. The dominant driver of climate change is the emission of greenhouse gases, predominantly carbon dioxide ($CO_2$), by human activities. About 90 per cent of anthropogenic $CO_2$ emissions originate from the burning of coal, oil and gas.[15]

## Conclusion

There are several important take-home messages from an analysis of the science behind the massive fires of 2019–2020:

These fires were unprecedented in terms of the extent of forest burned, and probably also in terms of the intensity of the fires.

The antecedent weather conditions across eastern Australia — record-breaking extreme heat in 2019 and the lowest rainfall on record for the 2018–2019 two-year period — were very likely influenced by the longer-term changes in Australia's climate driven by anthropogenic emissions of greenhouse gases.

The 2019–2020 fire season does not represent a 'new normal' in terms of dangerous fire conditions. Temperatures will continue to rise for at least two decades, and probably longer, because of climate change, increasing the likelihood of even more dangerous fire weather in the future.

---

1. M.M. Boer, V. de Dios Resco and R.A. Bradstock, 'Unprecedented Burn Area of Australian Mega Forest Fires', *Nature Climate Change*, 2020, https://doi.org/10.1038/s41558-020-0716-1.
2. Ibid., and the references therein.
3. Bureau of Meteorology, 'Annual Climate Statement 2019', http://www.bom.gov.au/climate/current/annual/aus/. Last accessed 3 August 2020.
4. Climate Council, 'Summer of Crisis', https://www.climatecouncil.org.au/resources/summer-of-crisis/. Last accessed 3 August 2020.
5. Tom Beer, personal communication.
6. Bureau of Meteorology, 'Annual Climate Statement 2019'.
7. Bureau of Meteorology, 'Special Climate Statement 70 update — drought conditions in Australia and impact on water resources in the Murray–Darling Basin', 2019, http://www.bom.gov.au/climate/current/statements/scs70.pdf.
8. Bureau of Meteorology, 'Australian rainfall deciles in December 2019', 2020, http://www.bom.gov.au/climate/current/month/aus/archive/201912.summary.shtml. Last accessed 6 September 2020.
9. A.D. King, A.J. Pitman, B.J. Henley, A.M. Ukkola and J.R. Brown, 'The Role of Climate Variability in Australian Drought', *Nature Climate Change*, 2020, https://doi.org/10.1038/s41558-020-0718-z.
10. CSIRO and Bureau of Meteorology, Melbourne, 'Climate Change in Australia—Technical Report', 2015, https://www.climatechangeinaustralia.gov.au/media/ccia/2.1.6/cms_page_media/168/CCIA_2015_NRM_TechnicalReport_WEB.pdf. Last accessed 6 September 2020.

11. CSIRO and Bureau of Meteorology, Melbourne, 'State of the Climate', 2016, http://www.climatechangeinaustralia.gov.au/en/publications-library/technical-report/.
12. Ibid.
13. N.J. Abram et al., 'Coupling of Indo-Pacific Climate Variability over the Last Millennium', *Nature*, 2020, https://doi.org/10.1038/s41586-020-2084-4.
14. W. Cai et al., 'Increased Frequency of Extreme Indian Ocean Dipole Events Due to Greenhouse Warming', *Nature*, no. 510, 2014, pp. 254–8.
15. Friedlingstein et al., 'Global Carbon Budget, 2019', *Earth System Science Data*, vol. 11, no. 4, http://doi.org/10.5194/essd-11-1783-2019.

# Communities

11.02.20
It was a quiet and still evening with a distant rumble of thunder echoing through the streets of Tumut.
A few drops of rain. A red Batlow firetruck was parked out the front of the Colonial Pub.
A group of firefighters, some from New Zealand, were sitting together quietly, talking stories, eating food and drinking beers.

Text & Drawing • Hugo Muecke

# Grandmother Trees, Aboriginal Women and Fire

Vanessa Cavanagh

I remember brushing my teeth over the green enamel sink. I would gaze out the window at a prominent grandmother and ponder her age. This grandmother had soft pink skin, smooth and dimpled, and incredible curves that burled in places. She stood at least 25 metres tall. She was one of the sentinel trees which stood strong on the property where I grew up in Colo Heights, north west of Sydney, at the edge of Darkinjung Country. Belonging to the *Angophora costata* family, she, like me, is part of human and non-human kinship networks that connect us with Country.[1]

To begin to understand this connection, you might start by thinking about how every naturally occurring native tree on this property grows in its perfect place.[2] Thousands of generations of evolution caused for it to grow right there. Each plant belongs to that very soil, and under that particular sky. Each plant is connected to the next, also growing in its own perfect way. Just like this grandmother tree, the plants are all families to each other. A community that is woven together with every element of nature participating. This is Country. It includes the plants, the animals, the weather, rocks, fire, soils, waters, air, all of planet Earth. The powerful celestial beings too. They are all crucially important, in their belonging place. Humans are part of this community, evolving together. Our relationships with each other, human and non-human, helped us thrive as the longest continuous culture on Earth.[3] There is much to learn from honouring this connection.

These are not new thoughts. I am not trying to be a clever person. Indigenous people have shared this story for millennia.[4] Indigenous people have adamantly protested against greedy environmental destruction.

## A Layered Coincidence

I returned home to Colo Heights in the first week of 2020 to review the damage caused by the Gospers Mountain bushfire. The Rural Fire Service had done a brilliant job protecting the main house. But for this grandmother tree, the combination of ongoing drought and persistent flames ended her reign at the far edge of the yard. The sight of this old tree with her crown removed brought warm, stinging tears to my eyes. It was a deep hurt of losing someone far older and wiser than me. Losing someone who was respected and adored. Someone with knowledge I cannot fathom or comprehend. When I told my Mum that evening she reacted similarly, a personal and family loss. To others she might just be a big tree. Yet we know, too, that Country is powerful and will recover. These trees return to the earth, and their legacy will regenerate, we each have our cycles.

It's not inconsequential I'm having these experiences of fire right now. I'm an Aboriginal woman and scholar, researching the ways in which Aboriginal women are, and are not, involved in cultural burning practices in New South Wales. I explore and promote the layers of meaning that Aboriginal women's stories reveal — historical record, educational tool, and cultural expression. Such are present in my own story.

## A Childhood Immersed in Nature

Mum and Dad bought the 25-acre, heavily forested property in the late 1960s because they wanted their kids to grow up in the bush, to have that connection. They also wanted to have the security of owning a place of their own, away from departmental housing and government interference in Aboriginal cultural welfare. Thus, it became a place for extended family to come to, to avoid the controlling gaze of others. My late father, a Wonnarua man, started a forty-year career as a labourer and heavy-machine operator in the NSW Department of Main Roads, as it was known then. He also volunteered in the local Rural Fire Service (RFS) over four decades, and he was captain for some of this time. Mum is a Bungum Bundjalung woman, a life-long social justice advocate and a vocal feminist. Before having us kids, Mum was involved in the lead-up to the 1967 Referendum doing advocacy work and attending demonstrations. When I started high school, Mum returned to paid work in Aboriginal women's refuges.

I can't recall a childhood summer when my parents didn't spend days volunteering at the RFS shed. It was something most families participated in, and a real strength of our rural community. My brother still volunteers with Colo Heights RFS. He is one of many Aboriginal firefighters across the nation. My parents gave me my love of the bush, and a strong sense of justice, which undoubtedly inspired me to pursue a career in environmental conservation.

At twenty years of age I secured a job with the NSW National Parks and Wildlife Service. As part of the fire-fighting responsibilities of this role, I trained as a tree-feller and remote-area fire team-member, where I was getting winched in and out of fires by helicopter. I saw some amazing places while fire-fighting. I've seen first-hand the devastation bushfires can wreak. But seeing the land around my childhood home destroyed, brought a different type of grief.

## The Aftermath

It has been one month since the fire passed through Colo Heights. Returning has been an incredibly emotional journey. With me is my partner, our two kids and their cousin who was evacuated from his home. The fire burnt from our letterbox and across most of the property. The fruit trees my Mum and Dad planted — blood plums, pears, bush lemons — all gone. A farm shed, water tanks, pipes and electricity poles, also compromised. There is so much work to do. The blackened ground is blanketed with a thick layer of dead leaves, dropped by the grandmother trees and her kin. The two-toned fallen leaf-litter suggests some leaves fell immediately after the fire, while others died and fell later.

Walking sounds like stepping on thousands of brittle eggshells. I hope if it rains, the leaf-litter slows the erosion. This Country is wounded, it's sandy and fragile. As we follow the track that meanders towards the rear of the property, we notice a pink stain on the ground and low branches. During the fire-event a water-bomber plane dropped retardant to slow the fire's spread and ferocity. Despite these efforts, many trees have been stripped bare of foliage. Prior to the bushfire, the forest canopy would have created ample shade, making dappled light along the track. This time as we walk, the stark light of the brightly overcast sky causes me to squint as I look up at the non-existent canopy. I'm hurting for those old grandmother trees with their crowns removed.

There are signs of life, though. Familiar responses of native plants to fire: nuts bursting open and setting seed, vivid epicormic growth bursting through the charred bark. Birds are calling and we see a few small animals: beetles, a huntsman spider, a cicada shell hitched to a blackened tree. Occasionally there are patches of green. But the fire has stripped away the forest kilometre after kilometre, across ridges and into gullies. There's little for larger animals to eat, drink, or places for them to live. Country is so dry, I wonder if much will survive. Country is already sick from drought; this fire adds to the illness.

Sitting quietly, we hear a large tree crashing down and echo through the gully. Another granny whose reign had ended. 'Will it grow back Mum?' my son asks. The reassuring mother he needs in the face of all this devastation, replies: 'I really hope that it'll recover, but us humans need to do better in the way we live with Country. That's why I take you and your sister to those Indigenous Fire workshops and teach you about Country'.

## Time to Listen, Time to Reflect

Returning to the bushfire site makes me reflect on all the training I received in the National Parks and Wildlife Service, and how it was founded on Western scientific methods. At the time, I was one of only two Aboriginal people working in the department locally, and there were only a handful of women in these roles. The positions I held in this department changed over the years. As I moved into heritage management and research roles, I was able to promote greater inclusion of Aboriginal women. In undertaking my PhD, I continue to empower Aboriginal perspectives in my work, specifically highlighting Aboriginal women.

Indigenous knowledge and local expertise must take precedence in the forward management of natural environments both in Australia and globally.[5] The 'State of the Environment' report argues, 'the critical importance of Indigenous land management to the ongoing maintenance of biodiversity is increasing and becoming better understood'.[6] This is true for all of Country: river and sea Country, sky Country and astronomical Country, human and non-human. Indigenous knowledge and systems provide valid models of sustainable existence.[7] The success of this requires Indigenous people and systems leading the process, and more roles for Indigenous people across environmental conservation practice, policy and research.[8] Fundamentally, however, Indigenous knowledge should not be excerpted and cropped into models that don't suit. Fire will continue to be part of our relationship with Country.[9] We need to take notice of what isn't working. Indigenous people have been contributing to debates on fire over several decades.[10] There is growing interest in Aboriginal fire knowledge. Where cultural burning has been initiated, Indigenous people experience benefits, including in the south east of the continent.[11]

The need for stronger, fairer collaboration is obvious. Indigenous and non-Indigenous people can work together. For example, my PhD research contributes to broader bushfire research through its attachment to the NSW Bushfire Risk Management Research Hub. The preliminary results of my research suggest Aboriginal women are, and wish to engage in cultural burning in NSW. The Aboriginal women I have spoken to demonstrate an awareness of gendered influences to their full participation, such as trying to gain access into a male-dominated field. The women I've spoken to also want to respect cultural protocols and fire-knowledge integrity. Perhaps the greatest outcome of my research thus far, has been the opportunity to promote and amplify that cultural burning can and should involve Aboriginal women where appropriate.

Women's engagement must be encouraged for all Indigenous caring for Country activities. There must be opportunities made for Aboriginal voices, and Aboriginal women's voices to be heard and listened to.[12] The intricate network of kinship between humans and the non-human needs to be restored to help heal Country and protect it into the future. Although regulatory frameworks are challenging, conversations about fire can provide a space to share knowledge and spark conversations about nature, risk and healing. As an Indigenous person, researcher, auntie and parent, I want us all to take better care of our Mother Earth. Future generations need Indigenous leadership in this space and many other spaces, right now.

1. P. Dudgeon and A. Bray, 'Indigenous Relationality: Women, Kinship and the Law', *Genealogy*, vol. 3, no. 2, 2019, p. 23, https://doi.org/10.3390/genealogy3020023.
2. I use 'naturally occurring native tree' to delineate between: native species that have been planted by humans that are not local indigenous species, and plants that occur naturally in that environment.
3. L. Burarrwanga, R. Ganambarr, M. Ganambarr-Stubbs, B. Ganambarr, D. Maymuru, S. Wright, S. Suchet-Pearson, K. Lloyd, *Song Spirals: Sharing Women's Wisdom of Country through Songlines*, Allen & Unwin, Crows Nest, 2019.
4. I acknowledge the labels applied to define peoples are complex and problematic. In this chapter, I use the term 'Aboriginal' to refer to Indigenous peoples who identify as being from the lands now known as NSW. I use 'Indigenous' in a national and global context.
5. J. Altman, et al., *Indigenous Cultural and Natural Resource Management Futures*, CAEPR, Canberra 2011; F. Berkes, *Sacred Ecology*, 4th edn, Routledge, New York, 2017; M. Langton, L. Palmer, and Z.M. Rhea, 'Community-Oriented Protected Areas for Indigenous people and Local Communities', in S. Stevens, ed., *Indigenous Peoples, National Parks, and Protected Areas,* University of Arizona Press, Tucson, 2014; tebrakunna country and E. Lee, 'Reset the relationship: Decolonising Government to Increase Indigenous Benefit', *cultural geographies*, vol. 26, no. 4, 2019, pp. 415–34.
6. I.D. Cresswell and H. Murphy, 'Australia State of the Environment 2016: Biodiversity', Independent report to the Australian Government Minister for the Environment and Energy, Australian Government Department of the Environment and Energy, Canberra, 2017, p. viii.
7. V. Steffensen, *Fire Country*, Hardie Grant, Melbourne, 2020.
8. K. Maclean, C.J. Robinson, and O. Costello, eds, *A National Framework to Report on the Benefits of Indigenous Cultural Fire Management*, CSIRO, Canberra, 2018; M. Adams, 'Outlier: Earth-Writing as Survival Strategy', *Griffith Review*, no. 63, 2019, online only, www.griffithreview.com/articles/outlier-earth-writing-survival. Last accessed 16 March 2020; S. Muller, S. Hemming, and Rigney, 'Indigenous Sovereignties: Relational Ontologies and Environmental Management', *Geographical Research*, vol. 57, 2019, pp. 399–410.
9. R.A. Bradstock, M.A. Gill, and J.E. Williams, *Flammable Australia: fire regimes, biodiversity and ecosystems in a changing world*, CSIRO, Canberra, 2012.
10. M. Langton, *Burning Questions: Emerging Environmental Issues for Indigenous Peoples in Northern Australia*, Centre for Indigenous Natural and Cultural Resource Management, Northern Territory University, Darwin, 1998.
11. Maclean, et. al., op. cit.; M.B. McKemey, et al., 'Cross-Cultural Monitoring of a Cultural Keystone Species Informs Revival of Indigenous Burning of Country in South-Eastern Australia', *Human Ecology*, vol. 47, 2019, pp. 893–904; T. Neale, et al., 'Walking Together: A Decolonising Experiment in Bushfire Management on Dja Dja Wurrung country', *cultural geographies*, vol. 26, no. 3, 2019, pp. 341–59; J. Weir and D. Freeman, *Fire in the South: A cross-continental exchange*, Bushfire and Natural Hazards CRC, Melbourne, 2019; and J. Weir, S. Sutton, and G. Catt, 'The Theory/Practice of Disaster Justice: Learning from Indigenous Peoples' Fire Management', in A. Lukasiewicz and C. Baldwin, eds, *Natural Hazards and Disaster Justice*, Palgrave, Singapore, 2020, pp. 299–317.
12. J. Davies, J. Walker, Y.T. Maru, 'Warlpiri Experiences Highlight Challenges and Opportunities for Gender Equity in Indigenous Conservation Management in Arid Australia', *Journal of Arid Environments*, vol. 149, 2018, pp. 40–52; C. Eriksen and D.L. Hankins, 'Colonisation and Fire: Gendered Dimensions of Indigenous Fire Knowledge Retention and Revival' in A. Coles, L. Gray and J. Momsen, eds, *The Routledge Handbook of Gender and Development*, Routledge, London, 2015, pp. 129–37.

---

An earlier version of this essay was published online as 'This Grandmother Tree Connects Me to Country', *The Conversation*, 24 January 2020.

# We Face a Tipping Point

## Helen Szoke

A tipping point is the moment when a series of small changes or incidents become significant enough to cause a sudden, larger, more important change. I wonder whether the Christmas of 2019 and early 2020 will be viewed in history as a tipping point? The combination of unseasonable weather, massive bushfires, subsequent flooding rains and, just when we thought it was time to regroup, a global COVID-19 pandemic. What has brought Australia to a pause is not a world war, not a terrorist act, but the impact of our planet's beseeching us to act differently. Will history show that this was the moment when we made decisive decisions about how to protect our planet, how to rebuild our communities, and how to chart better individual and collective paths to the future? Will history show this as a period when political leadership and community courage were truly shown?

Like so many Australians, I will remember the summer of 2019-2020 for the bushfires. In August 2019, my husband and I travelled to Noosa. Already, the fires had burnt out an area to the south, near Peregian Beach. The countryside looked tinder dry and even then there were warnings about smoke haze. But the wind blew the smoke further south and we were unaffected.

Two months later, we drove up through the north east of Victoria and the south coast of New South Wales. It was cold and windy — early November! — and the warnings about the fires seemed out of place. How could this be when it was unseasonably cold? Canberra was windy and then the trip back through Jindabyne and Kosciusko brought freezing weather, rain and then light dustings of snow as we headed through the mountains.

Yet by New Year, all of these areas were ablaze, one fire joining another. There were unprecedented images of people fleeing to beaches for safety, animals and habitat destroyed and tragically, lives lost. And just in case those of us in areas not directly hit by the bushfires thought we were spared, smoke engulfed areas hundreds of miles away, wrapping cities and coastal areas in thick, menacing haze. While we were transfixed and horrified by the images being broadcast by the ABC throughout January, I kept thinking about the compound effect. Were we at a tipping point?

At the national level, we have lacked leadership and bipartisan agreement on the climate crisis and what Australia's contribution might be to the global targets. I was a member of the Oxfam delegation at the United Nations Climate Conference (COP) in Paris in 2015 and joined the non-government sector's contribution to realising the ambition of compromise in order to get a global response. We celebrated as 197 countries, including Australia, agreed to a modest target: to aim for the global average temperature to stay well below 2 degrees Celsius above pre-industrial levels, with an effort to limit the increase to 1.5 degrees Celsius. Each country was to set its strategy, its Nationally Determined Contributions (NDCs), and be reviewed regularly.

But what did Australia then do? We lost impetus and the will to realise this ambition through successive political leadership changes, polarised debate in the country around continued production of coal, and little real or genuine leadership.

A tipping point has come. There is no chance we will reach the two degrees target by 2030, even if the world were to ramp up its activities starting right now. But we still have time to protect this planet and prevent further, unnecessary disaster. The question is, how? Have we heard the messages of our burning country, as we send smoke signals around the world to share the pain of the fires?

As we head into recovery mode from the bushfires, we are now distracted by the global pandemic. Will we think about the compounding effects locally on communities still reeling from the fires, small rural communities like Corryong and Cobargo that have already gone through periods of redefining their purpose and their reason for being? These are towns that were once thriving farming communities where, even before the impact of the fire, people were living on the margins — multi-generational farming families on one property, people who had sought to live in those communities to access low cost housing in others, and people who were off the books and living without being part of the mainstream of Australia. These are communities where the widening inequality gap that is so much the story of the world was being demonstrated in real terms. Now these communities face the challenge of redefining themselves again. Why are they there, what is their contribution, how do they deal with the short-term trauma even while thinking about how to redesign their communities, to lower the chance of facing this battle yet again in the future? Cruelly, these are the communities that are likely to feel the greatest impact of the global pandemic.

One member of a long-term Corryong farming family shared this with me via text message when I asked how he was going:

> ... just back from Corryong ... so much to do. Still seems very disjointed ... David had a portable air conditioner delivered to his house that had been burnt down and we are all struggling to get fencing materials. Lots of people on the ground offering counselling. I don't know if this is a good thing or not? ... long term view is needed. In some instances ... rebuilding should not be an option. Re-invention is needed. Over the last 30 years the district has lost so much. Snowy wind-down, mills closed, butter factory closed and banking and government jobs

removed. The void left was filled by people seeking low cost housing, thus increasing the disadvantage gap.

Since sharing this message with me in January, he has lost a brother-in-law to a heart attack experienced in response to the fires, and a young man who fought the fires has committed suicide. Compounded challenges, and tipping points for communities.

The crises bring out the best and the worst of us as a country. We have seen the incredible generosity of the Australian public, the important role of the charities working with governments. We have also seen the frustration and cynicism that challenges the role that many groups are playing. Accountability is important and somewhere in this is trusting the expertise of those who are equipped with dealing with an emergency response. Charities become the target of criticism, when so many of the gaps that people are feeling are about the channels to have services reach them, and to be clear about the type of help that is required.

Having worked with a big charity that has been part of large-scale humanitarian responses, I felt protective as the domestic charities copped criticism, and I also knew the challenges they would be facing, wedged between angry, traumatised communities and governments at local, state and national level scrambling to understand their roles, and in a space where co-operation was not a natural fit. Ironically, it is charities that are the organisations both best placed and in the current environment, best regulated, to manage this response. There is a high degree of obligation, and the ethical and regulatory frameworks exist, to let these organisations get on with what they do best and what is their expertise in a crisis. It has been said: 'Grief and Determination' are woven into the DNA of charities'.[1]

There are challenges ahead as we deal with the new horizons of need and of development, such as addressing the immediate trauma, the longer-term impacts, the spikes in mental health and domestic violence, the economic considerations. In facing these, will there be charities, government agencies and businesses that are brave enough to take a long view? Will organisations hold their nerve by waiting to make a contribution that will allow communities to redefine their futures in a way that not only helps with the climatic impacts and the threat of fire, but also the human impacts and the changing development needs of rural and regional Australia? Will we listen to the lessons of our First Nations peoples who have shown through the Indigenous ranger programs in the north of the country that the land can be better protected? Tipping points to protect our land.

And just as we are coming to grips with all of this — as the rains come to finally douse the fires, as millions of dollars have been given by the generosity of Australians to help with the recovery of communities, people and animals

— another threat arises. I think about compounding effects. COVID-19. How could we predict that not only does the planet cry for attention as it warms and burns, but a virus evolves that is so virulent that it looks like temporarily closing down the world? Compounding effects that will reach every part of Australia — and the most vulnerable communities already traumatised by the bushfires. We know that the tipping point will further exacerbate the widening inequality gap. So many communities and people, particularly women and children, have been facing this tipping point through no fault of their own for so many years and with the harshest of consequences. This tipping point is where inequality hits home the hardest — both here in Australia, impacting First Peoples and disadvantaged communities and rippling across the globe.

We will not forget the Christmas of 2019 and the start of 2020. What will be important is that we remember the lessons and respond to the challenges in a way that commits to protection of our planet, our communities and our peoples.

1. David Crosbie, https://probonoaustralia.com.au/news/2020/01/good-grief/. Accessed 24 January 2020.

# An Unequal Flame

Maithri Goonetilleke

The gentle drive from Melbourne to East Gippsland is one I know well. Each week, as I make my way to the two clinics where I work as a doctor, I look out my car windows at vast, verdant expanses. I know by heart the places where the indolent cattle and brown horses will be, or the fields where, each year, a million little canola flowers will gently burnish the landscape in a blanket of gold.

A few months ago, on my familiar journey, nothing was the same. The ferocious fires burning across the East Gippsland region choked the skies with dense, grey smoke. It was hard to see even a few metres ahead. A ghostly shroud blanketed each little hamlet through which I passed. When I finally arrived at work, I could hear the shrill alarms on the clinic roof that kept sounding because the pervasive smoke was rising into the ceilings. Over the next few weeks, I saw several patients who had lost homes, pets, livelihoods in these fires.

In the prison clinic, I sat with patients who had watched their homes burning on the prison television. In those stark images they saw not only bricks and mortar burning, but the hope of new beginnings that could emerge beyond the prison walls. In the family clinic, I met young people who were immobilised not only by grief, but also by the fear that the fires could continue to worsen every year. Sadly, the scientific consensus agrees with them.[1] The Australian climate has steadily become warmer and drier over the last hundred years, providing the perfect conditions for ever wilder, more devastating bushfires.[2]

Vulnerable and marginalised populations such as the rural poor, prisoners and Indigenous Australians are disproportionately affected by climate events.[3] This is not only due to a disproportionate loss of assets and income, but also because many of these communities are already grappling with current and historical socioeconomic and health inequities. Calamities such as the recent Australian fires serve to deepen and entrench these injustices.

The insidious amalgam of structural injustice and disasters is not unique to Australia. Eswatini, is a small, mountainous nation in Sub-Saharan Africa with a largely rural population.[4] As a doctor and public-health researcher I spent a significant part of the last fifteen years working with Indigenous health leaders and local Swazi communities in parts of the Lubombo region that have been significantly impacted by HIV. Eswatini continues to have the highest prevalence of HIV in the world despite millions of dollars being invested in individual behaviour-change programs over many decades.[5] These programs often failed to appreciate the more proximal structural factors constraining the ability of local people to modify behaviours which might reduce risk of transmission or maintain health whilst living with the disease.[6] These factors are manifold and include not only social issues such as lack of effective transport to health services, food insecurity and lack of income but also larger national and global forces such as neoliberal trade agreements which affect drug availability, structural economic adjustment of African economies, and movements of foreign aid. In Eswatini, as in so many parts of the world, 'the fire' of HIV which ravaged the nation emerged from a field of structures which have amplified and enabled its growth.

Gilles Deleuze and Felix Guattari used the rich metaphor of the 'rhizome' when describing complex systems.[7] A rhizome is a subterranean root system which is decentralised and is constantly transforming itself. A rhizomatic system is comprised of structures which are in motion and constantly articulating and disarticulating with one another. It is highly differentiated in its constituent parts whilst maintaining coherence within the system.[8] Examples of this kind of system in nature include decentralised neuronal networks in the brain or a murmuration of starlings.[9] The myriad structures which underlie the emergence of a catastrophic event are often rhizomatically organised. Moreover, these factors cannot be considered in isolation or as single entities which have linear, monogenetic links to each other. Rather they are dynamic multiplicities whose collective impact is qualitatively different from the sum of their individual parts.[10]

Catastrophic events do not occur in a void. They emerge from a sociopolitical matrix which enables and amplifies them. Be it a pandemic or an environmental disaster, these events are merely the leading edge of a rhizomatically connected system. Rather than being limited to permutations in climate or health alone, the factors within this system are inter-sectorial and derive from geopolitical, socioeconomic, biological and environmental spheres. Moreover, the severity and distribution of harms felt across a population by a climate event at a given moment in time are also shaped by the rhizomatic connections between that event and a host of current and historical inequities.

Commensurate with calls for climate action must be the recognition and amelioration of socio-economic inequity across the population. The fires of climate change will touch us all, but due to a myriad of inter-sectorial, rhizomatic connections, it is the vulnerable and marginalised among us who will feel their effects most intensely. Inequities that are exacerbated by climate events remain insolvent when we do not understand the ontological multiplicity that underpins their origins and augments their harms.

1. I. Parise, 'A Brief Review of Global Climate Change and the Public Health Consequences', *Australian Journal of General Practice*, vol. 47, no. 7, 2018, 451–6.
2. R. Garnaut, *The Garnaut Climate Change Review*, Cambridge University Press, Cambridge, 2008.
3. J. Altman and K. Jordan, 'Impact of Climate Change on Indigenous Australians: Submission to the Garnaut Climate Change Review'; and Parise, op. cit.
4. UNAIDS, 'Country factsheets Eswatini', 2017, http://www.unaids.org/en/regionscountries/countries/swaziland, 2017. Last accessed 2 August 2020.
5. AVERT Global information and Education on HIV and AIDS, 'HIV and AIDS in Eswatini', https://www.avert.org/professionals/hiv-around-world/sub-saharan-africa/swaziland. Last accessed 2 August 2020.
6. J. Hickel, 'Neoliberal Plague: The Political Economy of HIV transmission in Swaziland', *Journal of Southern African Studies,* vol. 38, no. 3, 2012, pp. 513–29.
7. G. Deleuze, and F. Guattari, *A Thousand Plateaus: Capitalism and Schizophrenia*, Bloomsbury Publishing, 1988; and K. Robinson, *Deleuze, Whitehead, Bergson: Rhizomatic Connections*, Springer, 2008.
8. Ibid.
9. P. Patton, *Deleuze and the Political*, Routledge, London & New York, 2002.
10. I. Buchanan, 'Deleuze and cultural studies', *The South Atlantic Quarterly,* vol. 96, no. 3, 1997, p. 483.

# FIRE PLACE

## Catherine Larkins

It was New Year's Eve 2019, my 66th birthday. A carefully planned escape route from the south side of my home to the ocean shoreline took less than five minutes to traverse. The vast waters of Bass Strait were to be our fire refuge. Burnt gum leaves rained endlessly into the sea turning the white sands of the Ninety Mile Beach black as apocalyptic skies to the east, west and north encroached. Our survival was now at the mercy of the wind.

'Stay and Defend' is deeply etched into my family DNA. My father Alex Larkins survived the 1939 fires in Warburton, was appointed to the first position as CFA Regional Officer for East Gippsland and in the 1960s became Chief Officer of the CFA for Victoria. My maternal grandfather Sir Albert Lind was MP for East Gippsland for forty-five years, installing the first Fire Spotting Towers for Victoria in Gippsland. My brother Greg Larkins (dec.) received both the National Medal for Service to Fire and the rarely awarded and prestigious Australian Fire Service medal for his outstanding life service in East Gippsland and beyond. He and his crack Nowa Nowa fire crew became heroes when they saved Wilsons Promontory in the early 1990s.

But this 2019 fire threat was like no other. Drought had ravaged the bush and farmland. Rivers had stopped flowing months earlier and weather patterns were unprecedented. It was a fire season that would call on all those learned, practical, survival skills passed down to me from my family. Not only was my current family home at Lake Tyers Beach threatened, so too was my previous home at Clifton Creek, an hour's drive to the north west. This extraordinary 1970s mud brick home was being defended by my son, and my daughter (and her partner) working alongside their Dad. He was an aptly named 'hot shot' firefighter who had experienced extreme wildfire action for decades. Two hours' drive to the east in Mallacoota, my partner's home and the homes of many dear friends were also in the firing line as fire fronts joined to generate a holocaust of an unfathomable scale. In the hours and days to follow, my generational homes and those of my friends were furiously attacked at random. Many were engulfed and decimated by 'The Beast' as people were cast mercilessly into a state of homelessness.

In Gippsland, catastrophic bushfires are just one of many traumatic events that have impacted the 'home' lands, culture and wellbeing of our First Peoples. For them, being homeless through dispossession is a starkly familiar world, but for the non-Indigenous community a previously unimaginable state of homelessness was assumed through an uncanny reckoning.

Before colonisation Gippsland was the ancestral home of the Gunai-Kurnai people. Since colonisation it has also become 'home' to many more First Peoples who were forcibly moved from their 'home' lands into Aboriginal Missions. As a child growing up at my current generational home at Lake Tyers Beach, I was living near the Lake Tyers Mission. It was the late 1950s and I was to bear witness to a time of appalling racial discrimination and unthinkable treatment of Aboriginal people. For most non-Indigenous Australians the plight of First Peoples was out of sight and therefore out of mind. I was fortunate to have parents who welcomed Aboriginal people into our home. At this time the Assimilation Policy brutally threw Aboriginal people off the Missions to survive in the non-Indigenous world by whatever means. Homes were not an option, so they lived in bush camps hidden in the forest. My brother and I played and roamed freely in the bush, often visiting the bush camps of our Aboriginal friends. Cultural understandings were shared and nurtured between families. All our parents encouraged respect and friendship, a friendship that is ongoing and greatly treasured to this day.

In the early 1970s, I discovered my passion for art and attended Art School in Central Gippsland's Latrobe Valley. At this time the homes of Yallourn were being demolished as a once beautiful town was ruthlessly dug up and transformed into a massive open cut mine. Morwell Briquette Factory and Hazelwood Power Station (both now defunct) were monumental, smoke belching factories. Whilst daily exposure to this monstrous industrial landscape held some level of fascination, it also left a heavy visual imprint on the creative soul of every art student.

Many years later my visual imprint from life in 'The Valley' was re-awakened. The trigger was the catastrophic 2009 Black Saturday bushfires. Their magnitude generated an arts-led recovery project called *Illuminated by Fire* initiated by Regional Arts Victoria. I was one of ten artists commissioned to make a major work about fire for the 2011 Melbourne Light in Winter Festival. The concept for *Fire Place* was generated from my memories of the Morwell Briquette Factory and the bizarre phenomenon whereby chimneys are left standing after houses burn down. Working collaboratively with Gunai Monaro artist Frances Harrison, Bidawal cultural adviser Lennie Hayes and the broader community of Lakes Entrance, a cross-cultural story of fire was created.[1]

---

1. All three artists were recognised in the 2020 Queen's Birthday Honours, with the award of OAM.

**Fire Place is explained as follows:**

*Fire is integral to human existence. Our dependency on fire or even the illusion of fire is a comfort we cannot do without. At the heart of a modern home is the fireplace, a structure for containing fire, the giver of warmth and comfort. The unique architectural features of the fireplace — the chimney, mantelpiece and hearth are powerful symbols of our civilized society.*

*The GunaiKurnai people say that the Fire Tail Finch brought fire to their country thousands of years ago on its tail; a vibrant red patch of feathers on its rump is testimony to this feat. A flock of beautifully hand-painted finches circle the briquette chimney, overlaying an ancient story onto an iconic symbol of modern architecture. The chimney is built from briquettes, 15 million year old blocks of compacted coal from Gippsland's pre-historic forests. These are the last of the domestic briquettes made in Morwell's briquette factory in the early 1970s. Firing the furnaces of the Latrobe Valley power stations, coal brought the first electric fires to our lounge rooms, electric stoves to our kitchens,*

Above: *The Bush Lounge Room* 2011 Sculpture Installation by Catherine Larkins in collaboration with Frances Harrison (Gunai Monaro), Lennie Hayes (Gunai Bidawal) and the community of Lakes Entrance Lake Tyers Beach

Left: *Fire Place* 2011 Sculpture Installation by Catherine Larkins in collaboration with Frances Harrison (Gunai Monaro), Lennie Hayes (Gunai Bidawal) and the community of Lakes Entrance. *Illuminated by Fire* was a project by Regional Arts Victoria for Light in Winter, Federation Square Melbourne.

*briquette hot water and a myriad of other life-changing conveniences. Then, in an horrific twist of fate, our best friend became our worst enemy. Wildfires were ignited by power lines and driven by the ravages of climate change, incinerating our landscapes and homes. Ironically, often all that remains is the architectural monolith of civilization, the chimney.*

*Fire Place is a cultural overlay. Surfaces are transformed into a stunning canvas of stories from GunaiKurnai country about the timeless cycles of fire. The viewer is invited into a familiar space where the modern-day sits with the ancient-past. The* Fire Place *Installation includes a kangaroo skin couch with boomerang arms. A retro TV cabinet embellished with traditional hot wire burning screens Koori campfire footage. A briquette chimney encircled by firebirds houses a fireplace with a pseudo-electric log fire. Guarding the 'home' is a spirit dog, a Mirrigarn adorned with a hand-painted cloak of ochre.*

# Where is the Light? Black Saturday Speaks to Black Summer

## Arnold Zable

A month after the 2009 Black Saturday fires, I received a call from Sharron Batt, a librarian at the Alexandra library. Over the years I had run writing workshops in the library, and I'd come to know it as a community hub, a place to meet, a space for stories. During the fires, Alexandra had become a place of refuge, and the campground, a site for displaced people. There were survivors coming to the library, anxious to tell their stories and to express their grief and longing for what had been, what they had lost, their fears for the future. Sharron's call inspired the 'Black Saturday: Telling the Stories' project.[1] In the following 20 months, I visited six towns impacted by the fires and spent a full day, once a month, for up to six visits in each place. I conducted workshops in the morning for an ongoing group of writers, and recorded stories in the afternoons told by those who wished to recount them orally.

The workshops became a space of camaraderie and shared purpose, where people could talk — or remain silent — without judgement. The fires had brought us together and we learnt from each other. We witnessed intense shifts in mood, from bouts of despair to unexpected surges of elation, and came to respect each other's fluctuating responses.

I kept a journal of my visits in which I recorded my reactions to the stories, and to the changing landscape as I drove up in the early mornings and returned in the evening. On the first day of the project I wrote:

*Left Melbourne in pre-dawn dark for Alexandra ... A brooding sunrise of crimsons and dark clouds hover over the Great Divide shading into bands of glowing pale greys, the drama heightened by the black outlines of the mountains ... I am driving into Black Saturday country, charred trees by the roadside, some clad from top to bottom in coats of newly grown leaves. Epicormic growth, 'an emergency reaction', G was to tell me later. 'Nature's stop-gap measure to keep the trees alive ...'*

*The first workshop dictates its own course. The grief is palpable beneath the stoic surface. Life can never be the same is the overriding sentiment: the shadow will always linger. B speaks of being drawn to the forests, her special place, a kind of dreaming. 'This is where my spirituality lies', she writes. 'And this is where the loss is immediate'. M recalls, 'trees bending almost double'. G recreates the onslaught, the fence posts 'like burning candles'. He is facing the blazing mountains like Don Quixote, one man with a mop against the fire's fury ...*

Returning home that evening: *I drive in the descending dark after seven straight hours of listening, deluged by memories of startling images. I think of S, now returned to his music-making, living each day as it comes, befriending the outsiders in the campground, and his modest, unassuming wisdom. 'We look out for each other. I now live for the moment', he says. 'I have returned to my creativity'.*

*S has come to know the paradox: the song, and the line, that come to me as I wind through the forests in the rain and against the fogged lights of the oncoming cars, is of Janis Joplin singing* Freedom's Just Another Word for Nothing Left to Lose. *This is the gift I have received for my first day, in return for making my way to and from the mountains.*

A collective poem could be composed of the images that flared up in the recorded stories and workshops. Of cotton threads of ash, with trees like fallen angels, of twisted branches viewed against the skies after the long-gone fury. Of the deathly roar that rose from the eerie silence like a stampede of cattle coming over the mountain, the whooshing sound of gas bottles venting like flame-throwers, punctuated by abrupt explosions, and the silver snake-trail that had once been an aluminium ladder.

Of the balls of fire coming off the mountain, like someone was saying: 'Here mate, I got this one for you, catch it'. Of a house, one moment fully alive in glorious colour, and the next engulfed in flames, the colour draining, and the house transformed into a black-and-white negative before imploding into ashes.

A collective novel could be shaped out of the tales of epic battles to save a life, an entire community, fights unto utter exhaustion and beyond. The novel would be driven by an intensity I had rarely witnessed, by the image of the young man, recounting his story with his entire being, his face lit up, his senses fully alert, the words spurting out as his hands inscribe the details. 'It was frightening mate, frightening'. He was back there in the lead up to the fires, trying to keep cool in the furnace of a forty-degree day. 'I had no idea', he says. 'Then the roar, and I am running through the flames, whole paddocks exploding'.

A memoir might be shaped around one dramatic moment: of a woman sitting at the wheel of her car — behind her, visible in the rear-vision mirror, a wall of flame, her house burning — and in front of her, a wall of fire, a swathe of forest blazing. And she is thinking: the windscreen is so hot it's going to explode and damage my eyes. She closes her eyes, puts her foot down on the accelerator, and comes out on the other side. Alive.

There is enough black humour for a stand-up comic — the exhausted folks standing about on the oval that had secured their lives, the town exploding around them. The cricket club-house is burning. 'Never liked the old club anyhow', someone says. 'The curtains were awful anyway', adds a clubmate. And they all fall about laughing.

Several months after the fires, I am driving through a forest of blackened trees on the way to Flowerdale. The rising sun filters through the bare branches, clumps of leaves, a green halo of new growth. And I am thinking: you can wound a tree, you can traumatise it, but it takes a lot to kill it. Yet many trees *were* killed, people who had lived here for many years would later tell me. But a tree can be resurrected in unexpected ways. The people of Flowerdale commissioned a logo to commemorate the fires. On the day it was launched, three months after the fires, the community came together. Weeks later, Odette Hunter drove down to Melbourne to Vic Market Tattoos. She would never have imagined applying a tattoo before the fires. Odette wept and told her story as 21-year-old tattoo artist, Olivia Brumen, applied the logo.

Odette rolls up her sleeve and shows me the image: the stark black outline of a tree, with one green leaf protruding from the trunk. Olivia invited people affected by the fires to have the logo tattooed for free. Many accepted the offer. Some have it on their heart, others on their hands and forearms, another on her ankle in the form of a bracelet. They call themselves 'The Tree People'. The bond between them can never be broken.

In the depths of the second winter, eighteen months after the fires, a melancholic mood enveloped one of the workshops — a reflection perhaps of the winter cold and the dark clouds that hung low above the hamlet. There was bitterness over the allocation of grants, disputes with authorities, an air of resignation. We let it be. And we let it out. We had all learnt to sit with trauma.

'Where is the light?' someone asked. We wrote the words down. It became our heading for the day. With each story read out aloud after the writing period was over the cloud lifted a little higher: tales of weekly meetings in a pottery shed where friends spun their conversations and released their emotions as they turned the potter's wheel. Of a woman who returned home to her devastated town to learn that her house had been saved by friends. Of a town band composed of pots and pans, allowing survivors to beat out their frustrations. Of the fortnightly meal where the residents gathered to create 'a casserole of community' and to find solace in each other's company.

There were nuggets of hard-gained wisdom: reflecting back on the day of the fires, P realised that, 'I learnt a lot about survival, about human capacity. Knowing that no one's coming to save you, so you had to make a stand. I learnt about the second, third and fourth wind. About the will to live. No way I'm going to burn. We live. We live. We live', he had chanted.

Her township remained her paradise, said L, 'A place where humanity and nature walk hand in hand, teeming with life'. She speaks of the need to be with people who went through it. 'City folks tend to say, six months after the fires, "why don't you just get on with it", or even, "get over it"'. She writes a moving piece that resonates strongly with all present: 'Something has been taken away. It could be a simple object, a swing, a cubby house that once stood in the yard, or the memory of the woman in her apron who would walk down the drive to get her mail. In the place of that memory there is now an empty lot. Even now there are times when I feel great anger at the fire'.

Yes, there is no simple resolution, no neat ending. But time passes. On Thursday 7 February 2019, towards the end of the Black Summer, and ten years after the Black Saturday fires, I am on the road to Flowerdale, invited by the community for their memorial service. Black and green are still the colours that flank my way as I curve up the mountain. The late-afternoon sun lights the forests, spot-lighting eucalypt leaves the colour of jade, the white trunks of dead gums, and a row of trees lined up on the heights, side-by-side, like silver sentinels guarding the ridge tops.

It is one of those moments when it all comes together — the beauty of the community I am about to revisit, the profound sadness of their loss, and the compassion and resilience that had shepherded their recovery. And the love they had shown me, as they had shown each other. I have received the gift of their welcoming. And of the paradox: *Freedom's just another word for nothing left to lose.*

---

1. 'The Black Saturday, Telling the Story' project was administered by the Alexandra Library, and Writers Victoria, and funded by the Grace Wilson Trust.

---

# Bushfires in the Land of My Birth and in the Country I have Chosen

## Lionel Bopage

I grew up in Sri Lanka and have maintained a close connection with my homeland since coming to Australia in 1990. I am deeply concerned with issues of social justice and, along with many others, have worked — and continue to work vigorously — to support a process of social change that will bring reconciliation and a fair and equitable distribution of wealth to all people in that country. There are both differences and similarities between Australia and Sri Lanka. Australia is a wealthy country and, fortunately, has been able to avoid large-scale violent social conflict. However, there are also inequities here, and there is widespread social injustice. Another area of concern that is shared between the two countries is the destruction of the environment and its long-term devastating effects.

My first experience of a bushfire was in 1968, when I was still a university student. A hilltop in the Hantana mountain range in Kandy had been set on fire to catch wild animals. The entire hilltop was charred as a result of this human-made fire. Since that time, wildfires in Sri Lanka have become more frequent in many areas of the dry zone. Massive forest fires break out in the mountain ranges burning forests into ashes, and large resources are deployed to douse the flames.

Historically, forest fires in Sri Lanka were comparatively small with relatively short burning periods. Most were surface fires with crown fires being rare. The fires in forest plantations and grasslands rarely posed a threat to human life or property or health. Traditional knowledge and farming practices were based on a deep respect for the fragility of the natural environment and limited the extent and effects of any fires that did occur. However, all that has now changed. Human intervention has greatly exacerbated the risks.[1] Pine plantations are pyrophytic and, being grown on steep slopes of the central highlands, create a strong fire hazard. The plantations pose a threat to the natural springs, making the soil barren. Guinea grass — the most fire-prone of the grasses introduced to Sri Lanka as cattle fodder years ago — has now invaded almost every forest. Dry and windy weather conditions combined with flammable grass cause fires to spread quickly.

Using fire for forest clearing has become more frequent. Human-made forest fires have doubled, causing immense short-term damage to human settlements, flora and fauna and long-term impacts on the ecozone.[2] Fires linked to poaching, finding fodder for cattle, and accidents such as flinging cigarette butts are common. Some forests are set on fire for hunting and preventing incursions of wildlife into village perimeters. Despicably, some people set fire to the hills just prior to the rainy season so that the rain will wash the sand and deposit it in the streams at the foot of the hills, so that it can be collected and sold. Despite legal prohibition of this practice, hardly anyone is arrested for forest-fire related offences. But even so, all too often they avoid prosecution through devious, often corrupt, means.

Despite the great differences between society and culture and the climatic and geographical conditions in Sri Lanka and Australia, there are also some striking similarities. In Australia too, the risk of wildfires has greatly increased as a result of human intervention, or more properly, interventions associated with the colonial culture. Traditionally, the Indigenous people of Australia used 'cultural burning' as a means of rejuvenating and nurturing the land. Cultural burns were carried out on a smaller scale using minimal equipment during misty mornings or late afternoons, while carefully monitoring that such fires will not get out of control. Cultural burning dealt with right moisture and weather conditions so that burning fires are hot enough to consume lots of dry fuel, but not to exceeding levels of hotness so as to make the control of fires impossible. Such burns cleaned out invasive plants beneath the main forest canopies leaving the canopies unharmed. This careful approach assisted the growth of native grasses, herbs and different habitats, which entice a variety of flora and fauna.[3]

The shift from customary land-conservation practices to the colonial and capitalist commitment to the exploitation of environment combined with more recent global forces, has made Australia the most fire-prone continent on earth. The recent bushfires have burnt around 21 per cent of Australia's forest (excluding Tasmania). Several firefighters have lost their lives and thousands of homes and properties were destroyed. An estimated 1.25 billion animals (native and others) have perished.[4] The long-term damage to the country's sensitive ecosystems, the deleterious effect on the community psyche and the psychological impacts on thousands of individuals and their families are unfathomable.

On the face of it, Australia and Sri Lanka face vastly different geographical and climatic conditions, in the contexts of different histories and cultures. However, the underlying causes of the increased occurrence of fires in both Sri Lanka and Australia are global and systematic, combining both distinctive local phenomena and common global ones. Similarly, the responses to the fire threat in both countries show both similarities and key differences.

In Sri Lanka, some traditional practices for fire containment are still employed. Peripheral or internal firebreaks around plantations are commonly established. Cultivation of hemp, which does not catch fire easily, is considered a means of countering fires. Drawing on local cultures, forest user-groups are now involved in a new participatory style of management. Sharing the benefits of a forest with the communities appears to have improved the sharing of communal responsibilities. This has allowed greater co-ordination between agricultural and forestry activities. Local communities are given fire-control training and material incentives. These are some welcomed positive measures. However, co-ordination among diverse authorities responsible for forest fire management, adoption of organised approaches for incident control, and investments in research programs are still needed.

In Australia, the recent fire storms have demonstrated the futility of adopting fuel reduction as a tool of forest fire management. Fuel reduction burns undertaken since the 1980s have been found ineffective in reducing the intensity of uncontrollable fires. Extreme temperatures and high winds have helped even a negligible amount of fuel to produce an unsuppressible high-intensity fire. A lack of political leadership, according to which the matter of land- and fire-management is taken as merely an economic, cost-benefit analytic exercise has prolonged and exacerbated the risks. Against this, there is emerging, even if it is still in an early form, a renewed consciousness of the customary wisdom of the first occupants of the land. There is a renewed awareness of the need for emissions control and of the responsibility of Australians to advocate for this on a global scale.[5] The full effect of the shock of the recent events, however, remains to be seen and whether there is capacity in Australian culture to effect the deep change in the relationship to the environment that is required to avoid a repetition of this catastrophe remains to be seen.

What are the lessons that we can learn from the experiences of the two countries? In both, forests and their natural resources have played an important role in preserving environmental balance and, in both, natural bushfires have played an integral part in the forest life-cycle, clearing up the dried forest material and creating a rich nourishing environment for wildlife and fresh flora. However, in both also, economic development linked to capitalist culture have led to widespread devastation of the natural landscape and a greatly increased risk of further destruction. And both are affected by the global changes in climate, with the drier and harsher conditions increasing vulnerability to major environmental and ecological disasters.

Learning the lessons from the new conditions is proving difficult. Reintroduction of customary land management practices, such as early dry-season burning, could bring significant environmental and economic benefits.[6] Ongoing community support, sharing of information and resources, professional and volunteers' assistance, social cohesion and sense of belonging would help lower levels of psychological distress. However, the real challenge, of effecting lasting, deep social change in both countries, including the introduction of new, more equitable, cultural and economic structures, and extending these to the global level, is proving much more elusive.

While the geography and the cultures are different, ultimately the similarities are greater than the differences. With climate change becoming more prominent, prevalent, and intensive, both societies need to explore ways to mitigate risks due to natural calamities. In both, the destruction of customary cultures and their displacement by an industrial capitalist system that has little regard for the value and fragility of the natural environment, first in local and then in global settings, is a common process that unifies the experience of the two countries. This means that, despite the differences, the solutions will be closely aligned too: in both settings there is a need for a revaluing of nature, a rediscovery of traditional practices, the establishment of a global agreement on emissions controls, and a continuing struggle for social justice.

---

1. *Ceylon Today*, 'Adding Fuel to Wildfire', 25 August 2019, https://ceylontoday.lk/columns-more/715. Viewed 12 March 2020.
2. *Daily FT*, 'The Tragedy of the Ongoing Fires in the Ella Rock Region in Sri Lanka and Amazon Rainforest', 24 Aug 2019, http://www.ft.lk/other-sectors/The-tragedy-of-the-ongoing-fires-in-the-Ella-Rock-region-in-Sri-Lanka-and-Amazon-rainforest/57-684485. Viewed 12 March 2020.
3. L. Russell, 'Indigenous Knowledge Must Be Brought into the Bushfires Conversation', 8 January 2020, https://lens.monash.edu/@politics-society/2020/01/08/1379433/bringing-indigenous-knowledge-into-the-bushfires-conversation. Last viewed 12 March 2020.
4. Lisa Cox, 'Unprecedented Globally: More than 20% of Australia's Forests Burnt in Bushfires', *The Guardian*, 25 Feb 2020, https://www.theguardian.com/australia-news/2020/feb/25/unprecedented-globally-more-than-20-of-australias-forests-burnt-in-bushfires. Last viewed 12 March 2020.
5. D. Chow, 'Australia Wildfires Unleash Millions of Tons of Carbon Dioxide', NBC *News*, https://www.nbcnews.com/science/environment/australia-wildfires-unleash-millions-tons-carbon-dioxide-n1120186. Last viewed 12 March 2020.
6. J.G. Pausas and J.E. Keeley, 'Wildfire as an Ecosystem Service', *Frontiers in Ecology and the Environment*, vol. 17, no. 5, 2019, pp. 289–95.

# Mortalities

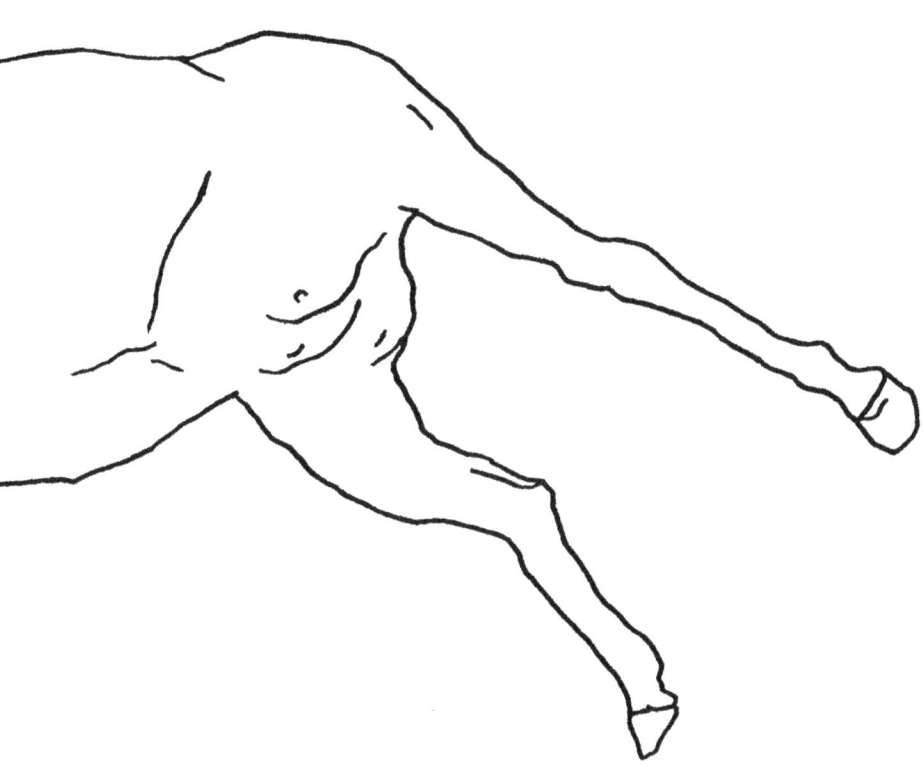

12.02.20
It started with rain.
The drive from Tumut to Tumbarumba was black in landscape with burnt trees and green shoots.
Large black trees were marked with big white crosses. Dead carcasses lined the road while workers in fluorescent vests were fixing the fences.

Text & Drawing • Hugo Muecke

# Water, Fire, and Ashes

Kieran Donaghue

'The sea! the sea! the open sea! The blue, the fresh, the ever free!'[1]

My father would invariably recite these lines as we came within reach of the ocean at Bermagui. Usually we'd drive from Canberra in the late afternoon, through Cooma and the old wool township of Nimmitabel, to the steep descent of Brown Mountain. Except in occasional times of drought, the Bega Valley would be green and lush, a striking contrast to the weathered colours and sparse vegetation of the tablelands. We would take the Princes Highway north until we reached the small village of Cobargo, then turn off to the coast. In those days the road to Bermagui was only partly sealed, and Dad would twist and turn the car to avoid the deep ruts. Impatient, I would urge him to speed up, but my pleas would make no impression on his stolid broad back and balding head.

In summer when we arrived, daylight still lingered; in winter, night would have fallen. But regardless of the season, the sound of the waves rolling in and smell of salt in the moist air would awaken in me feelings of freedom and adventure.

As a lover of the German language, I now regularly watch the television news from Germany through the Internet. Items on Australia are rare, and often when this country does feature it's just incidental, for example when a German tennis player has success at the Australian Open. On the occasions when Australia itself becomes newsworthy the report is usually of a natural disaster, with brief footage of tracts of land under water or bushland on fire. The Australian voices partially audible beneath the German translations often sound raw and rough, adding to the impression of a land where nature is overwhelming and human beings and their culture are fighting a losing battle.

So it was with the recent bushfires — but with some important differences. The first difference was that the fires were the top German news story for days at a time, with extensive footage and lengthy interviews. Another difference concerned the places that were featured, the coastal townships and villages that in my mind are so closely associated with carefree, happy times. But to me the most important difference was the shock of recognition as the camera showed the bridge we used to cross as we entered Cobargo before making the sharp right turn to Bermagui. The camera did not make this turn; it went straight on into the town, panning from side to side, showing destroyed buildings where we'd sometimes stopped for a cup of coffee or bought something superfluous because we were on holiday.

The camera then turned its gaze to a group of angry residents, picking out a young woman looking disdainfully at an awkward middle-aged man, his hand outstretched, the scene overlaid by a concise explanation in German of the woman's reluctance to shake the hand of the Australian Prime Minister. I was impressed by this woman's refusal to be used as a political prop, and I wondered what the German viewers would make of her.

Three people died as a result of the Cobargo fire: a father and son defending the family home, and an elderly man who died from burns after being transferred to a Sydney hospital. Many people lost their home or their business. For me, Cobargo will never again be just that little cluster of old buildings where you turn off the Princes Highway and head towards the sea.

My first close acquaintance with the destructive force of bushfires was on 18 January 2003. I can well remember the eerie atmosphere on that Saturday as a dark pall of smoke spread over Canberra, intensifying as the day progressed. We knew that fires had been burning during the previous week in the Brindabella Range to our west, but we were not prepared for these fires to join forces and launch a concerted assault on the city. In the middle of the afternoon I was standing in the semi-darkness with my eighteen-year-old son Toshio, looking out to the mountains, when suddenly we saw jagged flames leaping into the sky. Toshio asked whether we should be worried and I mumbled an evasive answer.

In no time, McQuoids Hill in our immediate vicinity was alight, then Mount Taylor to our east. The first embers appeared, tossed in the swirling wind. I was on the roof of the house, cleaning the gutters of leaves, when an emergency-services vehicle sped up the street and an amplified voice ordered everyone to evacuate. We quickly grabbed our cat Cello and a few valuables, got in the car, and left. The next three hours in the evacuation centre, not knowing whether our house was still standing, were a mixture of extreme anxiety and disbelief.

Around seven o'clock that evening we were finally allowed to return home. Traffic lights were not functioning and the scene was uncanny, with cars tentatively feeling each other out before proceeding through intersections. I was reluctant to turn into our street, fearing what we might find, but thankfully the house was intact. As I sat in the car trying to put my relief into words there was a loud bang, and once I got over my shock I confidently announced that it must be a gas tank exploding. Toshio countered that it was just the car door; he'd opened it too vigorously and slammed it against one of the steel uprights of the carport.

Memories of 2003 were at the front of our minds this summer. My wife Mariko and I had been in Hobart and returned on New Year's Day to a city shrouded in acrid smoke. But while the smoke continued to blanket Canberra for several weeks, it appeared the city would be spared the catastrophic impacts the fires were having elsewhere. But at the end of the month a fire broke out at Orroral Valley in the Namadgi National Park to the city's south and quickly reached 'out of control' status.

In 2003 we'd been ignorant of the seriousness of the threat until the fire struck, but this time we were all too aware of what might happen. Mariko sat glued to the computer and the radio, relaying to me every piece of advice offered on the ABC and every change in the alert level announced on the ACT Emergency Services Agency website. A large container with our important documents sat ready to be carried to the car, and bags with necessary clothing for several days were packed. We no longer had to worry about Cello. He died in 2013, after a long life of almost nineteen years.

Tidbinbilla Nature Reserve lies to Canberra's south-west. It was extensively burnt in 2003, and now it was under direct threat from the rapidly spreading Namadgi fire. The 2003 fire had taken an enormous toll on Tidbinbilla's animal population, and we were relieved to hear on the radio that this time the animals that are part of the Reserve's threatened species recovery program were being relocated. Animals moved to safety included small populations of endangered eastern bettongs (rat kangaroos) and brush-tailed rock wallabies, a breeding population of Northern Corroboree frogs (tiny creatures with striking black and yellow markings), the reserve's captive koalas and several platypuses.

The Namadgi fire burnt with enormous ferocity through 85,000 hectares of bushland, including 80 per cent of the Namadgi National Park. It menaced the township of Tharwa and Canberra's southernmost suburbs for several days, but did not reach the city. Just over 20 per cent of Tidbinbilla was burnt.

Tidbinbilla is a beautiful place. It has a quality of stillness and silence that invites reflection and instils peace. It is a special place for Mariko and me for this reason. It is also special for us because it was in Tidbinbilla that we scattered Toshio's ashes after his death in February 2010. Every subsequent year on Toshio's anniversary we have laid flowers from our garden on the unassuming spot where his ashes were spread, and Mariko has poured a cup of hot coffee on the ground in memory of his love of coffee.

On Toshio's anniversary this year Tidbinbilla was still closed as a result of the fire, so we will have to find another time to visit, perhaps the anniversary of the August day when we scattered his ashes. Hopefully by then all the animals that were moved to safety will have been returned.

---

1. From 'The Sea' by Bryan Waller Procter (pseudonym Barry Cornwall), 1787–1874.

# Signs but No Wonder

Lorraine Shannon

**6 January 2020**

My concentration is in tatters. I'm in the garden filling buckets with water, preparing for falling embers. Tears spill down my cheeks as the heart-stopping whump-whump of helicopter blades thunder overhead. Sirens shriek in the distance and my 'Fires Near Me' app blips yet again. I stumble about, trip on the hose, drench myself, curse and curse again. What other language is there in these circumstances? I grope for words but feel as if ash has invaded my core; silenced me.

All I have left are wretched sobs. How has our country arrived at a place like this: a place where a billion animals have perished horribly; where dreams and connections are shattered, the fabric of matter torn apart? How is it we ignored all the signs of what was to come? No wonder words have lost their substance. I ask myself, are we no longer able to listen and respond to the touch of the earth; to know that our interior world is folded in the earth, that each calls the other into existence; that our lives and the lives of other animals are intertwined? I ask myself are there tears pure enough to clear a pathway through the smoke? Words that can wash ash from the soul?

My neighbour leans over the hedge and comments laconically, 'Country's a bloody shambles, eh?' Silent, I nod helplessly.

Back inside, the phrase 'bloody shambles' echoes around in my head. Why does it resonate so strongly? In a rush, my mind returns to student days, to studying Pepys' *The Great Fire of London*. Admittedly, not a fire such as those engulfing the Blue Mountains heritage area where I live, but a city fire that started mundanely in a bakery. It burnt a large proportion of London's houses, but with little loss of human life. So why the 'bloody shambles'? This, I recall, was literally the name for streets where animals were slaughtered in the open air: the detritus such as guts, offal and blood were thrown into a gutter in the middle of the street — which is why we still refer to a mess as a shambles.

We have no records of how many animals died in the Great Fire of London although we do know that a great many animals were in the city. Thousands of cattle and pigs were brought there to live before being slaughtered and sold for meat. Great flocks of geese were kept for their feather quills, along with caged rabbits and poultry. Calves, deer and sheep were herded into the markets, destined to become leather, tallow and wool. Although Pepys pays scant attention to the fate of these animals in his writing, others were more vocal, describing animals panicking and running amok through the streets, traumatised by overcrowding and the sight of the shambles. Brother Jonathan wrote that, 'The scenes of cruelty here practised by the drivers towards the cattle and pigs, are of the most shocking kind'.[1]

Today, we do have records of how many animals have died in the bushfires although many more will undoubtedly perish from smoke inhalation and stress. Many animals are also known to lose the young they are carrying when under stress, while some of our native species may starve despite human efforts to provide on-going sustenance until the bush regenerates.

News and social media worldwide have exploded the silence around animal suffering in bushfires. For me, the most potent and moving image is the photograph that went viral on the Internet of a koala mourning a dead companion.[2] But it is not only native animals who are suffering and dying. Belinda Attree, a farmer in the Nariel Valley in Victoria's north was quoted by the ABC, saying, 'We had cows with calves at foot. Their teats are all burnt and they can't feed their calves ... walking these cows down to the yard — there were calves just dropping, falling down and not able to walk, we were having to go back and shoot them'.[3]

My own grief pales into insignificance. Unlike koalas, and other free roaming species who have survived, I am not living among the dead. Unlike domesticated cattle and sheep, I do not have to witness my kin lying dead around me, or shot before my eyes as the only solution under the circumstances.

> We find such scenes are confronting. And yet ...
> (there is always an 'and yet'.)

Are we sufficiently moved to change the stories we tell ourselves about animal lives, loves and grief? Are we capable of a change of heart, one that would see us attempting to establish a new eros (as Freya Mathews has suggested in *For Love of Matter*, 2003), a mode of relating to others, human and otherwise that is enlivening and dialogical rather than objectifying and dominating.[4]

Certainly, for Pepys and the majority of his fellow Londoners, the answer was no. The Smithfield market continued until the 1850s, although there were some who refused to be silent. In Dickens' *Great Expectations*, set in the 1820s, young Pip encounters the market, which he describes: 'the shameful place, being all asmear with filth and fat and blood and foam seemed to stick to me'.[5] Others wrote pamphlets, raised the matter in Parliament and eventually slaughtering was moved from Smithfield to a purpose built slaughterhouse.

Surely, if we fail to honour the animal deaths and grief that surround us now, we perpetuate the indifference to cruelty displayed at the markets in Pepys' era. If we continue to tell ourselves stories of 'livestock' rather than animal families, if we continue our stories of necessary commercial progress and ignore the human impact on the homes of native animals, we lose the possibility of a shared vocabulary of empathy, outrage and compassion, a vocabulary that despite our feelings of helplessness, refuses to collude with the silence of denial.

Generally we have paid little regard to the grief that animals can experience. It is considered of less import than human grief. Bowlby described human grief as, 'A peculiar amalgam of anxiety, anger and despair following the experience of what is feared to be an irretrievable loss ... ', and he differentiates it from separation anxiety, saying, 'Anxiety is experienced when the loss is believed to be retrievable and hope remains'.[6] There is ample evidence that farm animals experience separation anxiety when isolated or removed from their young. Such anxiety is expressed through distress calls, running about, attempting to escape and increased heart rate, among other symptoms. This, however, does not necessarily prove the existence of, or amount to, a despair reaction typical of human grief.

And yet ...

Darwin argued that there is continuity between the emotional lives of humans and those of other animals, and that the differences among many animals are in degree rather than in kind. In the *Descent of Man and Selection in Relation to Sex*, Darwin claimed that, 'the lower animals, like man, manifestly feel pleasure and pain, happiness and misery'.[7] Neuroscientific studies also suggest that all mammals have similar brain mechanisms that mediate grief reactions.

In her book *How Animals Grieve*, Barbara King argues that, 'Grief can be said to occur when a survivor animal acts in ways that are visibly distressed or altered from the usual routine, in the aftermath of the death of a companion animal who had mattered emotionally to him or her'.[8] King points out that manifestations of grief both between and within species vary widely — as they do between human individuals.

Although our ability to inhabit other animals' minds and feelings, to comprehend their coping strategies, is limited, we are more inclined to credit individuality and develop emotional attachment to free ranging animals such as koalas and wallabies, and to mobilise efforts to save them.

And yet, at the same time, we continue to destroy their habitat.

A similar paradox is in play with regard to domesticated animals. While we evacuate people under threat of fire, 'livestock' may be left trapped in sheds or fenced paddocks where they die. We rightly express empathy for farmers suffering trauma from having to shoot cattle, and assess affected individuals for psychological or emotional damage, providing counseling programs where necessary. Meanwhile, the surviving cattle and sheep are confronted with the sight of the corpses of their companions being buried by the army in mass graves.

## 6 March 2020

The garden is quiet now after the rain as if all that is good is nested in this tender lull. In this clarity I search for the power to break the silence, to find in our 'bloody shambles' the possibility of listening to the language of the earth as I listen now to birdsong bubbling in the trees; of humbly dwelling in grief with the animals in a shared, wordless space, casting myself into an animal place of howling, baying, whimpering, wailing.

But is this the answer? I look for a sign, a fire within myself, a spirit that burns with a passion of words. For surely, after all my animal keening is spent, it is words that transcend boundaries, nourish the heart, bolster the courage to convey knowledge.

The rain has returned, drops spilling from leaves, like tears, like ringing bells, inexplicably joyful. In this moment of wonder the heart of the world breathes again.

And yet …

---

1. Horatio Hastings, John Neal Weld, George M. Snow, Edward Stephens, *Brother Jonathan: A Weekly Compend of Belles Lettres and the Fine Arts, Standard Literature and General Intelligence*, vol. 1, Manhattan, New York City, 1842, p. 262. (free eBook, books.google.com.au).
2. 'Gripping Photo Shows Mourning Koala beside Dead Companion in Australian Bushfires,' www.sciencepagenews.com. Accessed 18 January, 2020.
3. Belinda Attree quoted in 'Farmers Impacted by Bushfires count "Heartbreaking" Costs as Livestock Losses Climb', by Sarah Jane Bell, www.abc.net.au. Accessed 18 January, 2020.
4. Freya Mathews, *For Love of Matter: A Contemporary Panpsychism*, New York, SUNY Press, 2003.
5. *literaturepage.com*, p. 181.
6. John Bowlby, 'Processes of Mourning', *International Journal of Psychoanalysis*, vol. 42, 1961, pp. 317–340.
7. Charles Darwin, *The Descent of Man and Selection in Relation to Sex*, The Modern Library, (Penguin Book Ltd), London, 1936, p. 448.
8. Barbara King, *How Animals Grieve*, University of Chicago Press, Chicago, 2013, p. 163.

# Her Date of Birth, 20 November 2019

Miranda Nation

On a sweltering January evening, I look down at my six-week-old baby asleep on the breast. Her tiny face is flushed, and we are glued together with sweat. Outside the window, the sun bleeds an apocalyptic red. Our old terrace house is a furnace. On day three of a heat wave, with no air-conditioning, we haven't been able to throw the windows open to the cool air of night. I check the EPA[1] app on my mobile phone for something like the fiftieth time today. The red peaks tell me that the air outside is still hazardous, among the worst in the world, second only to India. A month ago, I didn't even know the meaning of a fine particle count. The cracks around doors where the light bleeds in seem suddenly lethal. Cradling my sleeping daughter, I feel a sick anxiety in the pit of my stomach.

In November, megafires tear through old growth forest in New South Wales, the flames so massive they create their own weather systems. Frontline volunteers risk their lives, and friends in Sydney choke on smoke haze. In Melbourne, I am preoccupied with the final stages of my pregnancy. Our baby is measuring small. Statistics chase themselves in frantic circles in my mind. Coming to motherhood late, I'm defined as an elderly *primigravida* and, after three miscarriages, I'm all too aware of what can go wrong. For the moment, fears for my unborn daughter's safety outweigh all the other fears that accompany becoming a parent. Will she be better, kinder, more intelligent than us; or will she inherit all the traits we dislike in ourselves? How will we help her to navigate life's challenges? Will we be able to protect her from the evil that lurks in the world? And, always foremost in our minds, what will it look like, this world that she inherits?

Eco-anxiety has been described by the American Psychological Association as 'a chronic fear of environmental doom'.[2] This anxiety is a constant in our household, a kind of low-level, ever-present hum that gets drowned out in the everyday hubbub but keeps me awake at 3 a.m. And yet the desire for a family overrides all of my sensible concerns. This must be the epitome of selfishness, right?

As a film-maker, I'm passionate about telling stories from the female perspective, stories about our relationships with our bodies, our sexuality and the environments we inhabit. Much of my work to date has explored these themes and their intersections. I play with the metaphor of the female body as a landscape on which the scars of a patriarchal system are violently inscribed. It's not an original metaphor, of course. Mother Nature, the goddess Gaia, nature has long been understood as a powerful, female force, increasingly at odds with the dominant capitalist mindset. In her excellent book, *This Changes Everything*, Naomi Klein quotes Lord Francis Bacon who was instrumental in the shift from viewing Mother Earth as a revered, life-giving force, to one that could be enslaved and bent to one's will. 'For you have but to follow and as it were hound nature in her wanderings', he wrote in his *De Augmentis Scientiarum* in 1623, 'and you will be able, when you like, to lead and drive her afterwards to the same place again … Neither ought a man to make scruple of entering and penetrating into these holes and corners, when the inquisition of truth is his sole object'.[3] Hound, drive, penetrate. Harass, pester, molest. Rape, despoil, pollute. Violate, in the sense of desecrate: to treat (a sacred thing or place) with disrespect.

In late November I give birth to a healthy baby girl. While our first daughter took twenty-seven excruciating hours to crawl down the birth canal, this one arrives in a mad rush but the experience is no less profound. I'm in a state of fierce, fragile emotion as the first days of summer roll around and fires rage through East Gippsland. On Boxing Day, we retreat with family to our regular holiday spot on the Great Ocean Road. We check our news feeds obsessively. It seems like our little patch of coastline is one of the few not burning or choking. Blue skies and brilliant horizon contrast starkly with the images on our screens, of families crowding onto lifeboats on a beach in Mallacoota in a smoke haze so thick it blocks out the sun. I cry reading about the fathers of young children killed battling the blazes; about firefighters traumatised by the sounds of koalas screaming. And yet, selfishly, it's not until we get back to Melbourne that the terrifying reality hits me. Throughout January, smoke blankets the city. The official advice is for children and babies to spend no time outside. We're stuck inside our stifling house for days on end. The four-year-old, on kinder holidays, is climbing up the walls. I panic when I read that newborns don't sweat, that their bodies haven't yet developed the ability to cool themselves. I decide to buy face masks and an air purifier but when I go online I realise that everything sold out months ago.

Stealing out for an early morning walk to keep myself sane, each breath feels dangerous. I'm suffocating, the country is suffocating. I can't stop thinking about the blackened remains of ancient wilderness, the more than a billion native animals dying in terrible pain, the charred fur and blistered skin of those that survive, the tonnes of carbon billowing into the atmosphere. I'm overwhelmed with rage and distress. I can't shake the sense that the end of the world is nigh, that the apocalyptic future I feared handing to my children has arrived. I always imagined it as some distant, intangible horror, but these scenes of carnage are happening right now. There's a strange comfort in the fact that I am here to share it with my daughters, to protect them to the best of my ability.

Einstein spoke of the human being as 'a part of the whole called by us universe', and of the delusion we are in believing ourselves to be somehow separate from the rest. This delusion, he said, 'is a kind of prison for us, restricting us to our personal desires and to affection for a few persons nearest to us. Our task must be to free ourselves from this prison by widening our circle of compassion to embrace all living creatures and the whole of nature in its beauty'.[4] I think about Einstein's words as I witness the outpouring of support for those affected by the bushfires. As politicians debate the link to climate change, and accuse each other of politicising a tragedy, the people mobilise to help in whatever way they can. It is a powerful display of global goodwill, of our ability to band together in a time of crisis, demonstrating that our compassion can and does extend to those outside of our inner circle. Can we expand that 'circle of compassion' to embrace the natural world? I want to believe that we are kind enough, wise enough, strong enough. Can we reimagine our relationship with Mother Earth? Can we relinquish our need for power and learn to believe that all living things are of equal value? Are we capable of effecting the massive shift in our attitudes, belief systems, and behaviours that is required to save ourselves?

Torrential rains come in early February, providing relief to the exhausted firefighters and bringing all but a few fires under control. As the smoke clears, I start to breathe normally again. We throw open the windows and doors and the children can play outside. For those directly affected, who have lost family members, homes and livelihoods, the scars are immediate and acute. For those of us at a distance, clean air and blue skies bring a flush of relief and a risk of forgetting. I try to hold the trauma in my body without letting it overwhelm me. I try to focus on nature's potential for healing, on the resilience of the human spirit and our capacity for hope. To focus on the things of beauty that make it all worth fighting for. The promise of new growth after the rain. The call of a magpie on a cool clear morning. The quiet majesty of an ancient tree. The warm weight of my daughters in my arms.

---

1. Environment Protection Authority.
2. S.C. Whitmore-Williams, et al., 'Mental Health and Our Changing Climate: Impacts, Implications, and Guidance', https://www.apa.org/news/press/releases/2017/03/mental-health-climate.pdf, 2017, p. 68. Last accessed 6 May 2020.
3. N. Klein, *This Changes Everything*, Simon and Schuster, New York, 2014, p. 149.
4. W. Sullivan, 'The Einstein Papers. A Man of Many Parts', *The New York Times*, 29 March 1972. https://www.nytimes.com/1972/03/29/archives/the-einstein-papers-a-man-of-many-parts-the-einstein-papers-man-of.html. Last accessed 6 May 2020.

---

**Susan Norrie** *Undertow*, 2002, video still, installation detail. Six channel digital video, colour, sound, projection boxes.

# Elements

"... an uncontained oil-fire on water ..." Susan Norrie

# Undertow

## Susan Norrie

The image on the preceding page is of an uncontained oil-fire on water at Sakhalin Island (in the Pacific Ocean, north of Japan), projected as a large wall-scaled artwork. It is the feature screen of my 2002 installation *Undertow*.

The multi-channeled project comprised documentation of numerous disasters from around the world: the aim was to reveal the seemingly ongoing cycle of man-made catastrophes — often the result of the mismanagement associated with multi-national corporate energy exploration and technological advancement.

But the reality is that in the twenty-first century, as the recent unprecedented and catastrophic bushfires across Australia this past summer have shown, there is an increasing disconnect between natural cycles and the capitalist-driven, rampant demand on natural resources.

*Undertow* focused on real and challenging issues … the environment, delicate ecosystems, socio-economic behaviour and a disregard for humanitarian concerns.

It was my hope that viewers leaving this experiential installation would be alerted not only to present catastrophes but would also be concerned about the future: what the world could be like if we don't reconnect with its natural cycles …

It's disheartening: nearly two decades on with, firstly, an ongoing drought, then ferocious bushfires, and now the COVID–19 pandemic … it is clear that we have stopped listening to, watching for and taking heed of the signs.

Will we ever learn?

---

*Undertow* is held in the collections of the Laurence Wilson Art Gallery, Western Australia University and The Art Gallery of NSW.
See https://www.artgallery.nsw.gov.au/collection/works/266.2003.a-i/.

---

# Some Say the World Will End in Fire

Paul James

There have been three moments in my life when I have been overwhelmed by the possibility of our world ending. Mostly, such fears have gently informed my politics without being all-consuming. The first moment came as a teenage existential shock. I was at a youth camp by the Ocean Grove beach, and one of the leaders stood up at breakfast and said, 'A couple of days ago, the world almost ended … Fortunately for us, Israel backed down from using nuclear missiles against the Arabs'. I have never forgotten his faltering words from October 1973, nor how he stood on an old chair, his trousers hitched above white socks. The occasion prompted me to buy Doris Lessing's *Briefing for a Descent into Hell*, though not because the book was directly related to nuclear holocaust. It was because of its apocalyptic title and the linking of the boring administrative notion of 'a briefing' to the elemental evocation of hell. I became fascinated by the distressed amnesiac at the centre of the narrative who believed that heat-waves were making the ocean's water thinner.[1] This is not precisely accurate, to be sure, but what science tells us is more confronting: it is the shells of ocean crustaceans that are becoming radically thinner; the northern oceans are becoming less dense from melting Greenland ice; and global ocean currents slowing down.[2]

The second moment was at an Arena conference in 1981, called to respond to the nuclear standoff in Europe over Cruise missiles and SS-20s.[3] The Doomsday Clock symbolizing the potential end of civilization had just been reset at seven minutes to midnight — that is, two minutes earlier than its 1974-level when India acquired the bomb. The madness of the situation was captured in an essay by E.P. Thompson being discussed at the conference: 'Notes on Exterminism, the Last Stage of Civilization'.[4] That title stayed with me too. I read the subsequent book, and also Jonathan Schell's *The Fate of the Earth*, which came out soon after. There, the possibility of exterminism met the phenomenon of 'nuclear winter'.[5] That association added a new world of meaning to the prior definition of 'holocaust' — previously, a sacrifice by fire or the attempted genocide of the Jewish and Roma peoples. Now, it was also the grey-cold condition caused by the dust and smoke of fires blocking out the sun. The effect of these fires, long after they burned out, would slowly kill people through cold and starvation, leaving behind a republic of insects and grass.[6] This possibility involved elemental perversions: the light of the bomb, a thousand suns, would bring darkness; extreme heat would end in fatal cold.

The third moment was an afternoon, a few days after Christmas, 2019. I was driving home down Brunswick Street in inner-city Melbourne, listening to the radio. The air was acrid, and in a well-trained neutral voice the ABC newsreader said that Bundoora and suburbs to the north were being evacuated because of fire. Bushfires are not supposed to burn in our suburbs. This was too close to home, my home. Later that day a firefighter in a vehicle weighing around 10 tonnes was killed when his truck was lifted off the ground and dumped by a fire tornado — technically called a pyro-cumulonimbus event (see David Bowman and Greg Lehman's essay in this volume). The next day, smoke from Australia's eastern fires reached New Zealand's South Island and turned its skies murky yellow-grey.

These conjunctures are small personal expressions of global patterns. It is becoming clear that we are living through a period in which our relationships to the basic conditions of existence are being fundamentally unsettled.[7] Songwriters, poets and film-makers are increasingly setting their narratives in the end of days. Journalists go on journeys to the dark side to meet mid-western survivalists and purveyors of luxury underground bunkers.[8] Social theorists write about living through the end-times.[9]

The world is being churned. Ocean acidity is dissolving the shells of crustaceans, light is bringing darkness, and fires are creating cold yellow skies and changing the weather around them. What does it mean for climate change to intensify wild fires? And, in turn, what does it mean that intensifying fires cause their own weather patterns? It suggests that we are experiencing an assault upon the very elements of life. Until a bit over half a century ago, the disciplines of meteorology and climatology were based on the presumption that the climate was a stable phenomenon. Now, science tells us that the world could break the feared threshold of 1.5 degrees Celsius warming over the next five years.[10] In short, we are living through a time when prior worlds of meaning and practice are being overlaid and reconstituted by a new world of elemental perversions.[11] This new world is created by us, including through insatiable commodity fetishism, overproduction of things, technoscientific intervention in nature, and (perversely) through a constantly renewed hope for material progress and unsustainably comfortable lives.

In a once relatively stable world, thinkers on the human condition treated fire as one of the animating elements of being human. It was dialectically complex. In Aboriginal cultures, fire is variously healing, rejuvenating, protecting, teaching, connecting, *and* dangerous. In Greek mythology, Prometheus stole fire from the gods — and in the Vedic myth Matarisvan stole fire from the heavens. In the second century BCE, Plutarch wrote that, 'The mind is not a vessel to be filled but a fire to be kindled'. Again, in the first years of the Common Era, Luke's gospel treated fire as sacred and enlivening. He quoted John as saying in anticipation of Jesus, 'I baptize you with water. But one who is more powerful than I will come, the straps of whose sandals I am not worthy to untie. He will baptize you with the Holy

Spirit and fire' (Luke 3.16). From the same tradition in the fourteenth century, St Catherine of Siena linked creation and creativity through fire: 'Be who you were created to be, and you will set the world on fire'. And from around the same period but a very different tradition, the Persian poet and Islam jurist Rumi wrote, 'There are wonderful shapes in rising smoke that imagination loves to watch. But it's a mistake to leave the fire for that filmy sight. Stay here at the flame's core'. In this world, fire is red. Smoke is ethereal.

And so, the list could be elaborated. In this dialectical world (one, it should be said, that continues even as it is now overlaid by existential Anthropocenic destruction), fire can certainly be dangerous, physically and spiritually. In one tradition, the most wicked of us who cannot be saved by purgatory's purifying fires, will continue our way to hell's inferno. Nevertheless, the canonical writings and oral expressions of different traditions treat the fires of this world as dialectically animating and renewing; destructive and dangerous. Despite being beyond unmediated human control — a quality shared by all elements: earth, water, air and fire — fire, treated respectfully, brings warmth and comfort.

At one level, fire will continue to be a metaphor for struggle and energy. From Cornel West's ruminations on emotions and action, fuelling the fire of his soul,[12] to Bruce Springsteen's small-town blues: 'You can't start a fire; Worrying 'bout your little world falling apart',[13] fire is evoked as the metaphor for the necessary struggle that brings life. However, at an emerging and increasingly dominant level, in the new world of pyro-cumulonimbus events and end-of-the-world scenarios, fire has leapt beyond earth, and has perversely remade the elements of water and air.

It no longer brings glorious life in the long sustainable circle of life and death. For all the photographs after the 2020 fire season of 'whipstick stands of youngish re-growth eucalypts' (see Bill Gammage's essay in this volume), the new world of technically managed forests and audited quality-assurance fire-containing frameworks is taking over. For all of the hopes for making our lives better through technoscientific intervention and risk-management, our lives are more vulnerable than ever before. And, in the final irony, fire can no longer give more than forlorn and misplaced hope to our apocalyptic imaginations. In Cormac McCarthy's novel *The Road*, a dying father walks with his son across a post-disaster United States — a world rendered a wasteland by an unspecified extinction event. The sun is blocked by grey clouds and the landscape is covered in soft grey soot. Father and son talk about a future that will not happen:

We're going to be okay, aren't we Papa?
Yes. We are.
And nothing bad is going to happen to us.

That's right. Because we're carrying the fire.
Yes. Because we're carrying the fire.[14]

A few earlier thinkers felt the force of this new upside-down world. For them, fire offered a destructive warning — never a comfortable or even forlorn warming. In 1920, deeply affected by World War I, Robert Frost wrote a strange little poem called 'Fire and Ice'.

> Some say the world will end in fire,
> Some say in ice.
> From what I've tasted of desire
> I hold with those who favor fire.
> But if it had to perish twice,
> I think I know enough of hate
> To say that for destruction ice
> Is also great
> And would suffice.
> ('Fire and Ice', 1920)

The casual bleakness of the first line gives this essay its title, but the poem still only teeters on the edge of recognizing the new world that we face. Another poet writing at the same time, T.S. Eliot, gets much closer with his 'Fire Sermon' from his epic poem of despair, *The Waste Land*. Eliot's sermon reference here is to the third discourse delivered by the Buddha — the 'Fire Sermon' or Addittaparyaya Sutta. However, the difference implied by Eliot is that we will not achieve nirvana by deliverance from the fire of the senses. Eliot's despair derives from the limbo-land of consumptive waste, from the dulling emptiness of hungering fetishisms, and from the fiery hell-scape of failed connections; it does not come from meaning-making relations with others.[15]

Eliot ended another of his poems with the words,

> This is the way the world ends
> This is the way the world ends
> This is the way the world ends
> Not with a bang but a whimper.
> ('The Hollow Men', 1925)

This ending turns on a question that implicitly frames this whole essay. Will whimpering really be the way this world ends? Since that moment of Christmas 2019, I keep going back to reread T.S. Eliot's *Waste Land*. For me, that day has become more than just a moment of shocking realization; it has become an abiding concern. The possibility of the end of the world, at least as we have known it, has come to live in me as a constant return. If we do act now, and in a systematic way to change the way we live on this planet, the end of the world will come with further elemental perversions that we barely recognize. It advances flexibly and vigorously — without us taking in the momentousness of the challenges. It walks lightly and comfortably along the road of our desires for a comfortable life.

> Do not believe it is happening now.
> As long as the sun and the moon are above,
> As long as the bumblebee visits a rose,
> As long as rosy infants are born
> No one believes it is happening now.
> ('A Song on the End of the World', 1944)[16]

It is potentially happening now, but I no longer believe that this world will end in the red of fire or the quietness of whimpering. Rather, our demise will come with multiple voices, some defending, to the end, their contribution to maintaining our comfortable lifestyles.[17] It will come not with a bang, but with soft yellow-grey smoke.

---

1. D. Lessing, *Briefing for a Descent into Hell*, Granada, London, 1972. pp. 13, 14. What science tells us is that northern oceans are actually becoming less dense from melting Greenland ice, with global currents slowing down; it is the shells of crustaceans that are becoming radically thinner.
2. https://insideclimatenews.org/news/07052018/atlantic-ocean-circulation-slowing-climate-change-heat-temperature-rainfall-fish-why-you-should-care. Last accessed 10 July 2020; L. Fox, S. Stukins, T. Hill, et al., 'Quantifying the Effect of Anthropogenic Climate Change on Calcifying Plankton', *Scientific Report*, no. 1620, 2020, https://doi.org/10.1038/s41598-020-58501-w.
3. *Arena*, no 60, 1982, based on a conference held at Malmsbury in 1981.
4. E.P. Thompson, 'Notes on Exterminism, the Last Stage of Civilization', *New Left Review* (Series 1), no. 121, 1980, pp. 3–31.
5. The nuclear winter argument was incredibly controversial, dismissed by the Right, and challenged by other scientists. The tempered (in tone at least) dismissal from Russel Seitz in the then neoconservative journal, the *National Interest* is exemplary of the depth of damnation ('In from the Cold: "Nuclear Winter" Melts Down', *National Interest*, Fall 1986, pp. 1–17). However, later climate modelling, such as by Alan Robock, Luke Oman, and Georgiy L. Stenchikov ('Nuclear Winter Revisited with a Modern Climate Model and Current Nuclear Arsenals: Still Catastrophic Consequences', *Journal of Geophysical Research*, 2007, vol. 112, published online, no page numbers), confirmed the disastrous consequences of thermonuclear exchange, suggesting even that the blanketing effects would be probably longer-term than originally claimed.
6. The phrase 'republic of insects and grass' comes from Jonathan Schell's *Fate of the Earth* (London, Pan Books, 1982), first excerpted in *The New Yorker*. The concept of 'nuclear winter' entered the public lexicon with a bang through Carl Sagan's *Parade* article (30 October 1983, pp. 4–7).
7. The Doomsday Clock's original setting in 1947 was seven minutes to midnight. It has been back and forth 24 times since. In 1980, my second moment, it was again set at seven minutes to midnight. Now, at the time of the fires, January 2020, it is set at the closest to the end it has ever been: 100 seconds to midnight.
8. M. O'Connell, *Notes from an Apocalypse: A Personal Journey to the End of the World and Back*, Granta, London, 2020.
9. S. Zizek, *Living in the End Time*, Verso, London, 2010. I bought that book too.

10. https://public.wmo.int/en/media/press-release/new-climate-predictions-assess-global-temperatures-coming-five-years. Last accessed 9 July 2020.
11. A. Caddick, 'Will the Fires Change Everything?', *Arena*, Series 3, no. 1. 2020, pp. 2–3. Or, for a more extended discussion of what we call the 'Great Unsettling', see M.B. Steger and P. James, *Globalization Matters: Engaging the Global in Unsettled Times*, Cambridge University Press, Cambridge, 2019.
12. 'I must fuel the fire of my soul so my intellectual blues can set others on fire', says Cornel West in his *Brother West: Living and Loving Out Loud, a Memoir*, Smiley Books, New York, 2010, p. 20 (epub); See also his *Black Prophetic Fire*, Beacon Press, Boston, 2014.
13. Lyrics from B. Springsteen, 'Dancing in the Dark', released 1984.
14. C. McCarthy, *The Road*, Vintage, New York, 2009, p. 48.
15. T. Bruno, 'Buddhist Conceptual Rhyming and T.S. Eliot's Crisis of Connection in *The Waste Land* and "Burnt Norton"', *Asian Philosophy*, vol. 23, no. 4, 2013, pp. 365–78.
16. Czeslaw Milosz wrote this poem towards the end of World War II in the year of the Warsaw Uprising against Nazi occupation. In retaliation to the Uprising the Nazis completed their planned destruction of Warsaw, deploying flame-throwers, building by building. Hans Frank, the Governor General of occupied Poland, wrote in his diary, 'Almost all Warsaw is a sea of flames. Warsaw will get what it deserves — complete annihilation' (I.A. Karsten, 'Reconstruction of Historic Monument in Poland after the Second World War: The Case of Warsaw', in J. Bold, P. Larkham, R. Pickard, eds, *Authentic Reconstruction*, Bloomsbury, London, 2018, p. 50). At the moment of the uprising, Milosz's diary tells us that he was on his way to visit friends to discuss his new translation of an English poem, probably Eliot's *The Waste Land*, a poem that he had been working on for at least a year.
17. Comedian Mark Maron consoles his audience that the world may be ending but we were good: 'I think all of us in our hearts really know', he says, 'we did everything we could'. He pauses, as the audience tentatively titters. 'I mean, think about it, we brought all our own bags to the supermarket'. www.theatlantic.com/culture/archive/2020/03/marc-maron-netflix-special-end-times-fun-anxiety/607855/. Last accessed 31 May 2020.

# Is Fire a Feminist Issue?

## Sally Gardner

Fire is the ultra-living element. It is intimate and it is universal. It lives in our heart. It lives in the sky. It rises from the depths of the substance and offers itself with the warmth of love.[1]

Some women I spoke to during this past drastic fire season said that they were lost for words in their response to the bushfires: they did not know what to say and did not know if they felt anything or what it was that they may have been feeling. They seemed to be indicating a limit to conceiving in language. Alternatively, others have been all too articulate about what needs to be done. There has, for example, been alarming talk of our needing to further clear forests — whether burnt or not yet burnt — to reduce 'fuel load', to 'adapt' to drier hotter times, and other similar rationales coming from various quarters. This discourse was countered by other life-promoting and restoratively oriented voices, but it was forceful nevertheless. The discourse blamed nature, prolonging a hatred of nature itself, rather than recognising and taking responsibility for the effects of an unthinking exploitation of earth's bounty.

    The kind of punishing approach witnessed in this recent war-like and combative discourse is underpinned by deep values instituted in forms of language that have elicited profound criticism in the work of many feminists. In particular, the Belgian-born thinker and activist Luce Irigaray has over many years questioned Western rationality as the foundation of philosophical and scientific truth in terms of its underlying exclusions, unacknowledged debts, and blind-spots: that is, in the way this form of rationality is structured at the deepest levels of imagination. As a linguist, philosopher and psychoanalyst, Irigaray understands 'the house of language', historically, as a *de facto* patriarchal edifice instituting the values of masculinity while representing femininity only as the former's negative or binary opposite. Since it is not possible simply to leap to the outside of language, Irigaray painstakingly undertakes to unearth resources — symbolic, semantic, grammatical, poetic, and enunciatory — aiming to create another imaginary that would support the becoming of a sovereign feminine subject who would take part in a culture of at least two *different* (not just complementary or opposed) sexes and subjects.[2]

    One of Irigaray's numerous strategies has been to enter into a dialogue with individual male philosophers. By reading them in a questioning tone, from 'far away', she aims to 'jam their machinery' and self-proclaimed coherence. She has written a series of books critically but 'amorously' questioning key philosophers regarding their unconscious denial of certain elements and states of matter. This is a project that seeks a life-giving philosophy: it is philosophy as 'knowledge of love' rather than the more usual 'love of knowledge'. In *The Forgetting of Air in Martin Heidegger*, she argued that Heidegger's approach to thought, with its grounding in the origins of Western rationality as the means to truth, was unable or refused to think its own material and elemental conditions. In particular, she points to the elemental importance of air: 'does thought need an other air than the living do?'[3] Her claim is that an imaginary or phantasy exclusively of the solid underpins *presence*, and thus Being. She argues that 'metaphysics always supposes, in some manner, a solid crust from which to raise a construction'.[4] Beyond the solid crust lies only an 'abyss', that is, a space or hole without breathable air or other life-giving fluid substance such as water or warmth (fire): 'The metaphysical is written neither on/in water, nor on/in air, nor on/in fire'.[5] Thought or Truth in these terms does not acknowledge its material debt and denies matter in its fluidity, its non-graspable, changeable and intermixing capacities.

Irigaray has not to date produced a book on fire, although it has been noted that she originally envisaged a quartet of books on the elements. In *Marine Lover of Friedrich Nietzsche*, she questions the philosopher as to his avoidance and apparent fear of water, his desire to be on the heights, to be close to the sun: 'Perched on any mountain peak, hermit, tightrope walker or bird, you never dwell in the great depths. And as companion you never choose a sea creature'.[6] As for fire, in her discussion of Plato's cave, for example, Irigaray argues that, here at the beginnings of the Western canon in a myth where 'truth' and 'womb' are incompatible, there is a dissociation as far as fire is concerned between light and heat, vision and touch. Thus, we Westerners inherit a legacy in which a life-kindling, warming, sensual fire is no longer cultivated either in the mind or in reality.[7]

Irigaray's strategy of conversing with master texts are part of her commitment to the task of bringing into being a culture of sexual difference. Politically speaking, she envisages a sexed ontology where male and female would be understood along the lines of different species (hence different genres/genders) with specific rights according to their needs including for transcendence or the divine. Going well beyond seeking women's 'empowerment', Irigaray looks to a sexuate culture in which 'I' and 'you' denote a mutual relation of respect in difference, where man and woman are granted their uniqueness each as members of a different genre. Being able to create a culture where this primary difference amongst humans is cultivated can be the basis upon which multiple, different genres, species, genders, and relations or passages between them might also be imagined. A culture of 'the same', which includes the contemporary discourse of equality (women's equality, marriage equality,) is manifestly a deathly culture, a dystopia of an ultramodernist 'neutral' (but effectively masculine) sex which 'works towards the disappearance of women'.[8]

What this has to do with the recent 'watershed' moment of devastating bushfires in Australia and why some people cannot find words of response should be clear. We are living a great reduction of poetic resources for experiencing and thinking. The fires have been product of a culture based on the oppositional and instrumentalising language of a patriarchal subject who 'masters' and dominates others and the world. Because this subject understands difference as oppositional and tends to deny any limits to the self, s/he is unable to enter into mutually fecund relations with others.

This attitude and culture of domination underpins climate change. And it has not been difficult to discern the tendency during the fires to employ the language and imagery of war and its weapons: we've seen water fired from hoses and dumped from planes overhead; and we've heard the vegetal undergrowth named as 'fuel load' (along the lines of payload?). We've seen pictures of burned-out cars; helicopters circling; and we've seen the army mobilised. Of course, some of these events, actions and images have been necessary under the circumstances to attempt to save lives (animal and vegetable) and to honour those lost, but continuing to speak in terms of a weaponisation against nature perpetuates a deadly logic. Shouldn't we be seeking urgently now to cultivate our practices and discourses to recognise and put to work, as do some feminists, hitherto denied or submerged resources of difference?

Irigaray's approach draws on and mobilises at one and the same time rational, poetic, historical and spiritual dimensions of thought in order to further the possibility of a knowledge that does not 'lose touch with its sources'.[9] This idea of a knowledge not in denial of its material conditions of possibility or the sources of life and, for some, of language, finds an uncanny resonance elsewhere: this fire season has finally brought to the foreground and promoted wider acceptance of aspects of Australian Indigenous knowledges. In Indigenous burning practices, in order to promote life on Country, the lighting of fires occurs with attention to recent or coming rains and with careful observation of prevailing winds or flows of cool or warm air.[10] Fire, water, and air fluidly and abundantly embrace and touch one another. One does not move without the other.

---

1. Gaston Bachelard, 'Fire and Respect: The Prometheus Complex', *The Psychoanalysis of Fire*. Beacon Press, Boston, 1964, p. 7.
2. See Margaret Whitford, *Luce Irigaray: Philosophy in the Feminine*. Routledge, London and New York, 1991, Chapter 3, pp. 53–74.

3. L. Irigaray, *The Forgetting of Air in Martin Heidegger*, University of Texas Press, Austin, 1999, p. 6.
4. Ibid, p. 2.
5. Ibid.
6. L. Irigaray, *Marine Lover of Friedrich Nietzsche*, Columbia University Press, New York, 1991, p. 13. Whitford op. cit. writes that Irigaray 'takes Nietzsche's work as a point of departure for a meditation on the flight from water and from the unacknowledged nurturant element', p. 55.
7. L. Irigaray, 'Plato's Hystera' in *Speculum of the Other Woman*, Cornell University Press, Ithaca, New York, 1985, pp. 243–364.
8. J.-J. Goux, 'Luce Irigaray Versus the Utopia of the Neutral Sex', in C. Burke, N. Schor, and M. Whitford, eds, *Engaging with Irigaray*. Columbia University Press, New York, 1994, p. 185.
9. Whitford, op. cit., p.73.
10. V. Steffensen, *Fire Country*, Hardie Grant, Melbourne, 2020.

———

# Errinundra Shimmer

Kate Judith

Forests so lush that mosses seem to encourage each other towards greater densities and ever-more-surprising surfaces upon which to grow. Trees like teeming cities of diversity; lichens, spiders, moss, epiphytic orchids and ferns, twisting vines, birds, bats, so many ants, wasps and beetles; just listing is an act of wonder. Deborah Bird Rose, informed as always by the wisdom of her Northern Australian Indigenous teachers, has a beautiful word to describe the liveliness of complex ecologies — she calls it 'shimmer'.

Lively forests shimmer with the constant, complex calls and responses of all the meetings between, as spider catches fly, leaf chlorophyll transforms sunlight, beetle bores into wood and is in turn worried by ants and all the other accomplishments and celebrations occurring across the forest. Surely each beetle is an accomplishment — all the work of evolution and adaptation, all that eating and hiding, those skilful and lucky choices about which way to burrow and just when to emerge, that armoured jacket and those protected wings. Surely there are so many who celebrate that accomplishment in all their many ways — the fungus that colonises the chewed wood-waste, the mite waiting for a chink in an ageing beetle joint, the currawong listening for that quiet beetle chewing beneath the bark. The forest is full of brilliant accomplishments and their diverse celebrations. Rose describes shimmer as it occurs within the meeting of flying fox tongue and eucalyptus blossom: 'It is the great, expressive, demonstrative "yes"', she exclaims, as the 'lush, extravagant beauty, flamboyance, and dazzling seductiveness' of the blossom 'reaches out into the world … and for their part, the flying foxes come racing to respond'.[1] Shimmer is created in the spaces-between as living beings affect each other or interact with non-living things like water, sunshine and minerals. It is made in the thickness of relations, in meeting and responding: 'Life happens because sentient beings remain in communication with each other', Rose writes.[2] To make futures together that contribute the most towards shimmer, we meet in the middle, offering and inviting proposals, prepared to change in response.

Rose is clear that the great shimmer of life is not only about the 'yes' of accomplishment and celebration. Shimmer is not perpetual, dazzling brightness — it requires movement between darkness and light. Forests shimmer because they are complex and difficult, full of challenges that push accomplishment in ways that are often surprising and sometimes terrifying. Shimmer is both a wondrous and a troubled thing. As we know, fire, drought, invasive species and many kinds of human interference were pushing hard against the forests before last summer, but still the forests of the Great Dividing Range of eastern Australia were big with shimmer.

Once in 1986, seven of us with arms outstretched barely reached around one big trunk on the Errinundra plateau. And, all about, neither ground nor sky were locatable for all the layers of growing and decaying things. In those times, logging trucks were still sometimes coming out of that forest carrying only one big log that filled the truck's entire deck, though that was already rare. Not so unusual was to see them filled completely by only five or six large logs. The images stayed in my memory for years, like an assault. Now, our future-destroying habits seem to have suddenly leap-frogged over our more everyday violences and torn the forests apart.

It is hard to find ways to think about the losses from this summer's fires. I hear words like 'incomprehensible' and 'unimaginable' being used — the vocabulary is not available for what we feel we need to say. But here we are, trying to find ways to use words to approach and hold and share this loss. When Rose was writing about shimmer she was trying to find a way to describe the depth of loss that is extinction; the 'double death' of it, where even death itself — the future deaths that support the future lives — is defeated.[3] She was thinking about the blossom that calls out for a flying fox when there is no flying fox to celebrate that call, about the loss of all the celebrations without which life no longer counts as accomplishment. For Rose, the tragedy of extinction is its extinguishment of life's shimmer.

These fires have extinguished the shimmer of many forests and dimmed it across this country, which shimmered so much. They brought the death of billions of lives, all the results of such long and complex adaptive accomplishments, and the deaths of far more possible futures. Rose warns of the great 'no' that humans impose upon life's shimmer — a 'no' that is sometimes audible as the sounds of loud logging machinery or mining equipment — but is also the longer quieter 'no' of climate change. These fires were so extreme because of choices many humans made. We knew the climate of south eastern Australia would become hotter, dryer and more fire-prone as a result of human-induced climate change.

I know I am not the only one feeling now so sorry to have failed to have paid good enough attention, failed to celebrate those accomplishments even minimally enough to allow them to continue. I doubt I am the only one now speaking my sorrow and my sorries softly to the trees and birds as I walk around my dull suburban neighbourhood. These birds may not be refugees from the fires, but I am sorry all the same and seeking ways to find a between space of relations with those whom I have hurt so much. I seek a space of relation into which I can offer my willingness to continue the celebration of those accomplishments now lost by inviting that loss to change me. Shimmer needs its cycles of darkness, but these times are more continuously dark for Australia's tall moist forests. Can we find ways to allow even the current darkness to contribute at least a little to the ongoing shimmer of life? Perhaps if we meet it in the middle, with open proposals and a preparedness to listen and change.

How do we honour the loss? It seems to call for some labour, some time and effort that carries the shimmer of those forests into the future because it makes a difference. Caring for the surviving animals and plants is such a labour of honouring, and so is learning how to care for them better. But those of us in cities or countries far away need other ways. I have been writing into that middle, putting my thoughts and words into places where I spend some good long hours remembering the animals and trees of the shimmering forests I lived near and visited. Painting or drawing or spending time with photographs, telling stories to our children, or making music for the forests, all these may provide some openness that makes a difference. Our honouring may take many forms, labour together or alone that changes us as we celebrate the accomplishments of those great forests. If we live more attentively and celebrate life's accomplishments more fully, in changing us, our honouring carries some of the shimmer of those forests on into the future.

---

1. D.B. Rose, 'Shimmer: When All You Love is Being Trashed', in A. Tsing, H. Swanson, E. Gan, and N. Bubandt, eds, *Arts of Living on a Damaged Planet* (Kindle ed.). University of Minnesota Press, Minneapolis, paragraph 24, 2017.
2. D.B. Rose, 'Taking Notice', *Worldviews: Environment, Culture, Religion,* vol. 3, no. 2, 1999, p. 99.
3. D.B. Rose, 'Multispecies Knots of Ethical Time', *Environmental Philosophy,* vol. 9, no. 1, 2012, p. 128.

---

# Realities

13.02.20
Glassy eyes.
The women's shed had visitors. A group of women to knit and yarn.
Talking of evacuation and lost homes.
And at their feet, finches picking up the crumbs of the cake.

Text & Drawing • Hugo Muecke

# Creatures of the Earth

## Raimond Gaita

I was overseas in December 2019. I read, watched and listened to whatever I could about the fires. The news broke my heart every day. Like millions of people, I grieved for Australia, and because of the role that climate change played in the fires' severity, I grieved for the earth. But I won't write about the suffering, terror, and the heroism that I saw on television and read about. Many did at the time, and others will do so for this anthology better than I could.

Like many Australians who were overseas, I could not wait to go home. People across the world sorrowed over what Australians suffered. Perhaps millions grieved over the deaths of the animals, estimated to be over one billion. But no one grieved like Australians. I don't mean that we grieved more deeply. I mean that our grief was Australian coloured through and through. Though we are Australians by virtue of citizenship, the character of our grief as Australians didn't focus on the nation as a political entity: it focused on the country as we think of 'country' when we speak of our love of it, a love that is always mediated by local affections for a region, a town, a suburb, a landscape; by smells, light, literature, song and myriad inflections of actions and speech.

Many foreigners were scornful that a prime minister could go on holiday to Hawaii when fires, reported as perhaps the worst in Australia's history, devastated his country and traumatised his citizens, to return only after he had been ethically bludgeoned to do so. They were incredulous when they saw footage of a fire-ravaged community in which he took a woman's hand in a gauche attempt to shake it even though she had pointedly refused to offer it. Many Australians were also incredulous, scornful and embarrassed. More significantly, some were ashamed. To feel ashamed, you must be able to speak a kind of 'we' with fellow Australians that foreigners obviously cannot speak. Paul Keating spoke it powerfully in his Redfern speech.

My region is a part of Central Victoria where I grew up. My wife and I have a property there. An Aboriginal friend honoured me by calling it my 'country', intending at least some of the spiritual resonances of the word as Aboriginal peoples use it, without diminishing the significance of the fact that it is the country of which the Djadjawurrung people were dispossessed. Growing up, I came to love its summer colours. In deep and, as I still discover, unexpected ways, I was formed by my early life as an immigrant boy in its landscape and amongst the people who farmed it and worked in its towns. I now look at the summer beauty with a love that the threat of fire makes anxious. Only when the grass turns green do I relax.

When my wife and I landed at Melbourne airport on a flight from London, early on 5 January, we took our bags to our home in a Melbourne suburb and unpacked them. Immediately afterwards, though we were exhausted, we drove to our home on the property. I felt compelled to do it. The property wasn't threatened by fire, but the smoke from hundreds of kilometres away reduced visibility to about half a kilometre. The urgent imperative to go there was an expression of my grief for the earth and the living things that belong to it: its creatures, its trees and grasses, even the moss on the noble granite boulders. To explain this, or even for me to understand it, I would have to be a poet.

How deeply the meaning of being human is connected to our living and dying on the earth has been controversial in Western cultural history, sometimes bitterly controversial. Our connection to the earth has been lamented at least as often as it has been celebrated. To say that someone has been 'brought down to earth' has always been ambivalent praise: on the one hand it applauds sobriety and humility; on the other hand, it deplores betrayal of passion, of ideals to which we can remain true only when we look to the heavens.

For some — including myself — the fires took us to a visceral awakening to our creatureliness, to the full realisation that like the animals we saw fleeing the fires with terror in their hearts, we are creatures of flesh and blood. Their charred bodies forced us to acknowledge, not just in our beliefs, but to our living core, that we are essentially mortal beings. Unlike machines, we die rather than fall apart or break down beyond hope of repair. 'Dust to dust, ashes to ashes' is the manner of our ending. Yet, at the same time, as we seek to find a more awakened attention to our bodies and to the way our relations with other creatures and the earth defines our humanity, we continue to hope that science will enable us to replace damaged parts of our bodies with the same material from which we will make robots with whom we will 'live' in full ethical fellowship. Robot-makers have been saying for years that the interesting question is not, 'When will robots become like us'? It is, 'When will the replacement of our bodily parts with robot-stuff make us like them?' The conception of nature and our creatureliness that the fires awakened in many people looks to be at least in tension with what this assumes about the meaning of our embodiment. We enjoy our bodies more than many in generations before us did, but perhaps we are no closer to believing they are essential to who we are than they were.

What is the basis of that tension? An answer needs to unpack what I mean by 'essentially embodied being', but that is not possible in a short essay.[1] Instead, I'll appeal to the example of Australia's Aboriginal peoples. After the fires many people, including the Australian Prime Minister, were open to learning from them how to live more sustainably with the land in order to ameliorate the effects of climate change and to reduce the frequency and severity of fires. Others hoped to learn not only practical lessons, but also, inseparably from them, what it means to be human on the earth. They hoped that an essentially Western nation, profoundly affected by the spirit and astounding achievements of science, could look upon the earth and the place of human beings on it in a way akin to seeing it as 'country'.

Earlier I spoke of the spiritual resonances of 'country', as Aboriginal people use it. I meant nothing metaphysical or explicitly religious by the word 'spiritual'. Love of truth and the love of the beauty of the world are spiritual loves. Or, to put the point another way, these are examples of when the word comes naturally, carrying no religious or metaphysical baggage — just as 'soul' comes naturally when people speak of soul music, or of beauty as nourishment for the soul. As I understand it, the Aboriginal people's ideas of 'country', informed by and informing their 'Dreaming' stories,[2] expresses a perspective on what it is to be human from which the claims that we are only contingently bound to the earth, only contingently creatures of flesh and blood, that we would lose nothing of importance ethically and spiritually if we were made of robot-stuff, look literally unintelligible.

In the 1950s, some coffee table books in Australia counted Aboriginal peoples amongst the nation's fauna. People who found that unremarkable could not imagine a conversation between themselves and Aboriginal people from which they could learn more deeply about the meanings of things in their lives. Though some people respected Aboriginal practical skills as trackers and jackeroos they could not imagine how they might learn about living better, ethically and spiritually. Things are a little different now, but the nation is still far from listening to Aboriginal peoples. One cannot seriously converse with humbled and critically attentive engagement if one is not fully open to the pain of others, and to what they must do to assert their need of justice and human dignity. Most people in this country, including many who regard themselves as radical supporters of reconciliation, assume that if Aboriginal and non-Aboriginal peoples were to agree on what kind of 'we' they could speak as the expression of a form of political fellowship that is true to the injustices perpetrated against Aboriginal peoples, then it would be 'we, Australians'. But, it might not be. Or, the words 'Australia' and 'Australian' might take connotations and resonances different from any that most contemporary Australians could imagine. Or, more radically still, it might have to be acknowledged that it is not possible to speak truthfully and justly of a 'we' of national fellowship. For any of those possibilities to be taken seriously — not as aspirations to a just future, but as standards with which now to describe where Aboriginal and non-Aboriginal peoples of this land stand, morally and politically — discussion would have to be conducted in a radically different ethical and conceptual space from the one in which Australians now argue about Australia Day, constitutional recognition, the Uluru Statement from the Heart, or even treaty. I mean 'radical' in the sense of going to the roots. Until we go there, attachment to Australia as I described it at the beginning of this essay will be ethically compromised. The desire to learn from Aboriginal peoples about how to achieve a deeper relation to the earth will often be undermined by sentimentality.

It was the part played by climate change in the ferocity and extent of the fires that made many people throughout the world grieve for the earth rather than only for Australia. Climate change will test whether the nations of the world can constitute a global community in more than name only. Talk of a community of any kind is empty unless members of the community are concerned about the harms suffered by their fellow members — natural harms of the kind suffered by the victims of the fire, and, just as importantly, the wrongs done to them. The same is true of the idea of a community of nations, which can become an ethical reality that expresses the common humanity of all the peoples of the earth only if nations render themselves answerable to international criminal law. To find it unimaginable, as I believe most Australians now do, that one's political leaders should be answerable to an international criminal court for the wrongs they have done to citizens of other nations, is a sure sign of jingoism. We should therefore prepare ourselves for, and welcome, the day when there will be a new crime in international law, whose name we do not yet know, but whose ethical significance as a crime against the earth and all things of it will be ethically as grave as crimes against humanity now are. When that happens, I believe we will look back on 2019 as the year when the die was cast.

---

1. I try to answer that question in an extended introduction and afterword to my *The Philosopher's Dog*, Routledge, New York, 2017.
2. See https://theconversation.com/dreamtime-and-the-dreaming-an-introduction-20833. Last accessed 23 July 2020.

---

# The Taste of Reality

Philipa Rothfield

According to French philosopher, Jean Baudrillard, we live in a time of media saturation. Historical events are mediated by the circulating discourses of news, film, commentary and social media. As a result, we cannot access the real, independent of its representation. Baudrillard gives the example of the reactor meltdown at the Three Mile Island facility in the United States in March 1979. Twelve days before the real nuclear accident, a film (*The China Syndrome*) was released about a nuclear accident in the US. For Baudrillard, the historical reality of the accident merged with its fictional depiction.[1] What we experience is a mixture of these two registers, the imaginary and the real.

According to this view, representation not only sets the conditions for experience — our experience of actual disaster — but also, historical reality cannot be extricated from the fictional event. Could the same be said of our experience of the 2019–2020 bushfires: namely, that there is a sense in which the event of these fires had already 'happened' by virtue of its representation within the cultural imaginary? Could it further be said that 'the experience' of these bushfires was inextricably caught up in scientific prediction and analysis, in the political theatre of climate activism, geo-political and cultural critique, government policy and environmental practice?

In one sense, these bushfires were predicted, prefigured, feared and anticipated, in literary as well as scientific form. There is no shortage of media reportage, opinion and editorial, identifying the link between international events and global warming. To that extent, Baudrillard would be right to draw attention to the ways in which the figure of climate change is embedded in its experience. But for one thing: the taste of the bushfire smoke that blanketed Melbourne — in my eyes, in my nostrils, on my clothes, and in my hair. My experience of that smoke was corporeal, not semiotic, less a question of representation than a taste of the real.

On 14 January 2020, the Australian bushfires were such that Melbourne experienced the worst air quality in the world.[2] The smoke enveloping Melbourne turned the sun into a dusky orange disk, occluded neighbouring buildings, and wiped out the city's silhouette. It joined a procession of cloud-smoke that would make a full-circuit around the globe.[3] That smoke was my connection to history. Its conversion of life into particulate matter became more than a mere signifier for, once inhaled, the weight of climate change entered my body. The imaginary threat of imminent destruction had become real. It was inside me.

By incorporating the Australian bushfires, my body is put in touch with the destruction of swathes of bush, houses, people, animals, wildlife, entire life forms. I am part of this, this earth, this unfolding geo-history. Whatever my experience of these events, the smoke reminds me that I am not separate. Maurice Merleau-Ponty's conception of the flesh captures this sense of connection in the midst of (individual) difference.[4] For Merleau-Ponty, my perception is embedded in the world. To perceive is also to participate, to be part of that which I perceive. Merleau-Ponty stopped short of dissolution. I am still me — the subject and centre of experience — but no longer can I separate myself from what is happening. I feel like I am part of the earth's history. I no longer contemplate it as if from afar.

I feel sad, for the people, for the trees, for the animals and the wildlife. I feel responsible, individually and collectively. I feel for my daughter, for her future, for the future. I feel locked into a *modus operandi* destined to create more and more havoc. I feel for our First Peoples, having to bear witness to the effects of colonization, having to bear its impact on their person, on Country. I try to imagine how things would have been were this country not colonized, land not cleared, trees not felled. Only now are non-Indigenous Australians asking after Indigenous land care practices, a belated degree of respect born of self-interest.

Even though I want to acknowledge the sense that the body, my body, links me to the bush and to this land, there are historical factors that call into question a simplistic sense of belonging. Colonization, dispossession, genocide and the imposition of private property upon indigenous sovereignty pit time (history) against space (the land). Toula Nicolacoupolos and George Vassilacopoulous speak of our 'occupier being' on this land.[5] It is hard to imagine sorting out the way the Australian landscape is cared for without fully recognizing indigenous sovereignty. So while there is a sense of connection and continuity, of being part of something greater, there is also an ethical and political need to acknowledge difference, the production of difference and its attendant injustices.

Writing in the midst of the coronavirus pandemic, I am returned again to the question of air, if not smoke. According to Chinese medicine, the lung meridian enters into a relationship of exchange, between the inside and the outside. It embodies a mode of incorporation and expiration, ever moving between these states. I breathe the air that is part of the greater whole. Merleau-Ponty writes that 'we are the world that thinks itself'.[6] Is it possible to open up thought to a different kind of world?

Bruno Latour suggests we take advantage of our current situation to think critically and creatively about the suspension of global activities necessitated by COVID-19.[7] Latour claims the coronavirus has shown us 'that it is possible, in a few weeks, to put an economic system on hold everywhere in the world', something ecologists have been advocating for a long time.[8]

The question then is to resist a return to business as usual, to find a way to arrest 'the train of progress' so as to stage an ecological 'landing on Earth'.[9] Latour asks us to think through what it is that we would not like to see come back, how to support workers in such a transition, what activities to create and how. As with a mass elimination diet, we are to carefully monitor the introduction of new/old foods. Latour's challenge is to resist the idea that the best thing would be to have things just as they were. The point being, perhaps things were not so great, perhaps our obsession with production is injurious, not just to us but to life on earth. Also, that this moment of pause is also a chance to think and do differently, an opportunity to become otherwise, to create new possibilities and new relationships.

---

1. J. Baudrillard, *Simulacra and Simulation*, University of Michigan Press, Ann Arbor, 1994.
2. C. Webb and A. McMillan, 'Smoke Haze Makes Melbourne's Air Quality World's Worst, for a Time', *The Age*, https://www.theage.com.au/national/victoria/melbourne-s-air-quality-plummets-to-hazardous-levels-20200114-p53r7k.html. Last accessed 8 April 2020.
3. D. Keane, 'Bushfire Smoke Plume Destined to Reach Australia Again After Circling the Globe, NASA Says', ABC *News*, https://www.abc.net.au/news/2020-01-13/bushfire-smoke-plume-expected-to-lap-the-globe-nasa-says/11863298. Last accessed 8 April 2020.
4. M. Merleau-Ponty, *The Visible and the Invisible*, Northwestern University Press, Evanston, 1968.
5. T. Nicolacopoulos, and G. Vassilacopoulos, *Indigenous Sovereignty and the Being of the Occupier, Manifesto for a White Australian Philosophy of Origins*, re.press, Melbourne, 2014.
6. Merleau-Ponty op.cit., p. 136.
7. B. Latour, https://aoc.media/opinion2020/03/29/imaginer-les-gestes-barrieres-contre-le-retour-a-la-production-davant-crises/, trans. S. Muecke. Last accessed 20 September 2020.
8. Ibid.
9. Ibid.

# Koala Makes Us Australian

Freya Mathews

In Melbourne, where I live, the summer of 2019–2020 was unseasonably cool. For that reason, I felt at first somewhat removed from the fires. However, by the early days of January, I, like most of us, had become obsessed with the unfolding media spectacle of our nation in chaos — of thousands of people stranded amid infernos on the south-east coast; of people being evacuated by military vessels from lurid beaches; of highways choked with the traffic of fleeing holiday makers; and of community after community receiving the warning, 'you are in imminent danger and need to take action now', as towers of flame bore down on their homes.

    Over on the south coast, Kangaroo Island, iconic wildlife haven of over 4,000 square kilometres and home to a flourishing koala population of 50,000, was meanwhile undergoing incineration. Along with the rest of the world, I gazed transfixed with horror at images of blackened koalas, their still-living faces mutilated and scorched. I listened to them cry out in terrified little voices as they scrambled over glowing red ground on bare feet, their fur on fire. My heart cracked as I watched in video after video, desperately parched koalas approach a human stranger for help, reaching out to hold their benefactor's hand as they drank from the proffered water bottle. The shattered expressions of the little patients, bundled up in bandages and bunny rugs in the backyards and living rooms of saintly wildlife carers, were hard to bear.

    I remembered my own foray into burnt-out fire fields in earlier years, searching for survivors to deliver to carers. This was also koala country, and each charred body we found told the heart-rending tale of the animal's last moments. Particularly memorable was that of a mother koala, still gripping the base of a tree with one paw and the hand of her collapsed child with the other; also, that of a koala pressed into a slight excavation in the side of a stream bank, the depth of the excavation too pitifully small to provide protection. Koalas are more vulnerable to fire than most of the larger mammal species, being so slow-moving and so dependent for everything — food, shelter and safety — on the dangerously flammable eucalypt.

    There were of course videos and photographs of numerous other animals, grievously hurt or charred beyond recognition, and commentary about the tragic losses to conservation that had been incurred: six million hectares of threatened species habitat destroyed; the ranges of approximately 70 nationally threatened species reduced by 50 per cent; and, the figure that shocked the world, more than a billion mammals, birds and reptiles killed.

But, due to the circumstance of the Kangaroo Island fires and its impact on the last large colony of disease-free koalas in Australia, it was koalas that became the face of the Great Fires to the world.

Eventually, in February, cooler, wetter weather arrived and the fires abated. But we know that this is how it is going to be henceforth: that our forests are drying out and that our new climate might not be able to sustain forests any more. Forested areas might revert to the arid shrub land that occupies most of the Australian continent. It is hard to know what conservation might mean under these new conditions when the painstaking and expensive work of decades is cancelled out in a few days or weeks. The epic suffering that we have witnessed our wildlife endure is not over; it will be repeated endlessly into the future. Perhaps eventually we shall lose our heritage of wildlife altogether, the wildlife that, as Australians, we take for granted, abuse, trivialise, but clearly also love.

The outpouring of love was for me the most surprising response to the fires. In the past the deadly toll of bushfires on wildlife has been almost entirely ignored in news coverage and commentary. The impact of fires has always been measured in terms of asset loss (including the loss of so-called 'livestock') and loss of human lives. But now the plight of wildlife was being captured on phones and broadcast to the world in real time. Animal terror and torment was no longer backgrounded as a 'natural' part of fires, but seen for what it is — individual trauma experienced as we would experience it ourselves.

As the world outside looked on, and we were aware of others perceiving us and our wildlife as interchangeably Australian, we realised that that is indeed who we are. We are the Koala people — Kangaroo, Wallaby, Wombat, Kookaburra, Emu, Cockatoo, Platypus and Lyrebird people. For a hundred years, non-Indigenous Australians have asked the question, who are we? What makes us Australian? Was it Gallipoli and mateship? Don Bradman? Australian Rules football? Holden utes? The barbeque? It is hard to credit that we asked this question, when the answer was so obvious from the start. We are Australian because we inhabit the continent of Australia. The fact that we asked the question at all reveals our entire colonial history of erasure and denial, our blind determination to treat this continent — already at the time of European invasion a federation of innumerable human and other-than-human populations — as a blank slate on which to inscribe a new fiction: 'Australia'. This named fiction could not get beneath our skin, because all the while the continent itself was getting under our skin, and making us who we were — a people unconsciously shaped by the particular patterns of light and shade, sound and smell, wetness and dryness, form and, especially, life-form, that are unique to this particular continent. So, we prattled on about our institutions, our history, our sports heroes, our product brands, but as soon as those of us who were born here went overseas, we missed the smell of eucalyptus and the feel of summer on the beach or in the bush, and knew that we were Australian.

It is surely because we have been so blind to who we are, and have purposely built Australia as a fiction on that founding nullification of the entire variegated, intricately lived-in character of this land that we have from the very start treated the land so abominably. In doing so we have not only brought it to its present pass — desiccated, its soils exposed, cooked, eroded, leached of nutrient, polluted, blown away, its forest skin ripped off, its remaining wildlife battered, diseased and on the run. We have also betrayed ourselves. Because we are, at the end of the day, despite everything we have done, *of this place, this land*. It is because we are *here*, and not for any other reason, that we are Australian.

This land pre-existed us, by temporal orders of magnitude beyond reckoning. We did not make it. It made itself. It was made by Koala, Wallaby, Long-Necked Turtle, Kookaburra, Bettong, and a myriad of other species. They shaped it, with their feats of ecological engineering, at macro- and micro-levels, as it in turn shaped them, their anatomy, their adaptations, their ways of life. It was their country; its character was an expression of their character, as theirs was of its. In more recent aeons, the land was also of course shaped by Indigenous nations, who always acknowledged that theirs was a co-creation with that myriad of other species, each a nation in its own right. When Europeans arrived, their children too were born into Koala Country, Pobblebonk Country, Goanna Country, Cockatoo Country, as well as into the many Countries of the First Peoples. Whitefellas might deny this all they liked, but identity at the deepest level is not made by fiat, but by ontological realities.

Perhaps, as we watched these places, this continent — to which we belong in our ontological depths — reduced to ash without our consent, many of us did indeed realise that this is most fundamentally who we are. While the rest of the world wept for the helplessness of the adorable koala, we wept because Koala — along with our entire extended faunal family — is not only helpless and adorable but, beneath the skin, our kin.

So, Australia has been weeping, in a new way. Throughout the ordeal, people maintained their daily deadpan Aussie personas, their down-to-earth lives, but when talk turned to the fires, many of us found ourselves choking up, ambushed by a grief that lay deeper in our being than we could reach with our words. If the Great Fires have helped non-Indigenous Australians to connect with the ontological bedrock of our identity in this way, then perhaps there is yet hope for our ravaged continent. Identity is after all the deepest seat and source of our human values. If we can tap in psychically to the truth that, in belonging to Australia, we have become part of an extended faunal family, then perhaps the claims of kinship will induce us to set about, under the tutelage of our Indigenous countrymen and -women, the huge task of ecological reparation.

---

A longer earlier version of this essay appeared on the ABC *Religion and Ethics* web site, 9 March 2020, www.abc.net.au/religion/koala-makes-us-australian/12039676.

# It's the Greenies' Fault

## Stephen Muecke

He came from Abbotts Pest Control — was getting a bit old, walked with a limp. I'd called Abbotts to get the possums out of our roof, and Warren got up there on ladders, went in, and trapped them. He was gentle with the possums he caught, talked to them softly: 'Oh, you're just a baby one!' On the last day he came, the fires were raging around the country, and he'd just come back from a trip to Mildura.

'It's those bloody Greenies' fault', Warren said, getting into his HiLux. 'They let all that fuel pile up.'

'But, the Greens aren't in government, never have been.'

'No, but people just go along with their crazy ideas, you know.'

Who are these 'Greenies'? They are not necessarily the political party. They are ideas, abstractions. But we can see and feel the results of their efforts, because the Greenies are the ones who tried to do something, rather than sticking with the status quo. They tried to tell the truth, and even prophesy: 'If we don't do something, we are heading towards disaster'. The Trojans didn't believe Cassandra, either, that was her curse. There are other things besides the curse that make Cassandra less likely to be believed. She speaks in crazy, cryptic language. Sometimes young Trojans would tease her: 'Why are you speaking like an academic, Cassandra?' She doesn't have any formal authority. She's too far ahead of everyone else. She asks too much of the people.

'How's the Murray up at Mildura?' I ask Warren, changing the topic, 'any water in the Darling?'

'There you go again', he says. 'Green tape. All you have to do is put in a few more dams.'

'Nothing to do with cotton farming?' I say. But he didn't want to engage with that.

I imagine Warren as a Barnaby supporter. How do you argue with someone who was young in the 1970s, and things were great then, so why not forever? Dams, cheap petrol, uncongested cities. Clear the land for farming. Bike lanes in cities? Run them off the road!

Remember Cassandra: she asks too much of the people she warns.

'Did you ever catch a Murray cod, Warren? Those were the days.' (Engage at a shared emotional level, I'm thinking. I'm also trying to think of ways of narrating ourselves out of this toxic story.)

'Oh, yeah, fighting fish, them cod. I caught a big one once', and Warren's hands are spread wide.

And then I think, the toxic story I want to narrate our way out of has a long history. We have come to realise this through analysis of the consequences of modernisation. It is a bit like asbestos. Once our best friend for building, we welcomed it into our homes, until the facts about mesothelioma became undeniable and it was ejected from the democracy of things.

Those who continue to deny the history and continuities of climate change will not listen to facts that go against their narratives about how modernisation made their world wealthier, more comfortable, and even safer. If you prophesy that disaster is looming, and provide the facts to prove it, they will not listen because they are engaged at more than one ontological level. There is *factual knowledge*, there is *emotional investment* and there is *belief*, something a bit more metaphysical. The counter-narrative, what philosopher Isabelle Stengers calls a 'counter-spell', has to work at all those levels. And it has to be well-performed. The facts won't 'speak for themselves', they have to be re-created, re-crafted, suspended in networks of affect and knowledge.

If you can engage, through shared dialogue, and you can demonstrate that even people who are *not* toxic-story critics (people such as our populist Prime Minister) now say that they believe the climate facts, then you might be getting somewhere.

But there remains a metaphysical problem. Take war, for example. You can't just stop wars by pointing out that it is immoral to kill people. That kind of naïve pacifism comes across as moralistic. And no Australian larrikin wants to listen to a wowser telling them what they should do. You can only stop wars by engaging with the problem at every level, including killing the War God.

In our contemporary story, we are faced with the task of bringing the God of Modernisation down to earth. It is a god because it has so many ontologically distinct powers: it is factually real; it is abstract and fictional; it has invisible pervasive effects; it provides emotional comfort; it has massive financial backing; it provides collective identity. We need to rediscover the more pagan gods in every precious river, tree and mountain. We need counter-spells to escape its toxic stories.

---

# Perspectives from the Stanley Plateau on Fire and Food

Phillip Darby

Responding to the devastating bushfires in the summer of 2019-20 cannot be done in isolation. The fires interact with the coronavirus crisis, food production and the financial-ideological consideration of spending priorities. In a word, 'politics'. This essay is an overview of events and thinking on the Stanley Plateau, in the high country of north-eastern Victoria between Beechworth and Myrtleford.

My analysis has drawn on published material — mostly sponsored by the Stanley Athenaeum — and discussions with local activists and historians. The plan is first to consider how far the experience on the Stanley Plateau confirms the writing on Aboriginal burning practices as well as the understanding that the bushfire danger is now different in kind from before. Then we will address questions relating to food production. A short conclusion will reflect on the prospect of a major review of political norms.

In their essay in this collection David Bowman and Greg Lehman pay tribute to Victor Steffensen's book *Fire Country*.[1] It is indeed a landmark contribution to thinking for its inclusiveness, grassroots vision and passion. I was particularly struck with Steffensen's Kiplingesque discussion of the animals talking which adds another dimension to our understanding. (Think of Kipling's short story *The Bridge Builders* and also his dog short stories.) With regard to thinking on the Plateau, the much-respected Captain of the Stanley Fire Brigade, Royston Smith, told me there is much to be said for traditional burning practices and that recently the brigade has been working with two trained burners to follow up possibilities.

It is clear that traditional burning practices have the potential to substantially rework the existing firefighting regime, but there is a reluctance to question the high hopes generated by passionate advocacy. Again, it is a matter of the politically possible. For one thing, in our contemporary situation the great majority of people, including many Aboriginals, do not live as hunters and gatherers but are dependent on food obtained from modern animal production, crops and vegetable farms as well as horticulture. For another, the COVID–19 shutdowns pose enormous problems for fire control: cordoning cities from the countryside, closing borders between states and much depleted resources of governments does not augur well for fire control.

As I see it, it is also the case that easy distinctions between indigenous and non-indigenous species are in need of a good deal of rethinking. It appears to be the mindset of quite a number of usually well-informed writers that indigenous plants and animals are seen to pose little risk to the contemporary landscape and food production.[2] Certainly many introduced species such as pigs, deer and foxes are a problem for farmers on the Plateau. But a number of native animals and birds have enormously increased since white settlement. In the Stanley region sulphur-crested cockatoos in their thousands devastate orchards and more recently wombats have multiplied greatly, invading orchards and sheds, returning time and time again to dig out newly planted trees.

At this point I turn to the experience of the connection between fire control and climate change on the Plateau. Explorers and a few perceptive settlers noted the abundance of food as well as the lack of undergrowth which resulted in stretches of open grassland that attracted game. It was realized that this was not a natural condition but was the result of Aboriginal burning. Towards the end of the 19th century bushfires were becoming more common because of logging and the clearing of scrub along the creeks by gold diggers. As time passed, knowledge of Aboriginal burning practices was lost, trust being placed — especially in Stanley — on the cool climate and heavy rainfall. Later, the Government's refusal to allow local people to burn for fuel reduction and fire breaks was seen as a way to strengthen Stanley's natural climatic good fortune.[3] When a decision was made to establish a Stanley Fire Brigade in 1927 the myth was still widely held that a bushfire was most unlikely in Stanley. (In point of fact the Stanley CFA was not established until 1974.)

From the turn of the 20th century the experience of fires in Stanley was an awakening from much of the complacency of earlier years. Drought and very high temperatures during 2002 set the scene for fires of greatly increased intensity following lightning strikes. From the upper Kiewa valley, through the Ovens to Mount Buffalo and reaching the upper Murray, blazes were soon out of control with one merging with another. By the 21 January 2003, Stanley was seriously threatened. The Stanley Fire Brigade, supported by locals with utes and trucks were faced with a seemingly impossible task with fires springing up in multiple sites — including pine plantations — fanned by choppy winds. During the night reinforcements arrived. An Erikson S-64 air crane (Elvis) made some crucial drops near the cemetery before the winds strengthened making it too dangerous to fly. After being advised by police, some residents took refuge — with their animals — in the schoolyard and Stanley oval. Others stayed to protect their houses. A contingent of volunteers opted to feed the firefighters and one woman even set up her massage chair which was much appreciated. The fires were not contained until 27 January and putting out smouldering logs and ashes continued for another three weeks. In all, 2003 was a frightening turning-point regarding Stanley's vulnerability but worse was to come.

2009 was the year when the limits of what could be done hit home. The ferocity of the fires had to be seen to be believed. It could no longer be rationally denied that the Plateau was becoming drier and hotter due to climate change or that fires could be controlled as in the past. In my own area to the south of the village the flames appeared to be hundreds of feet high and spotting far ahead. Fire crews were stationed at a number of properties but there was nothing they could do. A bulldozer tried to stop the fire crossing the road but to no avail. It was not until the next day that crews and farmers could put out spot fires. I was shown a site where nothing remained: it was as if an atomic explosion had occurred.

More generally, with regard to climate change in my orchard, significant developments have taken place in the weather conditions in a very short period of time. Walnut trees in about twelve acres planted in 1938 lying between two hills were invariably hit by frost. Perhaps every third year we got no nuts at all and the trees would take a whole season to recover full leaf. Over the past eight or ten years we have experienced no frosts in the crucial spring period. Yet now we are faced with a new problem. We have to spray some varieties of nuts to protect them from sunburn in high summer.

This brings to our attention the role of Stanley in food production both for domestic and overseas consumption. Sadly, food production is now a shadow of what it was earlier. My guide here is Gif Thompson whom the community turns to for historical knowledge. After the demise of gold digging some locals took to planting potatoes and did quite well. Gif estimates that in its heyday there were more than 200 acres of spuds which were sought after for their quality and that they kept exceptionally well. Now there would be less than 10 acres planted for commercial sale. The collapse of the potato market in the late 1950s he attributes to the unsuitability of the Stanley climate for mechanical digging plus the swing in the market — or perhaps one should say supermarkets — to clean potatoes that are grown in sandy soil, not rich dark loam.

In the 1950s, growers turned to horticulture, the main planting being apples. Red apples were especially favoured because the very cold winters gave them a splendid colour and crispness. On Gif's calculations in 1950 there were 30 to 35 apple orchards. His own family farm loaded up three to four semi-trailers each day, whereas now one and a half semi-trailers would clean up the total crop. Again, there are various reasons for the collapse in production but I will illustrate by giving an example. Stanley excelled in producing a red apple named King Cole which had a tart flavour and was mainly shipped to the UK for consumption there. However, when the UK went into the common market on 1 January 1973 alternative markets could not be found. Some growers bulldozed out the trees. Others top-worked theirs to new varieties. A few went broke in the process. King Cole aside, the plight of the apple grower is graphically conveyed by a neighbour who bulldozed out two blocks of modern apples. He explained that when he had to sell them to major markets he got less than half their production costs.

A related issue is the enormously increased quantity of water now being taken off the plateau. The number of agricultural and domestic bores has increased dramatically. In addition, there is the commercial extraction of water for bottling sent off to Japan. After litigation that went to the Supreme Court of Victoria, the Stanley Rural Community Association was left with a $70,000 debt as the Water Act trumped the Planning Act.[4] It is telling that the volume of water now being extracted is a major concern of the Stanley Fire Brigade.

Another consideration is that the composition of the community has undergone much change over the past few years. Young people have gone to the cities and it must be at least a decade since anyone has taken a farming or horticultural apprenticeship. New people have arrived to enjoy the beauty of Stanley and to escape the noise and bustle of the city. Where I live is still mainly farmed by growers but elsewhere there is a good deal of tension between horticulturalists and new arrivals over spray programmes, scare guns and similar.

Despite the difficulties I have touched on, there are openings for nut and some fruit growers to expand production catering to migrant communities now settled in Australia. These people know about varieties and flavours with many remembering the foods grown in the mountains of their homelands. They are prepared to pay higher prices than Anglos (for whom nuts do not much feature in the culinary agenda). Leading the way were the Italians and the Greeks plus a smaller number of people from Poland and Germany. More recently the list has been extended to Turks, through the Middle East, India, and migrants from Southeast and East Asia. It is nuts that are particularly valued but I think some fruits as well.

Much of this essay has been concerned with the difficulties of negotiating a bushfire strategy for the future and with the obstacles to increasing food production on the Stanley Plateau. I would like, however, to conclude on a somewhat more positive note. There is reason to hope that the COVID-19 crisis may have changed the tenor of Australian politics in quite fundamental ways. The opposition in conservative quarters to interventionist government appears to have little support in the broader community. Closely associated is an accelerated movement for rethinking the ruling neoliberal economics of the past thirty years. To take one illustration, the campaign of the Australia Institute to reclaim a broken debate that prioritizes solving problems ahead of delivering surpluses. Hence new relationships appear to be emerging which were earlier unthinkable. But a caveat is needed. As I write in late May 2020 the Morrison Government shows every sign that it is returning to the market mechanisms of neoliberalism.

The present situation is perhaps best summed up by Sally McManus, secretary of the Australian Council of Trade Unions, who has been in daily contact with Industrial Relations Minister, Christian Porter, and the two have worked well together. Asked whether this will last, McManus replied:

"I don't think you can go through a crisis, no matter what it is — whether it's a personal or collective one — and ever emerge the same. What that means and what it looks like it's far too early to tell."[5]

---

1. Victor Steffensen, *Fire Country: How Indigenous Fire Management could help save Australia*, Hardie Grant Travel, Sydney, 2020.
2. Victor Steffensen is a notable exception. See Ibid, pp.157–9.
3. Here I am following Jacqui Durrant, *Fire on the Plateau: A history of fire and its management in Stanley*, Stanley Atheneum, 2019.
4. See the article written by Tony Wright, 'The town that fought the water merchants and lost', *The Age*, Feb 17, 2018.
5. *The Saturday Paper*, April 4–10, 2020, p.22

# The sense is porous to the thing
Anne Elvey

*after Paul Celan*

You say the thing is
ash; ash is the thing.
You defy Adorno, cut
the breath, say cinders

are in your eyes. To turn
the breath, you whet
the eye. When flesh opens
between fringed curves

a soft glass bends
the light. A child brings sun
to a point on the page. Retina
burns for an instant

to invert the grape mind decodes
as an eye, as love trodden
into words, as if to say
this thing survives otherwise

as if poetry were a bone-sliver
picked from ash. Your thought
if not joy is a tendering of flesh
deprived of saying that says

write me where cells
become breath to char
the page. A wild fire
is another thing. When wind

arrives from the bush, a cornea
itches. A retinal stamp is turned
upright by the synapse that links
and sifts the organ of memory

for a word that might turn
the breath. It is time, you say.
It is time. Time is this sliver
between ash and the thing.

---

First published in Anne Elvey, *On arrivals of breath: poems & prayers*, Montrose: Poetica Christi Press, 2019, pp. 54–55.

---

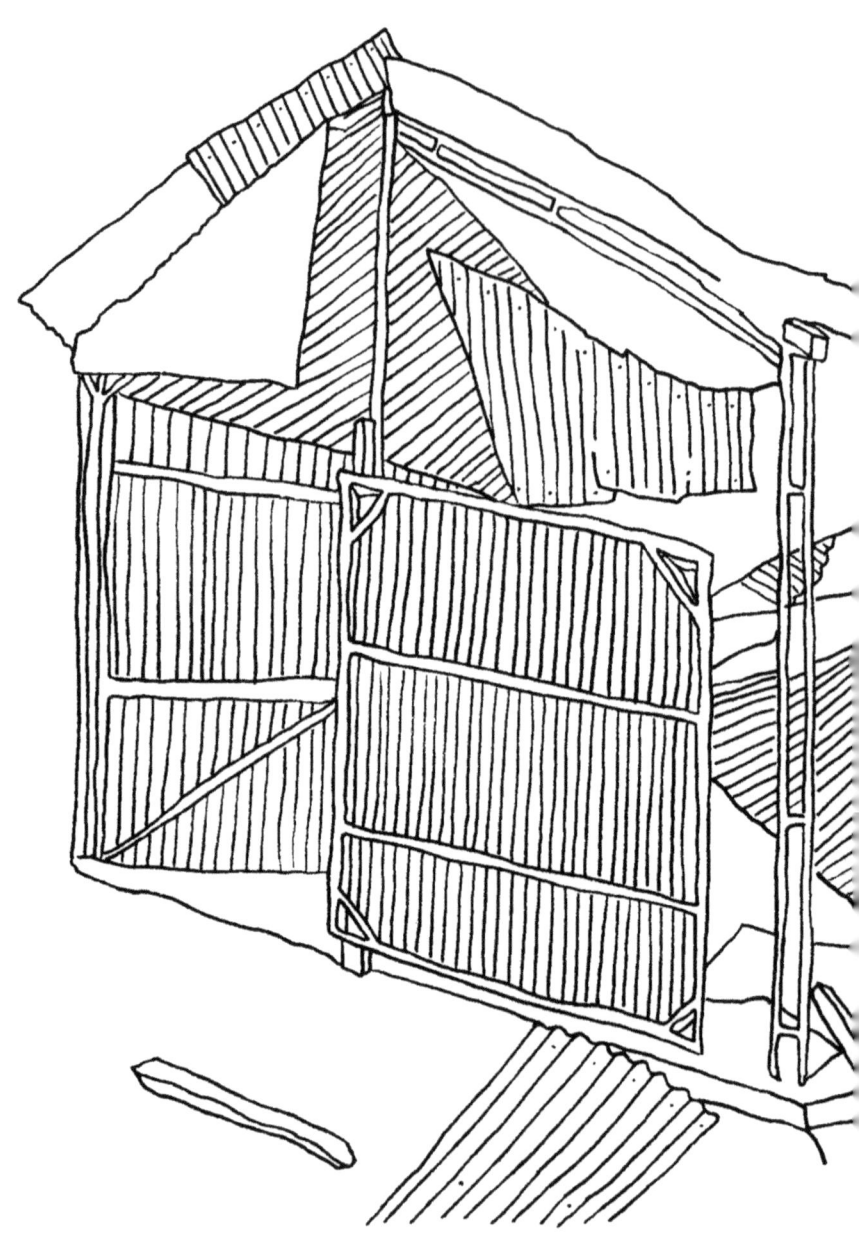

# Traumas

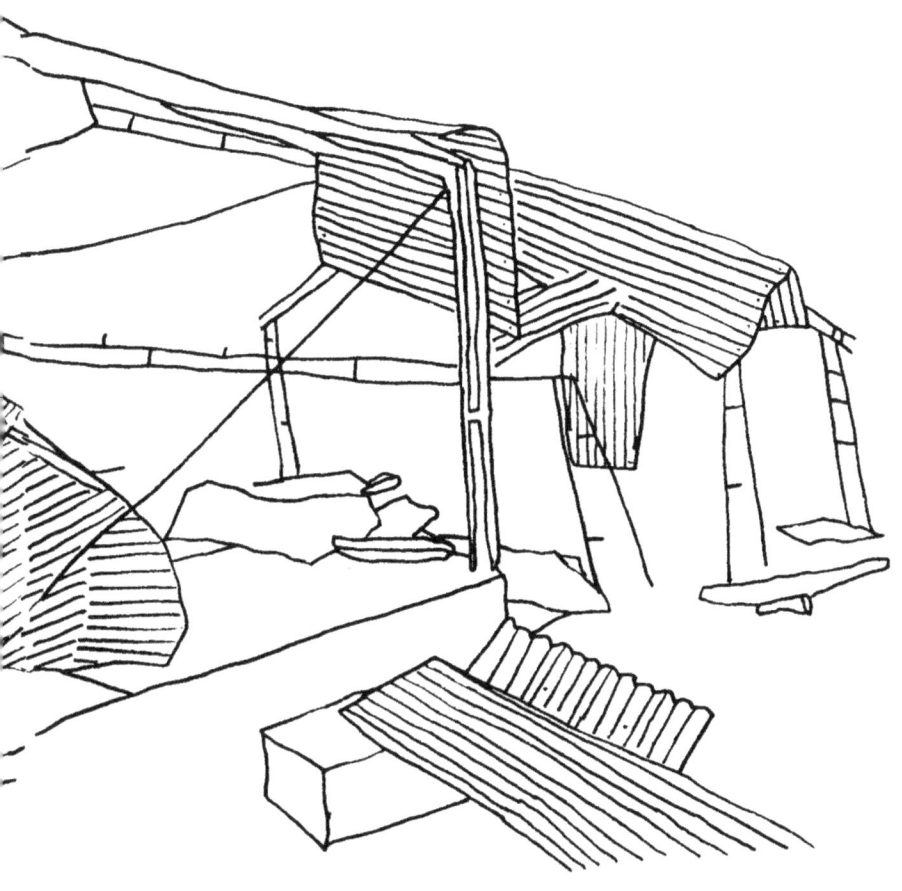

14.02.20
The burnt leaves on the trees. The crisp ground cracking under my feet, the walk around a burnt shed. The corrugated iron all twisted and bent.

Text & Drawing • Hugo Muecke

# Aboriginal People Find Strength Despite Perpetual Grief

Bhiamie Williamson, Jessica Weir, Vanessa Cavanagh[1]

How do you support people forever attached to a landscape after an inferno tears through their homelands? The latest fires decimated native food sources, burned through ancient scarred trees, and destroyed ancestral and totemic plants and animals. The fact is, the experience of Aboriginal peoples in the fire crisis engulfing much of Australia is vastly different to that of non-Indigenous peoples.

Colonial legacies of eradication, dispossession, assimilation and racism continue to impact the lived realities of Aboriginal peoples. Added to this is the widespread exclusion of our peoples from accessing and managing traditional homelands. These factors compound the trauma of these unprecedented fires. As Australia picks up the pieces from these fires, it's more important than ever to understand the unique grief Aboriginal peoples experience.[2] Only through this understanding can effective strategies be put in place to support our communities to recover.

Aboriginal peoples live with a sense of perpetual grief. It stems from the as-yet-unresolved matter of the invasion and subsequent colonisation of our homelands.[3] While there are many instances of colonial trauma inflicted upon Aboriginal peoples — including the removal of children and the suppression of culture, ceremony and language — dispossession of Country remains paramount. Dispossessing people of their lands is a hallmark of colonisation.[4] Australian laws have changed to partially return Aboriginal peoples' lands and waters, and Aboriginal people have long worked to advocate for more effective management of Country.[5] But, despite this, the majority of our peoples have been consigned to the margins in managing our homelands. Aboriginal people have watched on and been ignored as homelands have been mismanaged and neglected.[6] Oliver Costello is chief executive of Firesticks, an Indigenous-led network that is re-invigorating cultural burning. As he puts it: 'Since colonisation, many Indigenous people have been removed from their land, and their cultural fire management practices have been constrained by authorities, informed by Western views of fire and land management'.[7]

In this way, settler-colonialism is not historical, but a lived experience. And the growing effects of climate change compound this trauma.[8] It's also important to recognise that our people grieve not only for our communities, but for our non-human relations. Aboriginal peoples' cultural identity comes from the land. As such, Aboriginal cultural lives and livelihoods continue to be tied to the land, including landscape features such as waterholes, valleys and mountains, as well as native animals and plants. The decimation caused by the fires deeply impacts the existence of Aboriginal peoples and, in the most severely hit areas, threatens Aboriginal groups as distinct cultural beings attached to the land. As *The Guardian's* Indigenous affairs editor Lorena Allam recently writes:

> Like you, I've watched in anguish and horror as fire lays waste to precious Yuin land, taking everything with it — lives, homes, animals, trees — but for First Nations people it is also burning up our memories, our sacred places, all the things which make us who we are.[9]

For Aboriginal people then, who live with the trauma of dispossession and neglect and now the trauma of catastrophic fire, our grief is immeasurably different to that of non-Indigenous people.

## Bushfire Recovery Must Consider Culture

As we come to terms with the devastation of this summer of bushfires, Australia must turn its gaze to recovery. The field of community recovery offers valuable insights into how groups of people can come together and move forward after disasters. But an examination of research and commentary in this area reveals how poorly non-Indigenous Australia, and the international field of community recovery, understands the needs of Aboriginal people. Often 'community' is understood to be a single socio-cultural group of people, where people's individual needs broadly reflect each other's.[10]

Research in Australia and overseas has demonstrated that for Aboriginal people, healing from historical and contemporary trauma is a cultural and spiritual process and inherently tied to land.[11] The failure to include the influence of culture in community recovery, means that these differences are not acknowledged. Without considering the historical, political and cultural contexts that continue to define the lives of Aboriginal peoples, responses to the crisis are likely to be inadequate and inappropriate.[12]

The long-term effects of colonisation have meant Aboriginal communities are accustomed to living with catastrophic changes to their societies and lands, adjusting and adapting to keep functioning.[13] Experts consider these resilience traits as integral for communities to survive and recover from natural disasters. In this way, the resilience of Aboriginal communities fashioned through centuries of colonisation, coupled with adequate support, means Aboriginal communities in fire-affected areas are well placed not only to recover, but to do so quickly. This is a salient lesson for agencies and other non-government organisations entrusted to lead the disaster recovery process. The community characteristics that enable effective and timely community recovery, such as close social links and shared histories, already exist in the Aboriginal communities affected.[14]

## Moving Forward

The agency in charge of leading the recovery in bushfire-affected areas must begin respectfully and appropriately, and so too the different enquiry and review processes. To do so, they must be equipped with the basic knowledge of our peoples' different circumstances. It's important to note this isn't 'special treatment'. Instead, it recognises that policy and practice must be fit-for-purpose and, at the very least, not do further harm. As Aboriginal woman, scholar and co-author Vanessa Cavanagh wrote during the fires: 'I hope that Indigenous knowledge and expertise takes precedence in the forward management of natural environments. This requires Indigenous people and systems leading the process, not being tacked on, or our knowledges excerpted and cropped into failing models'.[15]

If agencies and non-government organisations responsible for leading the recovery from these fires aren't well-prepared, they risk inflicting new trauma on Aboriginal communities.[16] At the same time, we need to support Aboriginal peoples' own organisations and leadership. For example, two Aboriginal-led responses have emerged to provide direct support to south coast Aboriginal families in New South Wales. These are the joint Illawarra Aboriginal Medical Service and Dr Marlene Longbottom appeal,[17] and the Indigenous Crisis Response and Recovery appeal.[18] Central to both of these fundraising initiatives is the importance of culturally appropriate support.

The National Disability Insurance Agency offers an example of how the public sector is learning to engage with Aboriginal people in culturally sensitive ways. Whilst imperfect, their Aboriginal and Torres Strait Islander Strategy includes thinking about Country, culture and community, and working with each community's values and customs to establish respectful, trusting relationships. This demonstrates that a large national agency responsible for administering a complex and long-term policy can set out to embed different ways of working within its structures and recognise the uniqueness of Indigenous peoples.

The new bushfire recovery agency must use a similar strategy. This would acknowledge both the historical experiences of Aboriginal peoples and our inherent strengths as communities that have not only survived, but remain connected to our homelands. Similarly, the enquiry and review processes must learn and adapt.[19] In this way, perhaps the bushfire crisis might have some positive longer-term outcomes, opening new doors to collaboration with Aboriginal people, drawing on our strengths and values and prioritising our unique interests.

1. Where we have used 'our' in this text, Bhiamie and Vanessa are speaking from their standpoint as Aboriginal people.
2. A.C. Willox, S.L. Harper, V.L. Edge, K. Landman, K., Houle, J.D. Ford, and The Rigolet Inuit Community Government, 'The Land Enriches the Soul: On Climatic and Environmental Change, Affect, and Emotional Health and Well-being in Rigolet, Nunatsiavut, Canada', *Emotion, Space and Society*, vol. 6, no. 1, 2013, pp. 14–24.
3. B. Pascoe, *Dark Emu: Black seeds Agriculture or Accident?* Magabala Books, Broome, 2014; T. Alfred, and J. Corntassel, 'Being Indigenous: Resurgences Against Contemporary Colonialism', *Government and Opposition*, vol. 40, no. 4, 2005, pp. 597–614.
4. A. Moreton-Robinson, *The White Possessive: Property, Power, and Indigenous Sovereignty*, University of Minnesota Press, Minneapolis, 2015.
5. S. Hemming, D. Rigney, S. Bignall, S. Berg, and G. Rigney, 'Indigenous Nation Building for Environmental Futures: Murrundi Flows through Ngarrindjeri Country', *Australasian Journal of Environmental Management*, vol. 26, no. 3, 2019, pp. 216–35.
6. M. Faa, 'Indigenous Leaders Say Australia's Bushfire Crisis Shows Approach to Land Management Failing', ABC *News*, 14 November 2019, https://www.abc.net.au/news/2019-11-14/traditional-owners-predicted-bushfire-disaster/11700320?pfmredir=sm. Last accessed 14 March 2020.
7. Firesticks Alliance, 'Reinvigorate Australia's cultural fire knowledge', Media Release, 9 January 2020.
8. N.J. Turner and H. Clifton, '"It's so Different Today": Climate Change and Indigenous Lifeways in British Columbia, Canada', *Global Environmental Change*, vol. 19, no. 2, 2009, pp. 180–90.
9. Lorena Allam, 'For First Nations People the Bushfires Bring a Particular Grief, Burning What Makes Us Who We Are', *Guardian*, 6 January 2020.
10. For example, M. Moreton, '"We Needed Help, But We Weren't Helpless": The Community Experience of Community Recovery after Natural Disaster in Australia', *Australian Journal of Emergency Management*, vol. 33, no. 1, 2018, pp. 19–22.
11. E. Fast, and D. Collin-Vézina, 'Historical Trauma, Race-based Trauma and Resilience of Indigenous Peoples: A Literature Review', *First Peoples Child & Family Review*, vol. 5 no. 1, 2010, pp. 126–136; M. Feeney, 'Reclaiming the Spirit of Well Being: Promising healing practices for Aboriginal and Torres Strait Islander people', Discussion Paper, prepared for The Stolen Generations Alliance, 2009.
12. B. Williamson, F. Markham and J. Weir, 'Aboriginal Peoples and the response to the 2019–20 Bushfires', Working Paper, Centre for Aboriginal Economic Policy Research, Canberra, 2020.
13. K.P. Whyte, 'Indigenous science (fiction) for the Anthropocene: Ancestral dystopias and fantasies of climate change crises', *Environment and Planning E: Nature and Space*, vol. 1, no. 1–2, 2018, pp. 224–242.
14. R. Tiwari, J. Stephens, and R. Hooper, 'Mission Rehabilitation — a Community-centric Approach to Aboriginal Healing', *Australian Aboriginal Studies*, vol. 2, 2019, pp. 19–33.
15. Twitter 7 January 2020.
16. R. Howitt, O. Havnen and S. Veland, 'Natural and Unnatural Disasters: Responding with Respect for Indigenous Rights and Knowledges', *Geographical Research*, vol. 50, no. 1, 2012, pp. 47–59.
17. S. Wellington, 'Donations flow to fire-ravaged Indigenous communities on NSW south coast', NITV *News*, 7 January 2020. https://www.sbs.com.au/nitv/article/2020/01/07/donations-flow-fire-ravaged-indigenous-communities-nsw-south-coast. Accessed 16 March 2020.
18. Go Fund Me, Indigenous Crisis Response and Recovery, 11 January 2020. https://au.gofundme.com/f/indigenous-crisis-response-amp-recovery. Accessed 16 March 2020.
19. Williamson et al, 2020, op. cit

An earlier version of this essay was published online at *The Conversation*, 10 January 2020. https://theconversation.com/strength-from-perpetual-grief-how-aboriginal-people-experience-the-bushfire-crisis-129448.

# From Powerlessness to Agency During the Bushfires and COVID-19

Jane Fisher

I was away from Australia when the bushfires took lives and destroyed homes and livelihoods, communities, and places of history and beauty. International print and broadcast media accounts were sparse and gave the fires low priority. Even Australian online news clips provided thin factual descriptions, but could not convey the scale and scope, the intensity and the horror.

I returned to the pervasive smoke, acrid and disturbing in inner Melbourne, far from its source on our southeast coast. I experienced an urgent sense of needing to act, to contribute, to assist, to ameliorate, but could find few ways in which this could be realised. I admired community groups who went to fire-sites to provide practical assistance to victims of the fire and to the firefighters and frontline workers. Images revealed the active generosity of the Sikh Volunteer Group who had travelled to prepare and give meals, people caring for injured animals, police and naval personnel braving appalling conditions to rescue people who had escaped the fire by fleeing to the beach, and so many others. None of these required assistance from an urban academic in public health, a clinical psychologist.

Financial donations were necessary, but to whom and for what? There were detailed public accounts of the complexities and expenses of administering large funds, of monies that did not reach easily to people in need. Debates about how to govern funds and apportion them fairly, abounded. I recalled the paralysis that had followed Black Saturday (2009), and the deliberations about how to estimate and place a financial value on injury and loss. I know too how essential, but inadequate, financial contributions are to enabling people to integrate such horror into their life narratives, and find capacity to re-engage with a future, to participate and regain hopefulness.

I felt powerless. Power is most commonly considered as a capacity to exert authority or control over others. However, it can also be understood as an ability to act in relation to your own life, to apply skills or express values, contribute intentionally to the community or for the public good. Powerlessness is an absence of agency, a sense of incompetence, being unable to imagine a solution.[1] I reflected on my powerlessness in relation to the bushfires and wondered about the potential for psychosocial research to contribute to understanding the immediate and longer-term consequences for the psychological health of people who had been affected directly.

I had conversations with colleagues in the Department of Health and Human Services about the heightened needs of women who are pregnant and their growing foetuses during natural disasters, and the opportunity to understand this through collaborative research. I was invited to write a concept note, which was submitted and passed to those making decisions about the distribution of public funds for community reconstruction. Some sense of agency returned, there was potential that my skills could be useful even if applied in a way that was peripheral to the primary effort.

However, all of this was engulfed by the COVID-19 pandemic and the essential public health response to prevent the spread of the infection. The pandemic touched everyone, while the bushfires affected some people profoundly and others minimally. In the face of the pandemic, we all needed to do things: adjust to working from home while maintaining productivity and collegiality, maintain a physical distance from others, meet online and not in person, avoid visits to people living in aged care homes, cancel milestone events and travel arrangements, and be vigilant about health behaviours and signs of infection. Much of this was socially costly, but there were opportunities to act.

With colleagues, I found two opportunities to contribute. First, was to offer a way of understanding the psychological impact of the profound alterations to daily life and the threats either of illness, or of fines and public criticism, that pervaded media accounts and civic messages. I was struck by how many of these experiences incurred loss — not the publicly recognised loss of bereavement, but rather, unacknowledged loss. Disenfranchised grief applies to experiences of loss which might not be recognised, either by the person or by others.[2] Like grief following bereavement, disenfranchised grief is accompanied by disbelief and shock, yearning for reality to be different or as it was before the loss, and then uncertainty and sadness. The process is more difficult because unrecognised losses tend not to attract increased social support, or give rise to ceremonies and rituals.

With a fellow psychologist, I wrote a short article about disenfranchised grief in the context of COVID-19.[3] We argued that the losses of liberty and autonomy; of privacy, as our behaviours were subject to increasing scrutiny; of trust, as our potential to infect each other was made prominent; and, paradoxically, of participation, enforced through required isolation and seclusion, were sources of grief. More obvious, was the grief of being prohibited from joining the events that mark life progressions and draw people with whom we are affiliated together: weddings and funerals, milestone birthdays and celebrations of transitions. All were made worse by the lack of access to interactions with others and their potential to soothe and distract, assist with problem solving, comfort and encourage. We argued further that appreciating the impact of disenfranchised grief by speaking empathically and appreciatively about what had been lost, might improve uptake of public messaging.

It is not possible to quantify reach, impact and influence, but the open-access article was read apparently by thousands of people. We were contacted by agencies we had not previously heard of, to ask whether they could make it available to their constituents, for example, people living in public housing in inner-city Sydney, and members of an advocacy group for families affected by foetal alcohol syndrome. All told us that it explained to them how they were feeling and provided a language to communicate about their experiences.

We realised, then, as a research group that we had capacity to enable many people to contribute their experiences of the virus, the restrictions, and the psychological consequences of the pandemic, so that these could be drawn together to represent a collective voice. Also, that through the research and research-translation processes, this summary of population wellbeing and vulnerability could be made available to political and civic leaders and the community. This data could inform recovery strategies and policies and where these should be targeted, and represent what Alicia Yamin describes as a rights-based approach to improving human health through promoting participation.[4]

We designed a brief anonymous online survey launched in the first week of the Stage Three restrictions. It asked about experiences of the virus, the restrictions, and low mood and anxiety, but we also asked in open-ended questions about what had been gained as well as lost, and how optimistic people were feeling about the future. We partnered with the ABC who linked it in online stories and television and radio discussions.

In a month, nearly 14,000 people from all states and territories completed the survey. Respondents contributed quantitative data and hundreds of thousands of words describing individual experiences of loss and gain. Together, these enabled a snapshot of the psychological burden being experienced by the whole population to be developed, and the identification of groups within the community experiencing the highest needs, but also unexpected benefits of the emotional closeness of shared adjustments to this unanticipated life change.

Meanwhile, the people who experienced bushfires have been rendered invisible by the pandemic: people whose homes or farm buildings were burnt are still living in temporary accommodation as the remains are assessed for insurance and cleared; there is slow regrowth of animal feed, insufficient yet to support livestock; and farmers are waiting for the right seasonal conditions to replant crops. This is all occurring under distancing regulations that counter the need for gatherings to discuss experiences and find solutions or ways to advance. Very few news reports now describe the plights of these people. They have experienced profound losses — for some bereavement; for all, disenfranchised losses — which deserve recognition and active responses from the research community and policy-makers.

A sense of agency can counter disenfranchised grief and the demoralisation of powerlessness. As we recover from the natural disasters of fire and pandemic our civic leaders need to hold in mind the value of restoring autonomy for individuals, but also finding ways for people to contribute to the whole, the public good, in order to restore societal wellbeing. Co-designed, participatory and equitable psychosocial research is essential to achieving these processes of restoration.

---

1. R. Bright, *Grief and Powerlessness: Helping People Regain Control of Their Lives*, Macmillan, London, 1996.
2. K. Doka, *Disenfranchised Grief: Recognizing Hidden Sorrow*, Lexington Books, Lexington, 1989.
3. J. Fisher and M. Kirkman, 'Recognising Disenfranchised Grief amid Covid–19', Monash Lens https://lens.monash.edu/@medicine-health/2020/03/26/1379888/coronavirus-recognising-disenfranchised-grief-and-Covid–19.
4. A.E. Yamin, 'Suffering and Powerlessness: The Significance of Promoting Participation in Rights-Based Approaches to Health', *Health and Human Rights*, vol. 11, no. 1, 2009, pp. 5–22.

# A Fire Symphony of Traumatic Stress

Paul Valent

The recent bushfires, from which we are now attempting to recover, reinforced once again the point that major disasters have a widespread human toll. Understanding that toll facilitates healing. Here I want to describe a framework that evolved out of the 1983 Ash Wednesday bushfires, which has facilitated understanding consequences of disasters generally. Hopefully, it will also help recovery from the recent bushfires.

'Guilt', a man blurted out after a brief silence, following my question asking what was the worst aftermath of the fires.

'Guilty for what?' I asked in astonishment.

'For my house still standing, and my neighbour's having burnt.' The group around the man nodded in agreement.

A man sought us out in great distress. 'I have severe chest pain', he said.

We suggested taking him to hospital. 'No, no! You see, I took all care and my house is gone. My neighbour is a slob, but his house stands. The pain came on when he asked if he could help me.' The pain faded as the man expressed his fury.

A mother at the community centre screamed at her son because he refused to come to her. When we took him aside, the six-year-old boy confessed to us that his mother was a witch. 'How do you know?' He had asked her to retrieve his teddy bear. With flames behind her, she had screamed, 'I'll kill you if you don't shut up'. The child curled up on the floor of the escaping car and took a magic pill to protect himself against his mother. He still took magic pills. We negotiated a reconciliation between mother and child.

We found three firefighters hiding in an attic. They told us that they were totally exhausted. They were hiding from any reminders of the fires. They reminded me of combat fatigue.

An old man was severely depressed. He rose from his bed to open a curtain in the dark room. 'Look at this moonscape. Everything is gone, and I'm too old to see it rebuilt.' We concluded that he could serve as a base when rebuilding started. His depression lifted under our eyes.

Attendances at local doctors soared. Patients complained of a variety of physical symptoms. Others experienced uncontrolled emotional states that made them believe that they were going mad. Car and home accidents increased; so did alcohol consumption and domestic and sexual discord. Children regressed and some became antisocial.

And the strangest thing: although to us the physical, psychological, and social symptoms were obviously connected to the recent fires, people who were suffering those symptoms lost that connection. The above cases indicated that when we helped people to reconnect their symptoms to the distress they had experienced in the fires, the meaning of the symptoms could be understood and reconfigured with beneficial results.

Our team produced a pamphlet under the auspices of the Red Cross called *Coping with a Major Personal Crisis*. It stated that fear, helplessness, sadness, longing, guilt, shame, anger, let-down, and hope were universal normal feelings in disasters. So were fatigue, nightmares, fuzziness of the mind, loss of memory and concentration, and physical symptoms such as dizziness, shakes, palpitations, pains in head, neck and back, and digestive, menstrual and sexual disorders.

The pamphlet advised to not bottle up feelings, to talk, to maintain routines, seek support, and confront reality. It warned that accidents and reliance on drugs were common after disasters and that family and social relationships were at risk. Modifications of these pamphlets have been distributed by the Red Cross in Australian and overseas disasters over the years, and were available in the current bushfires.

In the first flush, we believed that we had found the means to solve post-traumatic disorders: that is, make people realise that their physical, psychological, and behavioural (biopsychosocial) symptoms were hangovers of disaster responses, which they could discard in current normal conditions. This accorded with the then recently formulated post-traumatic stress disorder (PTSD) approach, which suggested that rather than reliving or suppressing fight-and-flight symptoms generated in traumatic situations, these responses could be relinquished in safe situations.

However, PTSD did not explain the depressions, the physical and behavioural symptoms, moral guilts, angers, and outrages, nor cognitive distortions ranging from denials to magical explanations. Further, people needed to understand their specific distress. Why do I feel guilty because my house is still standing? Why does my neighbour give me chest pains as severe as a heart attack? Why am I so exhausted that I don't even want to lift a finger? Why does my son seem to hate me? Why is my husband running around like a chicken without a head? Why is my marriage breaking up? It seemed that almost any symptom was possible. How to understand this apparent chaos?

Fight and flight were not enough. Other survival instincts had been at play too. Firefighters and others were driven to help and rescue others even at high risk to themselves. Had they not done so, their guilt would have been extreme. Similar guilt spurred those we had encountered with standing homes to provide shelter to their homeless neighbours. Reciprocally to rescue, the attachment bond to rescuers was intense. But like the child who saw his mother as a witch, people were angry if rescuers fell short. Apart from rescuing, firefighters bravely combated the fires, but beyond their limits, combat fatigue set in. People had to adapt to and grieve their losses, but if this seemed too hopeless, depression could set in, as it did with the man surrounded by moonscape. The media extolled the co-operation, generosity and communal feeling among survivors, though in time competitive rivalries emerged. The man with the chest pain could not bear the injustice of his neighbour 'winning out'.

Eight survival instincts: rescue, attachment, goal-achievement, goal-surrender, fight, flight, competition, and co-operation: all these instincts were well known. I saw them as an octave of survival drives. Their positive and negative physical, psychological, and social expressions formed what to us seemed at first a fragmented chaos, but in fact it was a highly sophisticated and mostly effective symphony of survival.

This symphony contained many harmonics and overtones, which played out in different dimensions. The parameters dimension included the type of disaster and its context in time, place and person. Persons involved children and adults, and groupings from individuals through families, communities, and nations to the world. Like a symphony with different movements, disasters have a process through different phases. In time, looking after others may give way to looking after oneself. In the recovery phase frequent conflicts arise with insurance companies, bureaucracies, and politicians, who may divert their attention to new crises (currently COVID–19). The last dimension is a moral, exclusively human, one. Its judgements fine-tune one's own and others' instincts through intense feelings of guilt, shame, justice, self-esteem, and existential meanings and purpose.

I call these eight survival instincts in three dimensions a wholist perspective. It is more complex than the original perspective of PTSD, but people are complex creatures. Akin to, and indeed overlapping with taking a medical history, the wholist perspective can identify, orientate, and trace a variety of symptoms to their origins, make sense of them, and resolve them.

Let me conclude with an important question, which seems to have found a solution since the Ash Wednesday bushfires. Why do survivors present symptoms that are disconnected from their origins? Well, when we cannot resolve stresses and overcome traumas, we disconnect them from consciousness, so that we can move on with other necessities. We now know that the disconnection (sometimes called repression or dissociation) is into the non-verbal, non-thinking, timeless, self-unaware (unconscious) right hemisphere of the brain.

Partial release of traumas into the self-aware left hemisphere of the brain appears as symptoms, like those that inundated doctors' days after the bushfires. People may require help to reconnect these symptoms with their traumas and to emotionally as well as cognitively realise that they are over.

Time passes. Trees regenerate. Houses are rebuilt. Even pregnancies increase. But symptoms that were not resolved soon after the trauma may become entrenched and give rise to morbidity and even mortality, which are often increased after disasters. We may require the wholist perspective for a long time after disasters.

I must emphasise that each note in the symphony of traumatic stress must be recognised because discordant notes at any point can lead to severe consequences. Lack of clear warnings and information in the pre-impact phase can hamper application of appropriate survival strategies. Ignoring post-impact needs of firefighters can lead to these strong, brave people later succumbing physically, mentally, socially. Not recognizing sources of symptoms can lead to them acting as chronic abscesses. Not recognising the significance of events can lead to denials, scapegoating, and magical fantasies. Not recognising global meanings of the current huge bushfires can lead to lack of dealing with deteriorating climate conditions.

Each irrationality must be countered by facts and science. I believe that the wholist perspective is a useful scientific tool to help orientate, understand, and heal the wide variety of traumatic stress symptoms in this and other disasters.

# Fire

Rimona Kedem

**Rimona Kedem** *Fire*, 2019, oil on canvas, 40 x 60 cm.
Courtesy the artist and Qdos Galleries, Lorne, Victoria.

# Responding to the Catastrophe, Psychologically and Culturally

James Collett

When asked to provide media commentary on Australia's bushfires, there was one word that would inevitably come to me: 'catastrophic'. The word 'catastrophe' is often used in an abstract sense. Catastrophes are sometimes narrowly avoided possibilities, or we catastrophize when we anticipate an event to be worse than it is. But make no mistake, the bushfires of the summer of 2019-2020 were absolutely and irrefutably catastrophic. They were catastrophic for the environment, and catastrophic for us.

Better informed people than myself have written about the extent of the damage, the disruption of ecosystems, and the ravaging and probable extinction of flora and fauna. I will not repeat that information here. I am a psychology educator, so instead I will use this background to outline a selection of lessons that the Australian community can carry from this catastrophe. These lessons are not complex science, but are instead basic psychological principles that we will need to work with or around in order to protect Australia from the threat of bushfire.

## Suggestion 1:
## We need to think of bushfires as events that are relevant to our way of life across the whole year.

Individuals are more likely to bring to mind a thought that is readily available, a process called the 'availability heuristic'.[1] Why is this important? A heuristic is a mental shortcut, a way of thinking designed to conserve effort in our busy world. Bushfires have long been treated as a seasonal problem, and because of this, with the onset of autumn, they disappear from the news-cycle and from the forefront of the public consciousness. Instead of relying on the 'availability heuristic', we need to spend mental effort in thinking about bushfires in autumn, winter, and spring. By the time summer arrives it is already too late. There are many tragedies associated with bushfires, and one is that outside of fire services, environmental departments, and those living in regional areas, the general public stops talking about them when summer ends. We need to defy this mental shortcut and make the bushfires something that we talk about all year round.

… /

## Suggestion 2:
## While the fires may well be intensified by climate change, we should orient our claims about these connections to focussing on what can be done positively.

The increasingly destructive capacity of Australia's bushfires is attributed to climate change by many researchers and lay people, including by me. However, there are those for whom climate change is a controversial topic, or a political issue with unsettling ramifications. Research tells us that changing a person's attitude towards climate change is difficult, partly due to the far-reaching and gradual nature of the problem. Refusal to acknowledge climate change is not entirely due to ignorance. In fact, research tells us that providing information on climate science will not necessarily shift attitudes.[2]

Our bushfires bring with them the terrifying realisation that climate change is no longer a distant threat to be forestalled. But perhaps there is an opportunity for positive change here? Instead of spending energy attempting to convince those who cannot be convinced, perhaps that energy can be directed towards action-oriented solutions to the immediate danger posed by bushfires. Even those most dismissive of climate change projections cannot help but to understand the gravity of the bushfires, and we are likely to find that solutions to one are ultimately solutions to the other.

## Suggestion 3:
## We need to return to ideas of intrinsic worth in thinking about the value of nature.

Debate on the preservation of nature tends to swing between an ecocentric point of view — the perspective that the natural world is inherently important — and an anthropocentric point of view, the perspective that humans should control and draw resources from the natural world.[3] These poles of debate parallel the idea that motivation can be intrinsic, where behaviour is motivated by internal feelings such as happiness, satisfaction, and altruism, or extrinsic, where behaviour is motivated by external incentives, such as food, resources, or money.[4] Unfortunately, psychological research suggests that when we introduce the practical issue of money into a debate, it can shift people away from the intrinsically motivated, value-driven mindset to an extrinsically motivated, practical, business-like mindset.[5] This is unhelpful, as short-term financial savings at the expense of the environment mean little if future generations are deprived of the opportunity to experience nature. We need to approach public discourse around land-management from the perspective that the Australian country is of inherent value to our entire community, and that the Australian people have an obligation to be altruistic towards nature, to give of themselves for the preservation of the land.

Having lived through the destruction wrought by the bushfires, we cannot view caring for the environment as an optional luxury, or allow financial considerations to be a barrier to action. We cannot let money blind us to our values.

## Suggestion 4:
## We need to build attachment to place and empathy for the land.

The damage from the bushfires was felt in regional communities touched by flame. The smoke, however, touched all of Australia. A pall was cast over our cities, presided over by a sun resembling a hovering orange egg yolk. If there was one silver lining to this all-pervading smoke, it was that it imprinted on our metropolitan centres that bushfires have an impact. That this is not just a rural problem, or a political problem, but an Australian problem. The haunting atmosphere that the smoke carried perhaps did more to build a personal emotional connection to the bushfires for city dwellers than any piece of media coverage thus far.

Many psychological theories look at how to motivate behaviour change to solve problems.[6] One thing that needs to be in place is self-efficacy, the belief that our behaviour can affect positive change in the world, can have the corrective impact we desire.[7] Another is the need to combat avoidance, our human tendency to shy away from the unpleasant emotions that surround tough decisions.[8] Beyond all of these higher-level components of behaviour motivation, however, is personal meaning. Unless we do more to nurture and nourish our connectedness to the land, then we risk being apathetic to the problem that bushfires represent.

In this sense, the smoke was a bridge to empathy, as suddenly the bushfires had an authentic sensory impact on individuals far beyond the bushfire perimeter. But we need to do more to build a positive connection between city-dwelling individuals and the Australian bushland. One term for this connection, drawn from environmental psychology, is attachment to place.[9] We can foster attachment to place through direct experience with nature, so encouraging individuals and families to get out of their city and experience what Australia has to offer is one way that we can motivate more of our community to act to protect nature from bushfires and other climate-related disasters.

## Moving Forward: Growth from Destruction

When people work together, they are capable of tremendous feats, and I am optimistic that managing our bushfire risk and preserving the land is one of them. My hope is that the lessons that I have outlined, grounded in environmental psychology, inspire actions small and large to protect our world. The bushfires were frightening because of their scale, but remember that environmental destruction occurs in smaller ways every single day: when gardens are uprooted to make room for housing developments, when goods are shielded in unnecessary plastic packaging, or simply when you take steps outside your home without looking down and seeing what you risk trampling on. There is a lot of work we as a nation can do to protect our land, but at an individual level, it all starts with looking around, breathing in the air, feeling the sunlight, and purely noticing that there is something there worth preserving.

---

1. A. Tversky and D. Kahneman, 'Judgement Under Uncertainty: Heuristics and Biases', *Science*, vol. 185, 1974, pp. 1124–31.

2. D.M. Kahan, E. Peters, M. Wittlin, P. Slovic, and L.L Ouellette, D. Braman, and G. Mandel, 'The Polarizing Impact of Science Literacy and Numeracy on Perceived Climate Change Risks', *Nature Climate Change*, vol. 2, 2012, pp. 732–35.

3. S.C.G. Thompson and M.A. Barton, 'Ecocentric and Anthropocentric Attitudes Towards the Environment', *Journal of Environmental Psychology*, vol. 14, no. 2, 1994, pp. 149–57.

4. M.R. Ryan and E.L. Deci, 'Intrinsic and Extrinsic Motivations: Classic Definitions and New Directions', *Contemporary Education Psychology*, vol. 25, no. 1, 2000, pp. 54–67.

5. J.W. Bolderdijk and L. Steg, 'Promoting Sustainable Consumption: The Risks of Using Financial Incentives', in L.A. Reisch and J. Thøgersen, eds, *Handbook of Research on Sustainable Consumption*, Edward Elgar, Cheltenham, 2014.

6. I. Ajzen and M. Fishbein, 'The Influence of Attitudes on Behaviour', in D. Albarracin, B.T. Johnson and M.P. Zanna, eds, *The Handbook of Attitudes*, Lawrence Erlbaum Associates, Mahwah, 2005; L. Steg and C. Vlek, 'Encouraging Pro-Environmental Behaviour: An Integrative Review and Research Agenda', *Journal of Environmental Psychology*, vol. 29, 2009, pp. 309–17.

7. A. Bandura, *Self-Efficacy: The Exercise of Control*, W.H. Freeman, New York, 1994.

8. S. Roth and L. Cohen, 'Approach, Avoidance, and Coping with Stress', *American Psychologist*, vol. 41, no. 7, 1986, pp. 813–19.

9. L.C. Manzo and P. Devine-Wright, *Place Attachment: Advances in Theory, Methods and Applications*, Routledge, London, 2014.

# These Fires Have Consequences for Our Health

Stephen Duckett, Will Mackey, Anika Stobart

The year 2019 was Australia's hottest year on record. Temperatures across the country were on average 1.5°C degrees warmer than the long-term trend. It was also Australia's driest year on record. Areas of south-eastern Australia that subsequently burned had their lowest rainfall on record.[1] There had been extensive hazard reduction burns in the decade leading up to the 2019–2020 summer, but dry and hot conditions had limited the scope of hazard reduction burns during the winter before.[2] By the spring of 2019, the Bureau of Meteorology reported that most of Australia had the highest fire danger weather on record.[3] This extreme heat and dry weather had primed much of south-eastern Australia for bushfires.

Subsequently, hundreds of bushfires ravaged south-eastern Australia over the summer, burning more than 18 million hectares and billowing large plumes of smoke into the atmosphere. Both the fire and the smoke claimed many lives and caused health problems that will last. This bushfire season is not a one-off. Climate change is increasing the likelihood of ever more severe, intense, and longer-lasting bushfires into the future.

## 1. The fires were devastating

By early September, the fire season had kicked in, just five months after the previous season ended. By 9 September, more than 50 fires were burning in New South Wales, and 80 in Queensland.[4] The fires continued to burn into the New Year. By the end of January, 21 per cent of all Australian forests had been burnt.[5] It was not until 2 March 2020 that the NSW Rural Fire Service released a statement declaring there were 'no active bush or grass fires' in the state for the first time in 240 days.[6] The 2019–20 bushfire season had come to an end. The fires directly killed at least 34 people and destroyed 2,100 homes. A survey of 3,000 Australians conducted in January 2020 found that one in seven — nearly 3 million people — were directly affected by the bushfires through their property being damaged or threatened, or by being told to evacuate.[7] About 1.8 million people were forced to evacuate their homes. Three out of every five people living in Australia reported being exposed to bushfire smoke.

## 2. The bushfire smoke damaged people's physical health

As fires burned in the bushlands of south-eastern Australia, smoke rose, drifted, and blanketed towns and cities. On some days and in some places, air pollution was many times the 'hazardous' thresholds set by environmental protection agencies and health departments. About 11 million Australians reported some exposure to smoke from the fires.[8] It caused thousands of people to go to hospital.

Bushfire smoke is made up of a complex mix of particles and gases. This includes particles less than 2.5 micrometres in diameter ('particulate matter' known as $PM_{2.5}$) — about 30 times thinner than a human hair. Smoke from the 2019–20 Australian bushfires had extremely high levels of $PM_{2.5}$, in orders of magnitude above the 'safe' threshold stipulated by the World Health Organisation and the Australian National Air Quality Standards (see Figure 1). Canberra in the Australian Capital Territory (ACT) had the worst air quality in the world on New Year's Day.

Inhalation of particulate matter from bushfire smoke can cause many serious health problems.[9] The link between respiratory issues and particulate matter is well established.[10] Small particles can be inhaled deep into the lungs, causing difficulty breathing.

ACT and Victorian emergency department data show that the number of people going to hospital with respiratory problems increased significantly on days with poor air quality — by 27 per cent on days with $PM_{2.5}$ levels between 50 and 100, and by 70 per cent on days with $PM_{2.5}$ levels above 200 (compared to days with $PM_{2.5}$ levels below 25). Separate analysis estimated that the pollution from the bushfires resulted in 2,027 people being admitted to hospital with respiratory problems and 1,305 people going to emergency departments with asthma-related conditions. About 1,100 people were admitted to hospital with cardiovascular problems caused by the Australian fires. The bushfire smoke was responsible for 417 deaths.[11]

## 3. The bushfires damaged people's mental health

Bushfires destroy homes, livelihoods, and lives. People from affected communities suffer emotional distress, anxiety, and depression. About one-fifth of the people affected by the 2003 Canberra bushfires reported high to very-high levels of psychological distress three years later.[12] The 2009 Black Saturday bushfires in Victoria, which killed 173 people and destroyed more than 2,000 homes, also caused devastating and long-term mental health problems.[13] Three years after the fires, people in 'highly affected' communities — those in which people had died or properties had been damaged — were more than twice as likely to suffer from post-traumatic stress disorder (PTSD), depression, or severe distress than people in less-affected communities.[14] Although many people recovered, these communities still had higher rates of mental health problems than the general population five years later.[15] For people who suffer mental stress or confront difficulties with insurance or rebuilding their properties, these mental health problems can persist or get worse.[16]

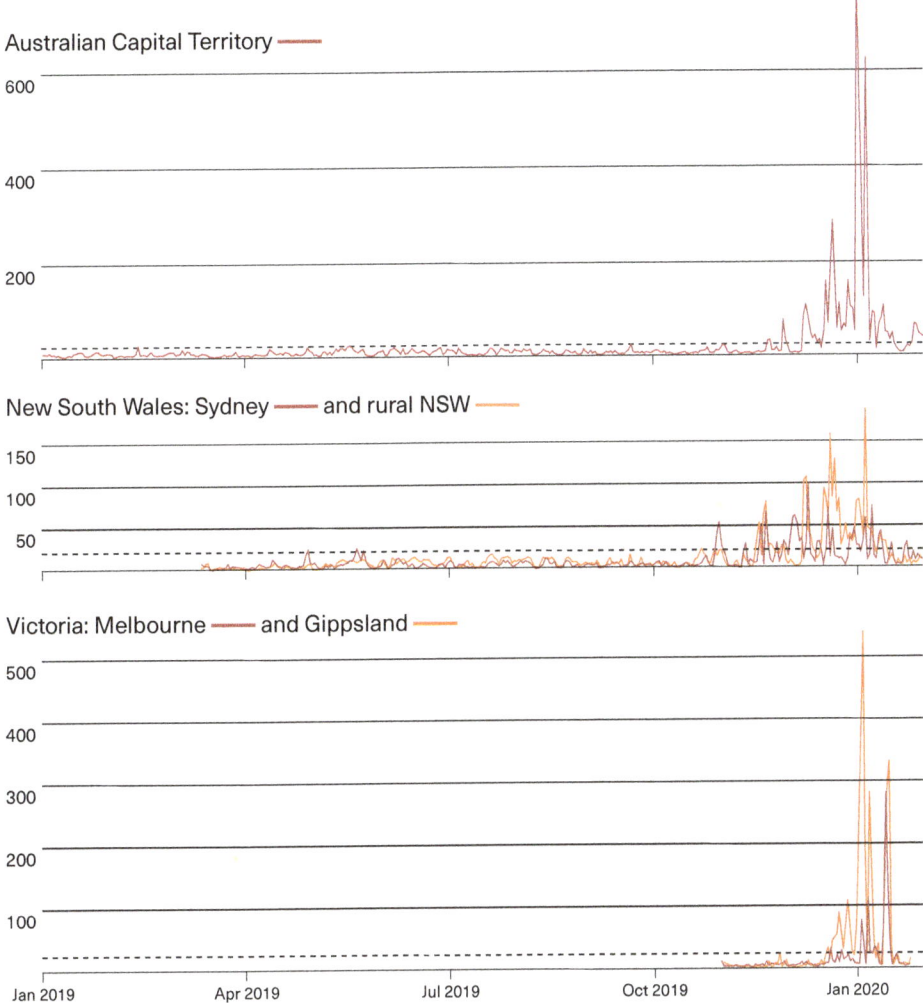

**Figure 1.** Air pollution from the bushfires was way above the 'safe' level in the Australian Capital Territory, New South Wales, and Victoria (PM$_{2.5}$ µg/m³ by region, 2019–20; the 'safe' level at 25 PM$_{2.5}$ µg/m³ on average for 24 hours is indicated by the dotted line).

Frontline firefighters are also at heightened risk of suffering mental health problems. Witnessing the devastating impacts of bushfires can cause them to feel guilty or helpless. About 15 per cent of firefighters suffer PTSD after fighting a bushfire, and the mental health problems can be long lasting.[17]

It's too early to know the full extent of the mental health consequences of the 2019–20 Australian bushfires. But a January 2020 survey of 3,000 Australians found that more than half (54 per cent) felt anxious or worried about the safety of themselves and others during the fires.[18] This equates to about 10 million people feeling an impact on their mental wellbeing — people living in both regional areas and cities.

Indigenous Australians may feel the effects of bushfires differently to other Australians. The bushfires affected regions that are home to one-quarter of the Indigenous population of New South Wales and Victoria.[19] The Yuin people from the south coast of New South Wales have reported that many sacred sites were feared to have been destroyed in the 2019–20 bushfires.[20]

## 4. Climate change means more frequent, more intense, and longer-lasting bushfires

Bushfires have long been a part of Australian life. But a warming climate means longer heatwaves and less rainfall — and these conditions mean there are more days of extreme fire risk, and therefore more chance of larger and longer-lasting bushfires.

A study released in March 2020 found that human-caused climate change had made the 2019–20 bushfires 80 per cent more likely to happen. It found that if global temperatures rise to 2°C above pre-industrial levels, bushfires in Australia like those of 2019–20 will be about eight times more likely.[21] As bushfires become more frequent and more intense, more Australians will suffer more often.

---

1. Bureau of Meteorology, 'Special Climate Statement 72 — Dangerous Bushfire Weather in Spring 2019,' http://www.bom.gov.au/climate/current/statements/scs72.pdf. Viewed 3 April 2020.
2. P. Hannam and L. Mannix, 'Australia Fires: What is back burning and will more reduce bushfire risks?' *The Sydney Morning Herald,* https://www.smh.com.au/national/prescribed-burning-what-is-it-and-will-more-reduce-bushfire-risks-20200106-p53paf.html. Viewed 3 April 2020; RMIT ABC Fact Check, 'Has NSW seen more than twice the amount of prescribed burning in national parks this decade compared with the last?' Fact Check — ABC (Australian Broadcasting Corporation) News, https://www.abc.net.au/news/2020-01-22/prescribed-burning-nsw-backburning-hazard-reduction/11878316. Viewed 3 April 2020.
3. Bureau of Meteorology, op. cit.
4. Bureau of Meteorology, 'Special Climate Statement 71—severe fire weather conditions in southeast Queensland and northeast New South Wales in September 2019', http://www.bom.gov.au/climate/current/statements/scs71.pdf. Viewed 3 April 2020.
5. M.M. Boer, V. Resco de Dios, and R.A. Bradstock, 'Unprecedented burn area of Australian mega forest fires', *Nature Climate Change*, vol. 10, no.3, 2020, pp. 171–172.
6. NSW Rural Fire Service, https://twitter.com/NSWRFS/status/1234360507919822849. Viewed 3 April 2020.
7. N. Biddle, B. Edwards, D. Herz, and T. Makkai, 'Exposure and the impact on attitudes of the 2019–20 Australian Bushfires', Australian National University, 2020, https://csrm.cass.anu.edu.au/research/publications/exposure-and-impact-attitudes-2019-20-australian-bushfires-0. Viewed 3 April 2020.
8. Ibid., p.5.
9. C.E. Reid, M. Brauer, F.H. Johnston, M. Jerrett, J.R. Balmes, and C.T. Elliott, 'Critical review of health impacts of wildfire smoke exposure', *Environmental Health Perspectives*, vol. 124, no. 9, 2016, pp. 1334–1343.
10. N.B. Arriagada, J.A. Horsley, A.J. Palmer, G.G. Morgan, R. Tham, and F.H. Johnston, 'Association between fire smoke fine particulate matter and asthma-related outcomes: Systematic review and meta-analysis', *Environmental Research*, vol. 179, 2019.

11. N.B. Arriagada, A.J. Palmer, D.M. Bowman, G.G. Morgan, B.B. Jalaludin, and F.H. Johnston, 'Unprecedented smoke-related health burden associated with the 2019–20 bushfires in eastern Australia', *Medical Journal of Australia*, 23 March, 2020, https://www.mja.com.au/journal/2020/213/6/unprecedented-smoke-related-health-burden-associated-2019-20-bushfires-eastern. Viewed 3 April 2020.
12. P. Camilleri, C. Healy, E.M. Macdonald, S. Nicholls, J. Sykes, G. Winkworth, and M. Woodward, 'Recovery from bushfires: The experience of the 2003 Canberra bushfires three years after', *Journal of Emergency Primary Health Care*, vol. 8, no. 1, 2010.
13. 2009 Victorian Bushfires Royal Commission, http://royalcommission.vic.gov.au/finaldocuments/summary/PF/VBRC_Summary_PF.pdf. Viewed 3 April 2020; R.A. Bryant, E. Waters, L. Gibbs, H.C. Gallagher, P. Pattison, D. Lusher, C. MacDougall, L. Harms, E. Block, E. Snowdon, V. Sinnott, G. Ireton, J. Richardson., and D. Forbes, 'Psychological outcomes following the Victorian Black Saturday bushfires', *Australian & New Zealand Journal of Psychiatry*, vol. 48, no. 7, 2014, pp. 634–643.
14. Bryant et al., op.cit.
15. R.A. Bryant, E. Waters, L. Gibbs, H.C. Gallagher, P. Pattison, D. Lusher, C. MacDougall, L. Harms, E. Block, V. Sinnott, G. Ireton, J. Richardson., and D. Forbes, 'Longitudinal study of changing psychological outcomes following the Victorian Black Saturday bushfires', *Australian & New Zealand Journal of Psychiatry*, vol. 52, no. 6, 2018, pp. 542–551.
16. Ibid., pp. 547–549.
17. C.S. Fullerton, R.J. Ursano, W. Leming, 'Acute Stress Disorder, Posttraumatic Stress Disorder, and Depression in Disaster or Rescue Workers', *Am J Psychiatry*, vol. 161, no. 8, 2004; A.C. McFarlane, 'Long-term psychiatric morbidity after a natural disaster. Implications for disaster planners and emergency services', *Medical Journal of Australia*, vol. 145, 1986, pp. 561–563.
18. Biddle op. cit., p.5.
19. B. Williamson, F. Markham, J.K. Weir, 'Aboriginal Peoples and the response to the 2-19-20 Bushfires', Australian National University, 2020, https://caepr.cass.anu.edu.au/sites/default/files/docs/2020/3/CAEPR_WP_no_134_2020_Williamson_Markham_Weir.pdf. Viewed 3 April 2020.
20. J. Perry and M. Hayman-Reber, '"Little hope" of curbing catastrophic bushfires unless traditional knowledge is utilised', NITV, https://www.sbs.com.au/nitv/article/2020/01/22/little-hope-curbing-catastrophic-bushfires-unless-traditional-knowledge-utilised. Viewed 3 April 2020.
21. G.J. van Oldenborgh, F. Krikken, S. Lewis, N.J. Leach, F. Lehner, K.R. Saunders, M. van Weele, K. Haustein, S. Li, D. Wallom, S. Sparrow, J. Arrighi, R.P. Singh, M.K. van Aalst, S.Y. Philip, R. Vautard, and F.E.L. Otto, 'Attribution of the Australian bushfire risk to anthropogenic climate change', *Nat. Hazards Earth Syst. Sci. Discuss.*, in review, no. 69, 2020, pp. 26, 27.

# Who by Fire?

Guy Rundle

The ABC radio was on in the summer heat of a January day, and we heard continuous coverage of the bushfires raging through south-eastern New South Wales. A mother and her adult daughter spoke of a burned-out town, and they were angry about the failure of emergency services to attend. Firies? Ambulance? None of these. 'There were no counsellors', said one of them. 'We asked for counsellors and they didn't send us any'. They were not talking about days after the fire-front had come through, but mere hours. Counselling was what they felt they needed in the moment.

It would be easy and wilfully stupid to sneer at such a response, as many on the political Right do. Right-wing think-tanks and parties are full of young men and women who talk about the 'real Australians', 'the nanny state', and so on, and summon up visions of stoicism and hardihood. The two women's distress and need were real, and expressions of such need were multiple through the summer. Across the media, trauma became a major talking-point in relation to the fires, an all-encompassing frame. It effectively rendered this extreme event — the walls of flame moving through the land and towns, trees exploding in heat, the skies red raw and then dark as death, the apocalyptic scenes of survival — as contained within the individual psychologies of the people experiencing them. Rather than being the raw and unarguable-with, the real, the scorching wall of nature and being, making us as one with regard to its indifference to our subjective being, the event was reduced to trauma. Nor would there be much recognition in the mainstream media, if one were to try and talk about this. High and low, trauma is all.

When trauma counselling was first introduced in the 1970s and 1980s, it was an external practice, derived from a specific set of theories by a newly expanded state-employed social care profession. Two generations have now grown up with that practice being part of their everyday lives, and it has become a known and regularly accessed resource. This is especially so in rural Australia, where decades of unnecessary decline created by neoliberal geographical development policies have hollowed out much of rural life. Furthermore, trauma counselling, and the idea of trauma as an organising principle of extreme events has now become generalised — especially in left-liberal media and culture, where an attention to it is seen as part of a duty to assist the disadvantaged and oppressed. It has become so generalised that much of the mainstream Right that would once have mocked it, has now adopted the trauma discourse almost entirely, leaving criticism of it to groups such as the yahoo Right who counter-pose a fictional self-reliant person, a more considered conservative response, or a minority response from sections of the Left.

The implicit assumption of such discourses, which dominated the coverage of the January fires, is that trauma is an understandable personal response. Sometimes this is rightly taken as a specific condition of our era, a product of modernity, but many people who now use it as a concept implicitly assume it to be transhistorical, and thus to have been 'discovered' by social science. This process rolled over from transhistorical notions of oppression, which are essentialised: women were always oppressed as persons denied full equality and humanity, and so on. At the root of the ethical demand for speaking about trauma in everyday life is the proposition that there should be state care structures in place, which specifically attend to such individual and collective life-predicaments with a systematic set of treatments, and guaranteed mitigation.

The idea of 'trauma' — from the Greek root for wounds, but also, significantly, echoing the German traum or dream — like 'psychic' and 'physical', predates modern psychology. It was integrated into modern concerns when Freud was drawn into the treatment of 'shell-shocked' Austro-Hungarian soldiers during the First World War. It became generalised in the 1970s, when social care becomes increasingly attendant on psychological dysfunction in the poor and excluded in modernity. When post-traumatic stress disorder (PTSD) is 'discovered'/'developed' in the treatment of Vietnam and Gulf war veterans, its use becomes generalised in a society that is both mediatised and where maintenance of psychological good health is necessary for employment in the service and knowledge industries. The 'loop-back' effect of this across two generations has been to change the structure and self-understanding of contemporary selfhood in a material fashion. Whereas people were once told to 'get over it', or expressed themselves in emotions and practices unreflexively shaped — anger, hysteria, going on a bender — or were at least shaped by a less structural account of extreme emotion, the contemporary populace has been raised and trained to process strong feeling arising from extreme situations as part of better psychological self-maintenance. One can see this as a clear division of the modernity of the twentieth century, up to the 1980s, and a postmodern approach to social and psychological management now. Part of the rush of popular culture focused on the mid-twentieth century — from Mad Men to the revived cool of the Beats, and back to Berlin Babylon — has been nostalgia for and fascination with, a period which was post-religious and steered by desire, but one in which structural psychological self-monitoring had not yet become generalised. That was the era of the 'nervous breakdown' rather than of PTSD. Paradoxically, it is occasioned by the retreat of death from the middle of everyday lives, as fatal heart attacks became fewer, cancer far more survivable, and fatal car accidents approximately six to eight times less likely now than they were in 1970. The residual fatalism that was once part of all social life has become less of an essential cultural feature — and, with this change, the capacity for extreme experience to structurally transform subjectivity may have increased in ways that provide raw material for the occurrence of PTSD.

If all that is so, people calling for counsellors (rather than having them imposed on them), aren't sooks, aren't bamboozled by the nanny state, and are very definitely responding to something real. Furthermore, the notion of a past stoic hardihood put out by a populist Right is neither fully accurate, nor, where it is true enough, an unambiguous virtue. It is clear that mid-century subjectivity was frequently hysterical (in their terms), traumatised (in ours), and that an earlier era substantially lacking in discourse about the self (aside from a bohemian/artistic sub-group) produced repression, transference and petrification of self, retroactively celebrated as stoicism.

But acknowledging the material reality of the demand and the process does not oblige one to accept the 'metaphysic' of trauma, or the proposition that all extreme experience should be professionally managed. Quite to the contrary, one would suggest that this process — which many in the social care professions, many policy-oriented public servants, health and social science academics take to be a true and transhistorical picture of the world — has been generalised to so many areas of life that the professions are now responding, in effect, to the vulnerable atomisation of everyday life not by exploring how we could make a world in which people are more self-reliant, but by (often unintentionally) making the vulnerable more dependent on externalised assistance. This is an invitation to infinitely reshape ourselves as victims and in need of support. In our society, where increasing numbers of people are being rendered surplus to essential requirements and feel increasingly vulnerable, such caring roles expand — even as they cannot offer an enhanced form of connection and a meaningful social role to those rendered surplus.

The problem with that process is not merely psychological debilitation, but existential thinning. Such a discourse, when generalised, prevents people from living their fullest lives. Here 'full' means an existence with opportunities to encounter raw experience and events, which open us to deep meaning and awe, and which anchor the capacity to love passionately, pursue projects and flourish in everyday life. Saying that is nothing like saying 'get over it'. And there is a time and a place for professional care. But, in general, those of us who want a world where more people get to live fully their one life on earth need to talk back to the generalisation of the life-as-trauma model. That starts at the academic level, where social science and social care training reproduce the model — partly as an unconscious form of maintenance of their own discursive power — and train the next generation of social care workers and policy-makers. It means challenging journalists not to simply reproduce the trauma framework when they do stories on people suffering extreme events. It means arguing with progressives in the social movements who see the discourse of trauma as in itself recognising a real structure of oppression, rather than as being a particular way of framing it. We will be trialled by fire again and again in the decades to come. In responding to the coming events, and to their character as a real presence of climate change, we will need to turn outwards, to the new walls of heat, rather than just withdraw into the cool interior.

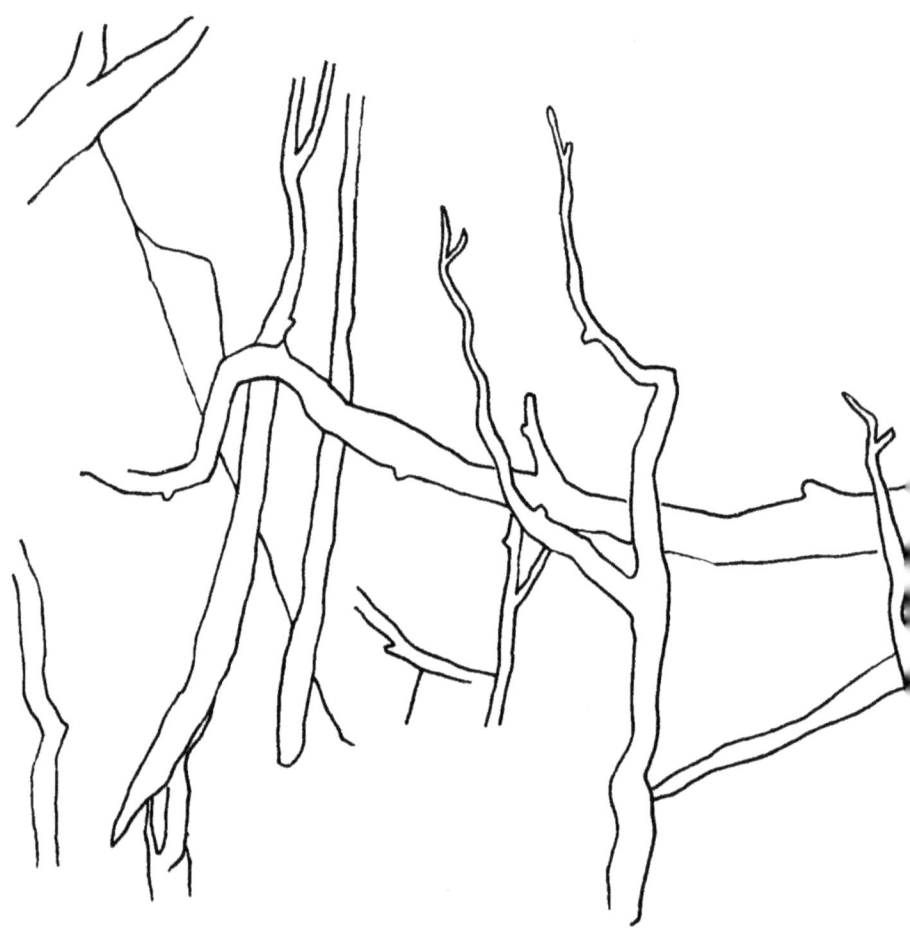

# Retro(pro)spectives

15.02.20
No birds and black trees, silence.
It came from all directions. I didn't have much time. The flames were high and it was hot and windy. I lost all communication. I left the house.

Text & Drawing • Hugo Muecke

# How Good are the Fires!

## George Browning

The country clearly owes a debt of gratitude to the Prime Minister Scott Morrison and his government for their sterling leadership, their visionary approach in vastly changed and challenging circumstance and for their assurance that under their leadership all manner of things will be well. There is no need for concern. How good are the fires! Let me try to summarise the reasons why the nation should be grateful:

> Thanks to the Prime Minister for coming back from his Hawaiian holiday. It is so reassuring to hear words of comfort like, 'Australians are resilient people, we have had bushfires before and will have them again, nothing to see here, this is all part of a normal cycle'.

> Thanks too for linking the efforts of firies and a host of volunteers to the magnificent effort of the cricketers. The connection must be obvious for all to see.

> Thanks for making sure that everyone is comforted whether they want comfort or not. Shaking hands or giving a hug to those who clearly do not wish to be touched might be considered assault from anyone else.

> Thanks for the continuing assurance that, while the government has always made the link with emissions and climate change, this is far too complex a crisis for any legitimate link to be made to the fires. Well, that is very reassuring. Of course fires are caused by lightning strikes and arsonists. Where I live on the coast it has refused to rain for months. Australia has been burning since the beginning of spring and we have been sucking in smoke every day for the last five weeks or more. Thanks so much for reassuring us that this is normal. I will probably fall off the perch before the long-term health implications affect me, so no need to worry here, let the younger generation look after themselves I say.

> Thanks to Minister Angus Taylor for complimenting Australia and Australians on how we are exceeding all expectations on emissions reduction. It is so reassuring that he is minister for something that is clearly so important to him. The fact that we have recently done our best to sabotage a broader and more effective global alliance is clearly a misunderstanding and we should have every confidence that the minister who has a Rhodes-scholarship reputation for fiddling facts on almost everything, is thoroughly trustworthy here.

Thanks for confirming what we feared: scientists, the Reserve Bank of Australia, fire chiefs, global consensus, the insurance industry, Defence Force chiefs, the Business Council of Australia, are all wrong. Climate change and global warming do not need to concern us, the little we might do will make no difference, so keep to present policy I say (in fact no policy at all), don't worry about wiping out the tourist industry, or large sections of agriculture, or even Australia's reputation internationally, all good here. (My overseas friends are saying international press are ridiculing our Prime Minister — how dare they).

Mr Morrison, let me bring you up to speed with life where I live. On New Year's Eve fires swept through our community with even more devastating consequence than three weeks ago. At midday, with no power and no telecommunication we needed a torch to get around the house. Many of our friends have lost their homes, whilst business after business has lost its livelihood. The devastation is beyond words and almost beyond belief. And now the community faces the same reality all over again tomorrow. We are of course but a small microcosm of the whole nation.

The team of volunteers at our local evacuation centre that my wife co-ordinates comprise those who have themselves lost their homes. They struggle to cope. With the roads impassable, others willing to help cannot get in. With deepest respect, some members of the government department oversighting the centre are beyond their capacity level in these circumstances. Too often the fall-back position is to rely on rules which should guide principle but not override need. We serve people not rules. Rules are of no value if they get in the way of service. More often than not, needs fall outside 'rules'.

One who has stood up as a leader is our local State member, Andrew Constance. He has had no smart words to offer. He has simply cried with his neighbours and is deeply respected.

Do I have hope? Yes, I have hope that young liberals, (who genuinely believe in and want to address the very serious situation we face), will oust the present crop of politicians and offer leadership which will restore respect and trust and take us down the path of new industry, technology and capacity. The time for fossils (human and mineral) is over. Those who occupy positions beyond their skill level should stand aside.

---

First published at https://www.georgebrowning.com.au/blog, 2 January 2020.

---

# An Ally Forsaken

Bill Gammage

Notice how many images of last summer's fires and black lands show whipstick stands of youngish re-growth eucalypts? No doubt amid such chaotic fury, cameras found it hard to reach old growth forest, but in southern Australia re-growth forest, burnt and not yet burnt, is common. If it were a plant category, as it usefully could be, it would be the most common category. Generations back whipstick country was grass or open forest. We let it run wild. Now we reap the whirlwind: a cascade of catastrophe which will scar our country forever.

Only the scale of catastrophe is new. Catastrophe is not. Over many past summers, people died and hectares burnt somewhere in southern Australia, including in suburbs of one or other capital city. We should never have accepted that, yet the fires have got worse. Last summer we spent millions fire-fighting and lost billions in homes and buildings, crops and fences, livelihoods and livestock. Fire-fighters risked and some gave their lives to save homes and communities in some places, to see hopes and dreams incinerated in others. Yet almost every fire was put out not by these stupendous efforts, but by rain — by chance. Until it rained, fires raged for months, burning an area two-thirds the size of New Zealand.

Notice something else. Last summer, and in most years earlier, the killer fires were all in southern Australia. There were no big uncontrolled fires in the north or centre. They do happen there, and they seem to have got worse recently, but they are escape fires, not a consequence of not burning at all, and they are not nearly as deadly as fires in the south.

People in the north and centre know fire as a friend, an ally they work with to protect habitats and species, keep country healthy, and make land beautiful. They plan and work hard to manage fire — to nourish it they might say. These people are Aboriginal, traditional owners and their families, who find it hard to believe that southern Australians think fire a fearsome foe. They look at country and see ground to love and nurture with fire and no fire, which repays their ceremonies and care a thousand-fold with comfort, abundance and beauty. Fire and no fire sustain not only them but every species, for all are equally entitled to the riches of the earth. Ceremony to care for country and burning after ceremony seek stability, but people know well that this can never mean doing nothing. All things change, so all must be kept in balance — not only humans, but every plant, animal, bird, reptile and insect (though the smallest of these may be grouped). Once it was like this in the south too.

In the north and centre, fire and no fire have many purposes: to reduce fuel, to protect camps and special places, to hunt or make ground ready to hunt, to harvest, to make plant mosaics for feed and shelter, to care for water edges, to clear tracks, to teach, to signal, to reassure neighbours and ancestors that country is being properly cared for. If people don't see smoke where it should be, they assume something is wrong, and look to see what it is.

Working with fire takes skill. Universal principles about maintaining habitats and protecting species must be applied via detailed knowledge of local plants and animals: where they are, how they behave, when their young are vulnerable, and whether they welcome or tolerate or dislike fire. Only locally is it possible to know when, where, how much and how often to burn. Working with fire is also hard work. Ceremonies must be properly prepared and presented, even little children are instructed on what and when to burn, and seasonal fire-control programs must be announced or negotiated — small fires within the family, big fires with neighbours and experts. Everyone is involved with fire, treats it with respect, and frees it knowing beforehand how it will behave.

The non-Aboriginal relationship with fire in Australia is primitive by comparison. Farms that I worked on in the early '60s always had a truck standing by in summer, water tank full, pump tested every morning. In the paddocks, eyes scanned for smoke, and if seen a hasty ring to the party-line switch located it, and anyone near enough raced to fight the flames. For generations white Australians fought fires that way, with branches or a flap of rubber nailed to a stick, with backpacks and back-burning, with days of hard work if necessary.

This did not stop frequent scarifying summers, especially in drought years, especially in forest country. Big fire years are stepping stones in white Australia's history. Rural fire brigades have largely supplanted farm tankers — obviously, since farmers can't serve both at once. The brigades remain the fire front-line in southern Australia. At the same time technology and command has been increased and centralised, on the face of it greatly expanding fire-fighting capacity: equipment, communications, planes, and publicity.

Yet, as fire trends worsen, while more equipment is assembled, local autonomy diminishes. Fire-fighting has become a state matter, and may become a national matter. As a result, fire management can't avoid focusing increasingly on fighting fires after they break out, sometimes days after. Key responses and equipment are centralised, letting fires get worse. Some of southeast Australia's big fires last summer could be diverted, but none could be put out. Not one. For that we prayed for rain.

The key to fire control is prevention. Here some local autonomy remains via control burns by brigades, farmers and volunteers — which in varying degrees state fire-controllers approve and add to. Since we have let so much fuel build since 1788, especially since the 1960s, this is sensible, though too many state-run burns are more for public relations than for fuel reduction. We would do better at fuel reduction by freeing local initiative. Even so we can't hope simply to chain fire up, to 'prevent bush fires'. We've tried that: it doesn't work. Learning to reduce fuel must take us further, teaching us to understand fire, to work with it, to see it as much a friend in the landscape as in the fireplace. Perhaps not a friend — that might be asking too much of whitefellas — but at least an ally, a tool pivotal to helping all Australia's plants and creatures to flourish, including us.

The contrast between 1788 and now is striking. In art, dance and song people then told many warning tales about what fire can do for good and ill, and either way the need to treat it respectfully. This was for good reason. How could they possibly have survived the raging furies we have endured in recent decades? They could not have outrun them, nor survived the black foodless wastelands which followed. They had to prevent uncontrolled fire; they had to make fire an ally.

Aboriginal fire-experts are willing to teach us how to do this. It is a way they can care for country they no longer possess, a way to resuscitate the safety, diversity and beauty their ancestors made. How lucky we are to have on offer such ancient skills! Surely, we should take advantage of them. Surely prevention is a role where Aboriginal expertise and local autonomy should lead.

We will fight big fires, worse fires, for decades to come. We must refine our fire-fighting. I trust we will find ways to put big fires out, otherwise our only refuges in the bush might become land already burnt. At the same time, we should take up the great gift 1788 offers us, and progressively shift the weight of our fire efforts from fighting to prevention. We can never go back to 1788, but we could learn much from it, and make a country which protects all its creatures, even a country of which the old people might approve.

———

# Reflections on Opportunities Lost

## Helen Caldicott

The dreadful and catastrophic fires which engulfed Australia this summer have evoked memories for me of debates and arguments in which I was engaged decades ago. In the early 1990s, I became keenly interested in what was then a relatively new science of climate change (although the language used then was somewhat different) and I wrote *If You Love This Planet,* published in 1992. I am now in my 80s, still living in a country town and still threatened by a bushfire disaster: my home-town of Berry was evacuated during the recent emergency and we had to remove to Sydney.

How much progress have we made and what do we have to do to avoid the next catastrophe, which could be even worse than those that have already occurred? Reflecting on these questions I dug out a speech I gave in Vancouver to a meeting of general practitioners in 1992. Reading it, I was struck by two facts: that most of the information about the dangers we face was already available then; and that, tragically, so many opportunities to avert the recent tragedy were lost. Here are some of the points I made in that talk thirty years ago that I would contend are still valid today:

- We have detailed and compelling scientific evidence that there is an imminent risk of collapse of ecological systems, including the extinction of many species and irreversible disruption of the life-sustaining environment.
- We are facing the destruction of the ozone layer and other effects which will lead to an increase in global temperatures. Although the full effects of global warming are difficult to predict it is likely to lead to major changes in crop growth, creating mass food shortages, a rise in the level of the oceans, massive weather events, destruction of many communities living at the current sea-level, and many other effects.
- Plant life will face devastating challenges. Destruction of the forests will affect every aspect of human and animal life and exacerbate the multiple other forces driving climate change and ecological destruction.
- The medical consequences of climate change and ecological destruction will be very far-reaching. There will be large-scale devastation of living environments, producing mass starvation, creation of ecological refugees and other social unrest, and uncontrolled spread of existing

diseases and development of new ones. There will be drowning people in their millions, starving people in their millions, epidemics of disease and the death of maybe one-half of the world's species.

- The international institutions either lack the ability or the support and resources needed to respond effectively to the approaching crisis. Capitalism is taking over the planet. Transnational corporations are seizing control in every country of the world and in all areas of social life, including the banks, telecommunications, the media, agriculture and transport. All our government will do is control law and order so that transnationals can continue to totally control us. But it is these corporations that are precisely the ones making the toxic products that are destroying the planet.

At the age of 81, I reflect upon my life of activism which I used to think of as 'global preventive medicine'. There were many of us, and we tried our best. But when we look out across the world today we see the same risks and dangers, only with the warnings actually starting to come true.

The risk of a nuclear holocaust has not passed. The threat of a climate crisis is more real than ever. Now we are experiencing bushfires on an unprecedented scale and the predicted novel epidemics are already starting to devastate the world. Our planet, which is itself a living, viable organism with an integument, a temperature, lungs and a blood supply, is in greater danger than ever.

Were we defeated? Have we failed future generations? Is there still the possibility that we will be able to rescue our precious patient? I am still hopeful, but recognise that I will probably not live long enough to find out the answers.

———

# Oracle of Fire

Paul Carter

In Memoriam, Andrew McLennan, 1940–2020 [1]

Fires are not only events; they prefigure other events. As flaming brands, they run in front of the larger fire to come. Burnt into history, they change the ethics of fire's production, its resourcing and manifestation. Even the fiery appearance of cloud-diffused light no longer looks appealing. A history as dry as tinder was going up in flames: the phenomenon of pyroclouds ushered in a new regime of self-reproduction. In the midst of this destruction life went on or, in the case of my friend Andrew McLennan, spiralled down, the last breathing embers extinguished a few months ago, by this smoke-bandaged departure running ahead of us, as it were, towards the next horizon: what could succeed this shortage of breath?

In 1996, AM and I created *Light* for the Adelaide Festival of Arts. It was a fire history of colonisation installed at Pinky Flat on the banks of the Torrens. It was designed by Hossein Valamanesh, performed by Chandrabhanu and members of the Bharatam Dance Company, all working inside the great lungs of a soundscape that permeated the entire night-time parklands. Named for William Light, Adelaide's original surveyor, the script crossed the phantasmatic emergence of the first houses with Light's difficulty in breathing. Oddly, his 'Last Diary', a record of advancing tuberculosis correlated, as I thought, with his morbid annotation of changes in the weather, began with a fire: flames from a neighbour's burning cottage engulfed Light's makeshift hut, initiating a new epoch in what remained of his life through the simple expedient of destroying all his papers. The documentation of his present activity, the evidence of his former lives, in Suffolk, in the Peninsula, in Georgetown, Penang or sailing under Etna — all, as they say, gone up in flames.[2]

In the Art Gallery of South Australia there is a self-portrait that Light began and left off, only to invert the canvas and begin a new self-portrait. A double self-portrait, it suggested what must happen now: a series of 'doubles' visits the dying Light, like revenants conjured up in séance, enabling him to bring back what, post-conflagration, has gone over to the other side, reduced to ashes. But naturally, springing from the fire, his doubles retrieve Light's life under the aegis of fire. Episodes of his life are told now in the key of fire, a parched pageant that grimly mimics his own difficulty in swallowing: Light is visited by a Chinese incendiarist who burns down the English factory in Junk Ceylon (and is tortured with fire); Captain Swing (he of the 'Swing' riots that 'illuminated the long-drawn misery of much of rural England' 'like a lightning flash'[3]); and a soldier wounded at the Siege of Burgos ('A ball entered my left side, below the heart./ Nothing at first then .../ Intolerable burning pain.'). Light deliriously remembers a Tyrrhenian storm ('The surface of the sea/ One continued blaze'). Returning through these earlier lives to the present, Light retraces his steps across the plain called Mikawomma. The moment is stressed where the newly arrived colonists began removing timber and burning it and the Kaurna felt this attack on the living body of the land as an asphyxiation of spirit.

When we performed *Light*, the dancer-choreographer Chandrabhanu created a fire-pit and walked through fire; artist Hossein Valamanesh, himself a fire-master, made a grid of elevated mirrors that reflected the sky through the trees like gobbets of cold fire.[4] Perched in his overheated van, AM orchestrated the ground rhonchus, the underground installation of sound recordings derived from volcanic vents in the Canaries which, transposed to Pinky Flat, made the roots of the Moreton Bay Figs shudder and the spreading branches recall the formation of lungs. There was no question that we were conscious of the fire motif, using it as a touch paper to ignite the passage from one scene to the next, but, looking back now, it was a flame being lit, not a fire to be extinguished. It arose, as often happened in those days, from the smallest spark, the mere coincidence of character and name — Light, when Light, as he knew (and as his double portraits showed) was, as they said, of brindled hue, his mother Siamese. In any case, light incarnate in matter was usually ambitious, touchy, passionate and capable of supporting a burning intellect: light as life was a passage through fire. But was there more to it, beyond the mere nominal coincidence, a deeper, fateful pattern?

*Light* rehearses a familiar irony of colonisation. The mimetic strategy plays into the hands of the destroyers. What was proffered as a consummation (peaceful coexistence) becomes consumption. 'Light: I pointed to the sun. Ten: They pointed to the sun. Light: They looked alarmed, then laughed. Ten: Imitating our every movement. Double 5: And soon after the whole country was on fire'. A direct comparison was made between the state of Light's lungs and the longing for drenching, sweet rain: 'Cumuli come, at first like a small spot, the nucleus on which it forms tuberculated'.[5] Associating 'colonialismus' — colonialism as a kind of medical condition — with wild fire, I understood the correlations made in *Light* between inner and outer states as a way of dousing the flames. The primary correlation is between the state of Light's lungs and the weather: 'Suffered much from debility occasioned by the atmosphere'.

When the rain did come to the Adelaide Plains, its relief was deceptive. In 'Memory as Desire', a radio-work I had scripted ten years earlier, the explorer Charles Sturt's response to rain is recalled. Trapped by drought at the 'Depot', he naturally welcomed rain: 'It burst in a tremendous crash immediately overhead. All the little hollows in the plain were chequered with water. The road northwards was thrown open to me'.[6] The road led to a greater desolation, but the dryness projected onto the Stony Desert was a function of colonial impatience. Light, perhaps, is wiser but the significance of rain coming is the same. On 5 September 1839, ventriloquising Light, Double 5 reports: 'At noon showery. Very ill all day. Showery all the afternoon. At night showery. Very ill. Westerly'. After this, in answer to the question 'Is he going to die?', Light's companion, Maria, replied matter-of-factly, 'Yes, my dear, very soon'. The Double takes Light's hand and promises to guide him back to the sea: 'Throughout Yerna there will be unto us a continuous road'. But Light is soon out of breath and in a moment, as it were, his life is snuffed out. 'Double 5: He were blowing out a candle. Light and Double 5: Where is the candle / To light me to bed? Double 5: Come back when the sun is in the west. Light: Monday, 9 September, moderate and fine … Westerly.'[7]

Sometimes, dreams can be put on notice. A vision has an internal logic but its relation to the common world is inscrutable. A 'poetic work of recreation' falls into the same category: in the tradition of '"hermeneutic" performance', *Light* does not settle the facts. Interleaving inner and outer states, they link what might have been to what is to come — what will happen when the poetic logic comes out. In the tradition of re-creation, such works are prophetic. They open the road to the future, inscrutable now because what they indicate has yet to arrive. Writing about the Yarralin people, Deborah Bird Rose describes a society in which history is not a record of facts, but the authorisation of the Law — that bundle of received stories that underwrite the present constitution of the people. What counts here is a tradition of illustration, parable and allegory whose value lies in their fulfilment in the future and in their renewal: 'an event happens, but to understand it fully one must wait to see what flows from it … People discuss events, try out different meanings, suggest alternative contexts and interpretations and, with time, sometimes arrive at a decision about what a particular event means'.[8] But, even when agreement is reached, so that people 'have understood the meaning' and are 'then able to say exactly what the event was', the 'event' only exists in its retelling.[9]

I never had the chance to discuss with AM what, exactly, *Light* was *about*. Had we spoken before his death about it, we would have talked about something else, the state of the atmosphere, and what the ear picks up, 'the ashes of sight,/ excrement of spirit'.[10] I would have wanted to praise him: 'Native genius/ Intellectual light/ All put out, douse/ Smothered, suffocated'.[11] But no decision would have been reached except that to find out what flowed from that distant collaboration we had to wait to these days of unresolved colonial delirium to see all the papers, all their prophecies, flung into the fire.

*Light,* the dying of the light, was an oracle of 'a dubious sort known as *kledon,* which at the moment of the announcement may seem trivial or irrelevant, the secret sense declaring itself only after a long delay, and in circumstances not originally foreseeable'.[12]

---

1. Andrew McLennan was an actor, broadcaster and audio arts pioneer. Instrumental in forming the Australian Broadcasting Corporation's Arts Unit (1984–1985), he was a driving creative force behind the now legendary acoustic arts programs *Surface Tension* (1985–1988) and *The Listening Room* (1988–2003).
2. A chapter 'Light Reading' was published in my *The Lie of the Land,* Faber & Faber, London, 1996, and contains all the biographical material. *Light,* however, remains largely undocumented and wholly unpublished. However, see 'Booking Guide, Telstra Adelaide Festival 96', March 1–17, p. 38. http://adelaidefestival.ruciak.net/archive/1996%20Booking%20Guide.pdf.
3. H. Hopkins, *The Long Affray,* Macmillan, London, 1985, p. 179.
4. See M. Knights and I. North, *Hossein Valamanesh: Out of Nothingness,* Wakefield Press, Adelaide, 2011, p. 85.
5. P. Carter, 'Light: A Séance Drama,' pp. 1–66, 54. Manuscript in author's possession.
6. 'Memory as Desire' was first broadcast in the *Images* series, ABC-FM, 9 June 1986. The reference is to Charles Sturt, *Narrative of an Expedition into Central Australia,* 2 vols, T. & W. Boone, London, 1849, vol. 1, p. 249.
7. Carter, *Light,* p. 53.
8. D.B. Rose, 'Life and Land in Aboriginal Australia', in M. Charlesworth, F. Dussart and H. Morphy eds, *Aboriginal religions in Australia: An Anthology of Recent Writings,* Ashgate, Farnham, 2005, p. 213.
9. Ibid., p. 213.
10. Carter, *Light,* p. 35.
11. Ibid., p. 38.
12. F. Kermode, *The Genesis of Secrecy: On the Interpretation of Narrative,* Harvard University Press, Cambridge, 1979, p. 1.

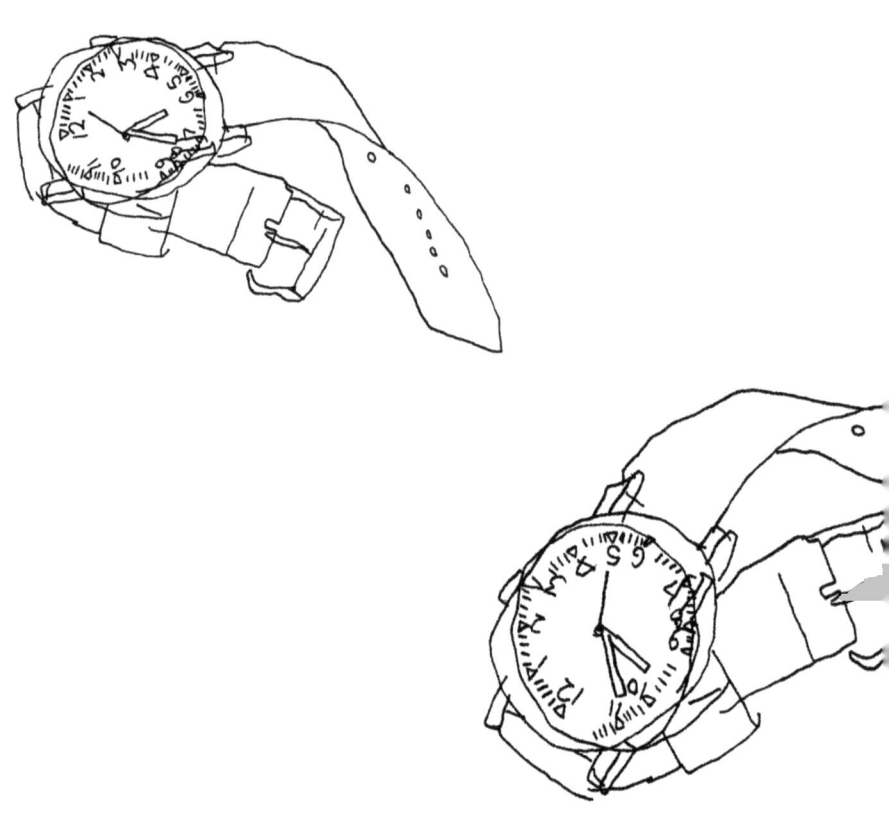

# Changes

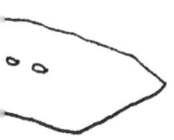
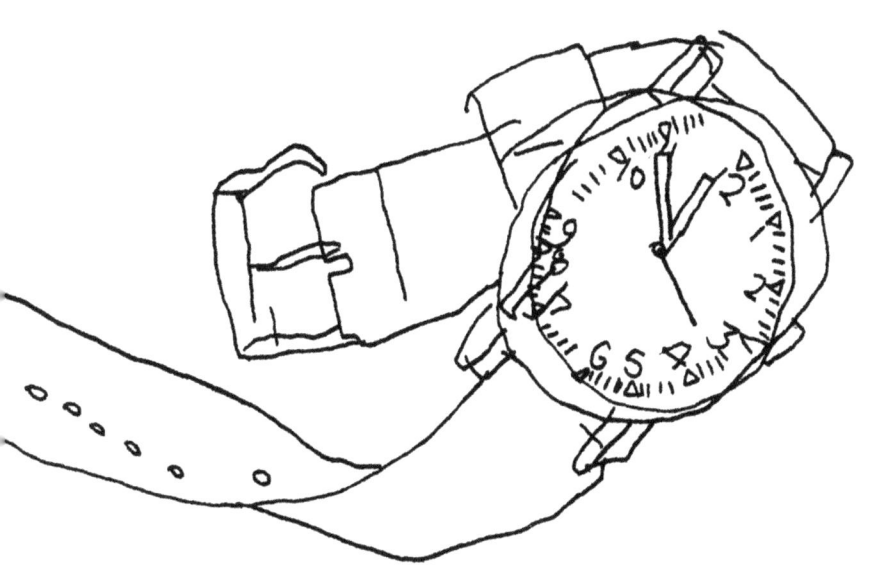

Drawings • Hugo Muecke

# We Can't Stop Climate Change by Refusing to Change

Ross Gittins

After Donald Horne's book in the 1960s, we all know we live in the Lucky Country. What we've forgotten until now, however, is the qualification Horne added: 'Australia is a lucky country run mainly by second-rate people'. We haven't been feeling so lucky this burning, smoky summer. But our present leader, Scott Morrison, has certainly been looking second rate. This summer we've had our Pearl Harbour moment. Just as the Japanese bombing of Hawaii in 1941 stopped Americans viewing World War II as some distant threat, so our season of unprecedented drought, heatwaves, bushfires and smoke haze has woken us up to the present reality of global warming.

There we were thinking climate change would be a problem for our children and grandchildren — who, we hoped, wouldn't remember our refusal in 2013 to pay a bit more for electricity so as to reduce greenhouse-gas emissions. Now we realise it's a problem for us — a level of harm and unpleasantness, and more likely to get much worse in the years ahead unless something decisive is done by all the major economies, including us, to reduce net emissions to zero over the next thirty years and stop us cooking.

It's a wake-up moment not just for us, however, but for the entire rich world. They've been watching in fascinated horror as global warming has punished the Aussies for their repeated refusal to take it seriously. Ostensibly, Scott Morrison has realised we need to change course. 'We want to reduce emissions and do the best job we possibly can and get better and better at it', he said when it dawned on him we were holding him responsible for the fires regardless of what the Constitution says about them being a state responsibility. 'In the years ahead, we are going to continue to evolve our policy in this area to reduce emissions even further', he said. But then he started adding qualifications. 'We're going to do it without a carbon tax, without putting up electricity prices and without shutting down traditional industries upon which regional Australians depend for their very livelihood.'

Really? Sounds like he's promising us all the benefits without any of the costs. Nothing needs to change to make things much better. Which, in this age of cynicism and distrust of our lengthening string of second-rate leaders, makes you fear all that's changed is the marketing spiel.

What we need is a leader great enough to seize our Pearl Harbour moment and turn it into a Port Arthur moment — the moment when a prime minister exercises true leadership and uses the horrible reality of death and destruction to win public support for big changes to stop such things becoming regular events. John Howard, Morrison's role model and mentor, saw such an opportunity and seized it. He did so not because it offered political gain, but because it was a leader's duty to deliver something great for those he led. He did so knowing that it would prompt great resistance from within the Coalition. But with the public behind him and his political opponents unlikely to oppose him, that was a risk he was prepared to take.

Just the same conditions apply to Morrison's decision on whether to turn us from laggards to leaders in the global effort to halt the rise in average temperatures to less than 2 degrees. Has he the courage to stand up to the noisy minority of climate-change deniers in the Coalition, who are now so badly out of step with public opinion?

There's a central lesson to be learnt from this appalling summer. The dichotomy Morrison has so far relied on — the environment versus the economy — is false. 'We'd love to help the environment, but not if that involves a cost to the economy.' Sorry, since the economy sits within the natural environment, anything that damages the environment also imposes loss — of property, businesses, jobs, wellbeing, lives and health — on the economy and the humans who constitute it.

It follows that, in our obsession with the cost of fighting climate change, we can no longer ignore the far greater cost of not fighting it. The one option that's not available is no change. We can refuse to change, but nature will change things whether we like it or not. The economy is always changing, as some industries expand and others contract. Jobs are continuously being lost in some fields and created in others. This is the very process by which we've become far more prosperous over the past two centuries.

So, the notion that our steaming coal industry can be preserved in aspic is laughable. Its days are numbered. But we don't have to kill it, the rest of the world will do that for us as — like us — they increasingly turn to renewable energy and away from fossil fuels. Business can see that; Morrison professes not to.

Second-rate leaders throw in their lot with those who fear losing from change, letting the rest of us suffer while they attempt to resist the irresistible. First-rate leaders seek out ways we can benefit from that change, restoring the luck of the Lucky Country. How? Watch this space.

---

First published as 'Our Pearl Harbour Could Become our Port Arthur Moment', Wednesday 22 January 2020. Reprinted with permission from *The Age*.

# Talking About a Climate Revolution?

Mark Beeson

As wake up calls go, they don't get much louder than the climate catastrophe that unfolded during the summer of 2019–2020. But to use another overworked phrase, will this actually prove to be the tipping point where enough people unambiguously understand the nature of the threat that the world is facing as a consequence of unmitigated climate change, and are prepared to do something about it? Despite the urgency of the problem — many climate scientists think we may have ten years at best to limit global warming to manageable levels — it is far from clear that our political class is up to the task. To be fair, we are collectively facing the greatest collective action problem the world has ever faced. It's not surprising that many leaders around the world are struggling to come up with feasible plans, even where genuine political will to 'do something' actually exists.

In Australia, we confront the additional problem that some of our most prominent politicians and business leaders remain in denial about the nature and urgency of the problem. Some of them seem genuinely incapable of understanding or appreciating the overwhelming scientific consensus about the drivers of climate change or the threat it undoubtedly poses to every aspect of our lives.

Of greater concern, however, are those who seem to understand the science, but who are driven by self-interest to ignore or actively undermine the efforts of those who are trying to encourage action before it really is too late. The coal industry is the quintessential example of an industry that is fundamentally incompatible with a sustainable environment. The industry's deep pockets and ability to influence the political process helps to explain why both the major political parties struggle to come up with coherent plans to deal with potential 'stranded assets' in electorally sensitive parts of the country.

So, what is to be done if politicians don't get the problem, don't have plans, or are reluctant to act despite a mounting sense of crisis and the increasing evidence of global warming's impact? I suggested recently that we need what might be called 'pressure from below'.[1] In other words, ordinary citizens need to mobilise, protest, and compel politicians to act. Unlikely as this may seem, there is some evidence that it is already happening. When I finished my book on environmental populism in early 2019, I had never even heard of Extinction Rebellion, for example. Now they have become a globally recognised phenomenon in little more than a year. Likewise, Greta Thunberg, was a very small dot on the political horizon, but now leaders queue up to listen to her, even if they don't always act on her advice.

Given that populism is usually associated with right-wing reactionaries and nationalists, many readers will no doubt be incredulous about the prospects of radical change being driven from below. But there is a long-standing tradition among left-wing political theorists who argue that the mass of the people is the key to revolutionary change. Again, there is some evidence that such movements are possible, even if translating that enthusiasm and momentum into meaningful and sustainable change is another thing altogether. The depressingly brief 'Arab Spring', and the '1 per cent' movement that called for reform in the aftermath of the global financial crisis are good examples of both potential and of the difficulty of realising sustainable change.

No doubt the language of radicalism will strike some as frankly alarming, especially given the unimpressive historical record of 'socialism' in places such as Russia and China. And yet a revolution in the way we live and think about our relationship to the natural environment and even to each other has plainly got to occur if human civilization is to have a future worthy of the name.

Alarmist? I certainly hope so. There are other contributors to this volume who know much more about climate science than I do, and I'm happy to listen to their advice and accept their analysis. What possible basis do I have for doing otherwise? That's the way the intellectual division of labour that allows people to become experts is supposed to work, after all. It is an unfortunate aspect of the era of 'fake news' and the problems we struggle with that 'expert' has almost become a term of abuse.

No single individual or country deserves the blame for the situation we collectively find ourselves in, of course, but some are arguably more responsible and more obliged to act than others. It is hard to imagine a more unfortunate person than the climate-denying, coal-supporting, divisive figure of Donald Trump to be the most powerful political figure in the world at this pivotal moment in history. Indeed, he and his supporters represent all of the more unfortunate and familiar aspects of populism. And yet it is important to remember that there are other, more inspiring and thoughtful, political figures in the United States than President Trump. Young congresswoman Alexandria Ocasio-Cortez is the face of a rising generation of leaders who understand climate problems and offer prospective solutions. Yes, there are plenty of problems with the Green New Deal, but at least it offers a plausible potential starting point for a conversation about possible futures that are sustainable in principle. Even that would be progress.

It is not only those in the United States who are important contributors to the climate debate, however. Ross Garnaut (see his contribution to this collection) has made a major and sustained contribution to our understanding of climate change and its likely impact on this country.

Equally importantly, he also has highly persuasive and plausible ideas about what could and should be done if Australia is going to survive — even prosper, perhaps — in a rapidly changing environmental context.

There is, in short, no excuse for inaction or ignorance, although that may not be enough to stop many of our alleged leaders from continuing to display it, of course. The frequent argument employed by defenders of the status quo is that if China, India and the United States don't act to reduce $CO^2$ emissions, Australia's 'sacrifice' will be in vain. Perhaps so. But if Australia, with all its advantages, wealth, capacities and compelling collective interest cannot act, why would we expect India or anyone else to take the lead given their compelling need to keep development going?

If achieving agreement on collective action in one country is difficult, one might be forgiven for thinking that it is well-nigh impossible at the international level. Perhaps it is. This is another sobering reality that we will all have to come to terms with if so. As last summer demonstrated, nowhere is immune from the impact of climate change, and certainly not the driest continent on the planet. No matter how implausible, utopian or out of contact with 'reality' the idea of collective action at the global scale may seem — and there's no doubt that it does seem implausible given the history of our species — that's what we have to do if we are to survive in circumstances that are desirable. And it's not just Australia, either: in a world still marked by appalling inequalities of opportunity and wealth distribution, we've got to persuade those less fortunate than ourselves to buy into it, too.

Unlikely as it may seem, this is where Australia — with more enlightened, and far-sighted leadership, perhaps — could play a useful demonstration role. Retrofitting the economy along more sustainable lines and building on our potential strengths as an energy superpower could benefit us *and* our neighbours.

Where's the money coming from, I hear you ask? For a start, I would suggest scrapping the new fleet of submarines — which even strategic types think will be obsolete if and when they are actually delivered — and concentrating on actually existing threats to our individual security. If the risk of being incinerated and losing all your possessions isn't a security threat, it's hard to know what is.

It's important to recognise that, even if you think such ideas are feasible or desirable, many in the policy-making and strategic communities that determine our collective public policy priorities (and spend our taxes) remain entirely unconvinced about the need for change. Indeed, they may actually be incapable of making the intellectual paradigm shift required to recognise where real threats and challenges lie. This is why widespread political activism — populism, if you will — is so vital. Even if we do mobilise by the million it may be hard to get the current generation of politicians to do more than pay lip service. The young are, as ever, the hope for the future. Unfortunately, they don't have long to make a difference, but the least we can do is to support them actively, with pressure from below.

---

1. Mark Beeson, *Environmental Populism: The Politics of Survival in the Anthropocene*, Palgrave, Basingstoke, 2019.

---

# Crossing the Bridge to a Safer Climate

Ross Garnaut

A pall has hung over south-eastern Australia since the extraordinary fires in Victoria, New South Wales and Queensland. It will lift to reveal a diminished natural and human heritage. Beautiful parts of Australia have been disfigured. The lift may also expose a changed political environment, in which all governments want to join the global action against the climate change threat to our security and prosperity.

There is a chasm between a world that quickly breaks the link between modern economic growth and carbon emissions, and a world that fails to do so. We need to build a bridge on which Australians can walk over that chasm, from policy incoherence, to hope and opportunity.

Yes, there is *hope* that we can avoid the worst outcomes from climate change. The greenhouse gases that continue to enter the atmosphere make the pall heavier on average as the years pass. The bushfires on average will come earlier and be more intense. The flows into the Murray and Darling Rivers will become weaker. The dams in Dubbo and Armidale will dry out more frequently and for longer. But how much worse it gets depends on how quickly the world moves to zero net carbon emissions.

And, yes, there is an *opportunity* for Australia to become the world's main trading source of metals, other energy-intensive goods and carbon-chemical manufactures in tomorrow's zero-net-emissions world. There are possibilities for a major new rural industry to emerge, as Australia becomes a major contributor to the world's absorption of carbon into land and plants. These are opportunities located in rural and provincial Australia. In *Superpower*, I describe this bridge across which we could walk to join the global effort against dangerous climate change.[1]

At the United Nations meeting in Paris in 2015, all countries agreed to reduce carbon emissions enough to hold temperature increases below 2 degrees and as close as possible to 1.5 degrees. That would require zero net emissions for the whole world by 2050 — earlier for 'developed' countries as some 'developing' countries would take longer. Each country sets its own targets along the way to the ultimate goal. These targets are not legally binding. Their purpose is to demonstrate that each country is doing its fair share in the global effort. Initial targets were never expected to add up to the ultimate goal. Periodic inter-governmental meetings review progress, place pressure on laggards and upgrade commitments.

Australia's 2030 target is the weakest of the developed countries. That makes us a drag on the global effort. Our position at the Madrid meeting on

Kyoto credits was also a drag on the development of mechanisms for international trade in carbon credits. That trade can reduce the costs of getting to zero net global emissions, while supporting a major new Australian rural industry. In UN meetings in 2021, we can choose to remain a drag, or to substantially upgrade our commitments.[2] If electoral promises block immediate upgrading in targets, it is still better to show that we will be beating those targets than just to meet them, pending revision of commitments in future parliaments. Australian actions will not determine global outcomes. But Australia moving from the discouraging to the encouraging side of the chasm would provide a substantial boost to the global effort.

Writing *Superpower* after the Coalition's electoral victory in May 2019, I accepted that the government through the current parliamentary term would avoid breaching its 2019 electoral commitments. It would not introduce carbon-pricing — the economists' preferred means of achieving climate objectives at lowest cost or largest gain. It would not take any steps that increased power prices above the giddy heights of early 2019, or take steps that led directly to diminution of the coal industry. Within these constraints, I proposed a set of policies that would lead to Australian emissions falling by 50 per cent on 2005 levels by 2030, and increasing the contribution of renewable energy to half or more of our electricity use. This would be a credible base for Australia to launch towards zero net emissions before 2050.

The role of the Australian Renewable Energy Agency would be expanded to support innovation across the range of low-emissions technologies. The role of the Clean Energy Finance Corporation would shift to cover the ACCC's 'Recommendation 4' on underwriting new supply of power to major users. Private investors in new unregulated transmission would be rewarded for their contributions to low prices, security and reliability in the regulated system. Measures would be taken to enhance electricity reliability. Australia's participation in the global trend towards greater use of electric vehicles would be accelerated by public provision of vehicle charging facilities. Reform of electricity-pricing rules would ensure that the electric car reduced the cost of electricity in other uses.

Recognising that the increase in Australian emissions in recent years has been driven by unconstrained release of methane and carbon dioxide from coal mines and gas processing, such 'fugitive emissions' would be reduced, and those that remained offset by purchases of credits from the Australian farm sector. This would be achieved through the Abbott Government's 'safeguard mechanism', phased in over a decade. Offsets for fugitive emissions would provide a major boost for sequestration of carbon in Australian soils, pastures, woodlands, forests and plantations. 'Carbon farming' would be supported by research and development to understand the opportunity and to lower costs of measurement. The Australian carbon-farming opportunity would be enhanced as we earned access to European and other markets for carbon credits. These steps would reveal large economic gains from reducing emissions.

Bumps along the way to low emissions will attract attention, but will be short-lived. Expanding supplies of low-cost renewable electricity place pressure on established coal generators. One after another, the coal generators will close. There is likely to be an immediate lift in electricity prices in the region of the closure. But these are temporary interruptions on a downward trend in prices driven by the rise of renewables. Much was made of the effects of closure of the Northern Power station at the end of 2015–2016 on South Australian (SA) wholesale power prices. SA prices had always been much higher than New South Wales or Victoria, because SA coal was poorer and located further from the capital city. On average over the decade before the Northern closure, 2007–2016 SA wholesale prices were 22 per cent higher than NSW and 32 per cent higher than Victoria. Immediately after the Northern closure, SA prices rose to 34 per cent above NSW and 63 per cent above Victoria in 2016–2017. But the rise of renewables, to over half total supply, set prices powerfully on a downward course, absolutely and relative to the big states. At the time of writing, in the current financial year so far (1 July 2019 to 15 January 2020), NSW prices have been 34 per cent and Victorian 63 per cent above those in renewables-rich SA. SA this summer has also had less reliability anxiety than the two big states.

*Superpower* explains four big changes that have reduced the economic cost of Australia playing its full part in the global effort to reach the Paris requirement of zero net emissions by 2050 — and turned them from an economic cost to a benefit. The cost of renewable energy and electricity storage has fallen dramatically — far more rapidly than anticipated in my 2008 and 2011 Reviews.[3] Australia has by far the richest endowment per person of renewable energy resources. This makes us naturally the country with lowest energy costs in the emerging zero-emissions world. Naturally, but not inevitably, as poor policy and business leadership could diminish the opportunity.

We also have exceptional abundance of fossil energy resources. However, these do not confer a large advantage on domestic industry, as coal and gas are traded internationally at prices that are similar to those in Australia. High costs of transporting electricity between continents, directly or as hydrogen, will make renewable energy permanently a source of large advantage for Australian energy-using industries in the zero-emissions economy. This makes us naturally the low-cost country for processing domestically mined iron and aluminium and other ores and raw minerals. The industries of the future can contribute many more jobs and much more income than today's coal and gas industries.

Capital is overwhelmingly the main cost of renewable energy. So, the costs of renewable but not fossil energy have been lowered exceptionally by the dramatic fall in the global cost of capital over the past decade. Progress in applied science has greatly increased awareness of the capacity to capture carbon in the landscape. Australian science and farming and forestry skills, and a *per capita* endowment of woodlands and soils suitable for carbon sequestration far greater than in other countries, mean that carbon farming can be a great Australian rural industry.

Similar endowments can make us a globally competitive source of biomass for plastics and other carbon-based chemical industries. This will be an important source of advantage in industry when the use of oil, gas and coal is blocked in a zero-carbon world. Australia also has advantages in a zero-emissions world from known geological structures of exceptional quality for securely storing carbon dioxide.

I am encouraged by Prime Minister Morrison's statements that we will be 'evolving' climate policies. We need not be discouraged by his statements that this will be done without introducing a carbon price, or raising the price of electricity, or destroying Australian jobs. I accepted these constraints in designing the bridge. Within these constraints, we can make a good start on doing what the Paris temperature goal requires.

Do it right, and faster progress on renewables and carbon farming and the electric car will make us more prosperous. That will change the political environment in which we can complete the journey across the chasm, to a place where Australia is an economic superpower of the zero-emissions world economy.

---

1. R. Garnaut, *Superpower: Australia's Low Carbon Opportunity*, Black Inc, Melbourne, 2019.
2. The 2020 meetings were postponed until 2021 because of the COVID–19 pandemic.
3. (Eds.) See www.rossgarnaut.com.au/climate-change/.

---

# Cosmic Calling with Christ

Archbishop Philip Freier

The events of the summer of 2019–2020 have cast into stark relief our human fragility — not just the vulnerability of our individual lives in the face of natural disaster, but the precarious nature of our society. With roads closed, and power and communication lost, whole communities were plunged into survival mode in the bushfire crisis of early January. It is of no comfort to realise that the bushfire season can continue well into the year. Australia is experiencing the intensification of the extremes of our environment. Droughts are longer and drier, fires rage with greater intensity, cyclones are more unpredictable and intense. If we ever thought that we lived in a world where we could control the impact of these forces, that assumption has surely been dispelled.

The prescience of the 2008 *Garnaut Climate Change Review*[1] and the failure of our national government to implement action informed by science impels us all to move our debate from opinion to the facts. Internationally, Australia is gaining a bad reputation for its climate scepticism even though we are said to be on track to meet the 2016 Paris targets. Our position at the recent United Nations Climate Change Conference (COP25) in Madrid disappointed many when we insisted on carrying over credits from carbon-emission reductions under the Kyoto protocol, thus effectively proposing actual reductions between 2020 and 2030 of only 10 per cent of the Paris target amounts. This can sound technical and even meaningless to the ordinary circumstances of our daily lives but it is evidence of the 'loophole' positioning, so named by Greta Thunberg in Madrid.[2]

For Christians, the degradation to our planet brought by climate change has the same implications it does for all humans, but it also has theological implications. The Christian understanding of creation brings us blessings and responsibilities, as well as an eternal perspective. The Word — or, in Greek, *Logos* — is present at Creation according to John's Gospel and is wonderfully known to us in the person of Jesus the Messiah. Jesus through his incarnation has a vocation of bringing Creation to its fulfilment and ultimately renewing all things in the new heaven and the new earth. As people gathered into the Body of Christ, Christians have a share in that cosmic vocation. It is a vocation that is relevant to the circumstances of the world at this present time. I call it a *cosmic vocation* because it continues as long as time exists, because it is universal, and also because it is for the entire globe. Carbon dioxide, wherever it comes from, knows no borders and influences the atmosphere and its retention of solar heat equally.

I think that we should not accept arguments that Australia's emissions of carbon are only a small fraction of overall emissions and that our policies are not significant in the whole. This is an argument that we would never accept if it were applied to drunk drivers or those who suffer from disease. We know in these practical circumstances, including now from our experience of COVID-19, that policy frameworks that require participation from all, even though few may be responsible or ultimately affected, are vital. I suggest that we reframe our climate-change debates in Australia to look at the quest from this perspective.

In uncertain times, we can easily despair and lose sight of the mercies of God in both Creation and in Redemption. Many people have legitimate fears about how climate change will damage societies across the globe and end the quality of life we have now. But our cosmic vocation has something to offer here. Therefore, in these times, it is important that we strengthen both our personal discipleship and our corporate participation as members of the Body of Christ. These are both things that we can do out of our own spiritual discipline and, I suggest, are vital for us at this time. Bless you in this year of Grace 2020 and may you know our Saviour's love in the presence of the Holy Spirit.

---

1. R. Garnaut, *The Garnaut Climate Change Review*, Cambridge University Press, Cambridge, 2008.
2. https://www.wired.com/story/greta-thunberg-blasts-creative-pr-in-her-climate-speech/. Last accessed 5 January 2020.

---

An earlier version of this essay was published in the February 2020 edition of *The Melbourne Anglican*.

---

# Can a Phoenix Rise Out of the Ashes?

John Funder

It is a week from Easter Sunday, and two weeks from when we began our own COVID lockdown. Three weeks ago, I was in Box Hill Hospital, with a stent, recovering from a minor heart attack. I could have, should have, written on the bushfires months ago, and now suddenly there is all the time in the world.

My wife Val and I bought a small vineyard in the Yarra Valley in 2003, and have lived there ever since. We are surrounded by fruit trees, some eucalypts, many pines and cypresses, and what used to be called market gardens. The first time we faced a bushfire — albeit at a distance — was in 2009, the year of Black Saturday in the eastern and northern outskirts of Melbourne. Each day we listened to John Faine on the ABC[1], his finest hour. At night we could see the fire-front, some ten kilometres away to the north-east. Each morning we could pick up the embers (mercifully cold, often large) from the driveway and the lawn. We had friends whose house, restaurant and vines were burnt out by a rolling front of incandescent eucalypt vapour. With five minutes warning, as they farewelled the last of the lunch patrons, they got out via a back road in their Land Rover. All that was left standing was a hayshed full of hay. It was too much: they relocated to the southern highlands of New South Wales, ostensibly to safety. For a couple of weeks, I went to the centre set up in Healesville to deliver food parcels to those in need.

Fast forward ten years, when, in late 2019, parts of Queensland and New South Wales were ablaze, to be followed by the Adelaide Hills and Eastern Victoria. We stayed on jittery alert for several months. Where would we escape to if it came from the north, the most likely direction? What should we take: family things, bank statements, this year's tax stuff, jewellery, photographs? The flat roof was cleared, the gutters sluiced out, and the downpipes unblocked. The fire never came: it never came to loading all these things into the car and abandoning our home — for which we must be grateful.

The 2009 fires were horrific on many levels. The death toll was horrific, numbering 173, with, possibly, one or two hermits unaccounted for. It was small consolation that those who died would have done so very quickly. We may forget — or not realise — that prior to Black Saturday there were three consecutive days when the temperature in Melbourne topped 43 degrees Celsius, with scant respite overnight. Even if we remember the heat wave, we may not know that the mortality over those three days totalled around 600 more people than the same three days the previous week, or the previous year. Those who died were predominantly the elderly, particularly women living alone and without air conditioning. They died of dehydration — just like in the Paris summer a few years before. No drama, nothing to drink after three o'clock, and they silently slipped away.

Poorly maintained poles and wires emerged as the major culprits, maintaining dividends was deemed more important than maintaining infrastructure and replacing the 50-year-old telegraph poles. They resulted in massive losses of property over 4,500 square kilometres: houses, resorts, sheds, livestock, and fences. Rebuilding was slow, often rendered difficult financially by new (appropriate, but very expensive) regulations in the wake of the fires. The Royal Commission went on and on, as the one ordained by the Prime Minister in the wake of the more recent fires is surely bound to.

Now for COVID-19. In almost every sense, it is premature to be writing anything about COVID-19 that would stand up to long-term scrutiny, but here goes. Global fatality rates vary markedly between countries, but as viruses go, the corona virus is relatively stable. If the average death rate is truly between 1 and 3 per cent, and a highly probable eventual infection rate without a vaccine is somewhere between 50 per cent and 75 per cent of the current population of our planet, we are faced with tens of millions of deaths. There are a lot of things we don't know, and may never know — the exact date on which the whistleblowers signalled the outbreak; how one of their number, an ophthalmologist in his early thirties, met his death; whether the figures for infection, recovery and death rates are accurate; why the World Health Organisation was so gushing in their initial commentary; when China will return to pre-COVID-19 levels of industrial activity?

Not dissimilar caveats apply to Iran, where informed commentators suggest that the rates of infection and mortality may be up to ten times higher than the published figures. Sweden appears to have embraced the approach of allowing 'herd immunity', allowing the virus essentially free rein, with a substantial mortality rate to date. Germany went hard early, tested widely, and has a much lower mortality rate than Italy, Spain, France and the United Kingdom. Closer to home, New Zealand went in early and hard. On a population basis they have a testing rate equivalent to that in Australia, but only (as of 4 April 2020) one death, compared with Australia's 34. They are small numbers, but early and hard at this stage would appear to have been the way to go.

It is also very early to consider the ultimate effects of the pandemic, globally and nationally, on society. What this pandemic is doing is unprecedented — with the Spanish Flu a century ago in the tumultuous wake of the First World War not a particularly useful echo. Governments, from democratic states of varying degrees to autocratic ones, are plainly shaken. Work, education, communities, leisure activities are all affected. What might be the post-pandemic tax levels needed to right the ship? In the immediate aftermath of World War Two the top tax rate in the USA was 91 cents in the dollar.

My hopes are for a more reflective less growth-driven society in Australia. Business should be taxed on turnover, not on profits effortlessly transferred offshore. There should be a truly independent review and recalibration of personal income tax, and effective measures to counter avoidance as well as evasion. We need a revision of the media laws, which currently are a farce and an increasing danger. My list goes on.

In Australia, we've had a rolling series of crises, from the Great Depression of the 1930s onwards. Doubtless they had effects on health, but they have been relatively well handled. The HIV/AIDS crisis was squarely about health, and to the credit of our politicians, their advisors and the doctors it was impressively handled. I have a vivid memory of a colleague from seen-it-all San Francisco gawping at a Swanston street tram emblazoned by a twelve-foot-long condom, and the message, 'Tell Him if It's Not On, It's Not On'.

Australia's response to the Global Financial Crisis was rapid and targeted with an emphasis on productive investment in social infrastructure. No stockbrokers jumped out of eleventh-storey windows. Despite its inevitable glitches it worked, and we had the luxury of every financial quarter being better than the previous one. To be sure, the trash talkers never let the truth stand in the way of a good story, particularly in relation to the so-called 'pink batts disaster'. We should remember that the rate of electrocution of roofing workers was higher in the year before the introduction of pink batts than during the scheme implementation. The fact that the Catholic School system got twice the value out of the allocation to buildings probably reflected Father Flynn telling Danny O'Brien, 'Nothing more than 10 per cent over the itemised costings — and don't even think about padding them'.

My one abiding concern — among a welter of concerns — is that, in addressing the pandemic in the (neo-Keynesian) way it has, the Commonwealth government will be able to do even less to address climate change. In a far-sighted country, many of those displaced from their current jobs may be able to contribute to a substantial increase in infrastructural build and clean-power generation. It would be sensible to nudge the businesses whose staff have been saved specifically into such society-building, climate-sustainable roles.

I have one abiding hope. Out of the difficulties that we all face, I hope that we can develop a new sense of community. A couple of months ago, the fires united us in one way: donations flooded in, the volunteer firefighters were recognized as heroes and at last paid for their near-superhuman efforts; the communities cruelly afflicted were being counselled and helped to rebuild. What the fires and COVID–19 now perversely give us is the chance to build a fairer and more united society. We face a shared adversity. At the time of writing, Australia — despite all the hesitations and delays — is in a better place than most countries not to crumble in the face of the pandemic. This gives us the chance, if we put our minds to it in the long months that stretch ahead, to fashion the country that emerges, not unscathed, but fairer, more united and stronger.

---

1. Australian Broadcasting Commission.

---

# Ethical Lessons from the Australian Bushfire Disaster

Paul Komesaroff, Ian Kerridge

The havoc wreaked by the disastrous Australian bushfires in 2019 and 2020 caused great, enduring pain but also generated some critical lessons. The damage was unimaginable: over a period of three months more than 17 million hectares of forest were burnt, nearly 500 human lives were lost directly or indirectly, thousands of homes were destroyed, and over a billion animals were killed. Unknown numbers of rare indigenous species of plants and animals were rendered extinct. During the crisis, vast areas of Eastern Australia, including the entire Alpine area, were evacuated. In addition to the suffering, loss of life, and property damage, the entire country experienced massive disruption to infrastructure and the economy, and unprecedented levels of air pollution.[1]

The sheer extent and ferocity of the fires was stunning: never before has a large part of an entire continent gone up in flames. It was the nature of the fires, however, that was so truly terrifying. With gale-force winds and tornado fireballs producing their own thunder and lightning, they behaved like hideous science-fiction monsters, ruthlessly annihilating everything in their paths.[2] The images of red-and-black skies, of terrified animals silhouetted against the obliterating forest, of whole communities huddled together in fear and despair, are now pictured permanently in the national psyche.

The entire country went into shock and mourning. While the horror of the terrible events — evocatively described by one bushfire victim as an 'apocalyptic nightmare' — will undoubtedly resonate for generations, the damage already runs deep. The all-pervasive threat of bushfires has produced a cultural reversal in a place where the bush and the outback could formerly often represent an apparently endless expanse of harmony and peace. From now on, for anyone in Australia the bush will never be able to be separated from threat and danger.

In its immediate aftermath, the national trauma provoked vigorous reflection and debate, along with some anger and recriminations about the causes, mistakes and omissions that gave rise to the catastrophe. When the COVID–19 pandemic supervened, producing massive disruption to the daily lives of particularly city-dwellers, public discussion of the bushfires was suspended, interrupting the national grieving process and leaving the business of recovery from the fires unfinished.

The two disasters have taken heavy, but different, tolls. As difficult as it has been, it is assumed with a resigned confidence that the COVID epidemic will ultimately abate, even if its final passing may be subject to delays in securing control of community spread or developing a vaccine. In contrast, the damage wrought by the bushfires is widely perceived to be irreversible. It suffuses the forests, the rivers, the mountains and the plains; it hangs in the skies; it permeates the history and the culture, and contributes to a newly uncertain future.

The smoke haze that engulfed almost the entire country over December and January well symbolised the blindness and lack of vision of public policies, in Australia and elsewhere. Despite mounting awareness of the effects of climate change over many years, successive governments had responded only with denials and refusals to act. In Australia, support for coal mining had been intractable.[3] At the COP25 meeting in Madrid, and elsewhere, Australia repeatedly joined with the United States to prevent any meaningful outcome.[4] Opportunities to build an alternative, forward-looking sustainable energy industry were ignored. Community concerns were dismissed with derision and contempt.[5] In notorious examples of base political opportunism, a former Prime Minister described climate change as 'crap'[6] and the current Prime Minister once brought a large piece of coal into the Federal Parliament to prove how safe it was![7]

These positions have historically been justified on the basis that in the global scheme of things Australia's contribution to warming is small compared to those of China and the United States, ignoring the fact that while Australia releases 1.3 per cent of the world's greenhouse gases, this is more than four times its share in terms of relative world population. More importantly, however, the scale of the destruction itself generated a profound boost to planetary carbon emissions, with consequences for human health around the world.[8]

The lessons to be learnt from the bushfire disaster, and the epidemic crisis that came after it, can be understood in critical political terms. The official responses to the fire emergency were widely recognized to be inauthentic and stage-managed, favouring parochial vested interests rather than public benefit. They were executed in a manner that lacked respect for individual Australians caught up in and affected directly by the bushfires, the friends and families on whom they depended, farmers and environmentalists, those who put their personal safety at risk to fight the fires, experts in climate science and health care, and the wider Australian community. Senior government members failed to demonstrate key qualities of leadership, such as compassion, personal courage, humility. Whereas the premiers of some states engaged directly with communities and victims of the disaster, the Australian Prime Minister not only was largely invisible but departed for an overseas holiday at a crucial moment.

Even in a time of despair and sadness, and the tragic failure of the political process, however, glimmers of hope were already emerging — some of which have, improbably, been sustained as the new emergency has taken shape.[9] Out of the traumas, strong ethical lessons have been learned that, hopefully, will help support a future of greater hope and confidence.

The first lesson is the most positive. It is that despite government neglect, the strength and resilience of communities remain intact. The heroism of voluntary firefighters, the countless stories of generosity, kindness and love, inspired awe.[10] We watched, too, with gratitude and admiration as overseas firefighters, mainly from the United States, arrived on our shores and moved resolutely to take up posts in disaster areas. Shopkeepers opened their doors to victims in country areas, and passers-by donated whatever skills they had to provide help to those suffering around them. Similar gestures of solicitude and care have been repeated many times during the COVID-19 crisis.

The second lesson is that we need to trust those with genuine expertise and knowledge. Scientists have been warning about the mounting dangers of climate change and untrammelled environmental damage for nearly fifty years, as the land itself was abused and the delicate balance between humans and other animal species was destroyed. By comparison, Australian Indigenous communities had effectively managed the environment, using sophisticated conservation techniques, for thousands of years before colonisation.[11] We know now that both ancient and modern knowledge has to be taken seriously if we are to avert even more terrible disasters than the present ones.

Lesson Three is perhaps the most fundamental, and applies forcefully to both the bushfire and the coronavirus disasters: it is the key realisation that we need to move from an assumption that the natural environment can be exploited and expended without limit to an understanding that we are no more than its custodians, with the responsibility to preserve it for future generations. The long tradition of the ruthless destruction of nature, driven by greed, money and power has to be replaced by a new ethic of nurture, sustainability, and respect.[12]

These three lessons, brought together with the political failure of the governing sphere, highlight the challenge we now confront. We face the question of how we — not just as a single nation but as a world community — can move forward to avert what Australians have experienced being translated, repeatedly and permanently, onto a global scale.

How can we reconstruct our institutions to mobilise the ethical insights above and discharge our responsibility to future generations? The vision of our continent aflame, we hope, may stimulate people elsewhere in the world to do whatever is possible to prevent further such catastrophes in the future. We must agree to limit emissions, to move to renewable energy-generation, responsible resource-management and effective conservation practices, and to a reliance on the complementary knowledges of Indigenous cultures and scientific research.[13]

Perhaps the ultimate lesson is the one we have taken too long to learn: in the age of globalisation, no continent 'is an island entire of itself'. The bell is tolling for all of us; this time we must take heed.

---

1. https://www.theguardian.com/australia-news/2019/dec/05/nsw-endures-longest-spell-air-pollution-record-bushfires-threaten-queensland. Last accessed 7 August 2020.
2. https://www.abc.net.au/radio/programs/pm/firestorms-create-lightening-and-wind,-but-rain-embers/11835014. Last accessed 7 August 2020.
3. https://www.theguardian.com/australia-news/2018/oct/09/australian-government-backs-coal-defiance-ipcc-climate-warning. Last accessed 7 August 2020.
4. https://www.news.com.au/technology/environment/climate-change/australia-is-among-a-number-of-countries-being-blamed-for-blocking-climate-agreement-at-cop25/news-story/730cb3aa0db89c0ce495482e3cbf02fa. Last accessed 7 August 2020.
5. https://www.sbs.com.au/news/pregnant-cobargo-woman-says-scott-morrison-turned-his-back-on-her-pleas-for-help. Last accessed 7 August 2020.
6. https://www.theguardian.com/australia-news/2017/oct/10/tony-abbott-says-climate-change-is-probably-doing-good. Last accessed 7 August 2020.
7. https://www.theguardian.com/australia-news/2017/feb/09/scott-morrison-brings-coal-to-question-time-what-fresh-idiocy-is-this. Last accessed 7 August 2020.
8. F.H. Johnson 'Bushfires and Human Health is a Challenging Environment', https://www.racgp.org.au/download/Documents/AFP/2009/September/200909johnston.pdf. Last accessed 7 August 2020.
9. P. Komesaroff, 'Not All Bad: Sparks of Hope in a Global Disaster', *Journal of Bioethical Inquiry*, vol. 17, no. 4, 2020, https://link.springer.com/article/10.1007/s11673-020-10011-0. Accessed Sept 13 2020.
10. https://www.news.com.au/technology/environment/hero-firefighters-surrounded-by-flames-in-new-south-wales-relive-horror/news-story/f4a536c38dbf258871837670878c2410. Last accessed 7 August 2020.
11. https://www.themonthly.com.au/issue/2011/december/1322699456/james-boyce/biggest-estate-earth-how-aborigines-made-australia-bill-g. Last accessed 7 August 2020.
12. P.A. Komesaroff, Ian Kerridge, Ross Upshur. 'Yes, We Need a Global Coronavirus Inquiry, but not for Petty Political Point Scoring', *The Conversation* 16 May 2020, https://theconversation.com/yes-we-need-a-global-coronavirus-inquiry-but-not-for-petty-political-point-scoring-138020.
13. https://www.un.org/sustainabledevelopment/climate-change/. Last accessed 7 August 2020.

---

An earlier version of this essay appeared in the *Journal of Bioethical Inquiry*, vol. 17, no. 1, 2020, pp. 11–14.

# Contributors

**Pat Anderson AO** is an Alyawarre woman, known nationally and internationally as a powerful advocate for the health of Australia's First Peoples. She has extensive experience in Aboriginal health, including community development, policy formation and research ethics. She is Director of the Lowitja Institute.

**Mark Beeson** is Professor of International Politics at the University of Western Australia and previously Professor of International Relations at Murdoch University. He has also taught at Griffith, York, and Birmingham universities. He is the founding editor of *Critical Studies of the Asia Pacific* (Palgrave).

**Lionel Bopage** was leader of the Sri Lankan People's Liberation Front (JVP). Bopage became its general secretary but left the organisation in 1984 due to its chauvinist position on the Tamil question. Today he lives in Australia where he works for intercommunal harmony in the diaspora community and in Sri Lanka.

**David Bowman** holds a research chair in Pyrogeography and Fire Science in the School of Natural Science, University of Tasmania. He explores the relationship between fire, landscapes and humans, and co-authored the book *Fire on Earth* (Wiley-Blackwell).

**George Browning** is a retired Anglican Bishop of Canberra and Goulburn. He is the Inaugural Chair of Anglican Communion Environment Network and President of the Australia Palestine Advocacy Network.

**Helen Caldicott** is an Australian physician, author, and anti-nuclear activist who founded several associations dedicated to a non-nuclear world. In the late 1970s and early 1980s, she was a leader in the anti-nuclear movement in the United States. Over decades, she has divided her time between the United States and Australia lecturing on nuclear energy, weapons and power.

**Paul Carter** moved to Australia from United Kingdom in the early 1980s. He is author of many books including *The Road to Botany Bay* (University of Minnesota Press) and *The Lie of the Land* (Faber and Faber). He has held research positions (University of Melbourne, 1994–2008; Deakin University, 2009–2011; and now RMIT). His collaborations with artists are described in his book *Material Thinking: The Theory and Practice of Creative Research* (Melbourne University Publishing).

**Vanessa Cavanagh** is an Aboriginal woman with Bundjalung and Wonnarua ancestry. She is an associate lecturer and PhD candidate in the School of Geography and Sustainable Communities, University of Wollongong. She has extensive experience in environmental conservation in NSW including as a Field Officer and national parks Ranger participating in remote area fire-fighting, and joint management of national parks, as well as managing the Georges River Aboriginal Riverkeeper Team.

**James Collett** is a lecturer in environmental psychology at RMIT University, specialising in compulsive hoarding, attachment, and multi-dimensional approaches to psychopathology. He is also a keen and experienced wildlife photographer.

**Phillip Darby** taught international relations and postcolonial studies, focusing on South Asia and Black Africa, for nearly fifty years. Together with Michael Dutton, he founded the independent Institute of Postcolonial Studies (IPCS), Melbourne, and was its director, retiring in 2018.

**Kieran Donaghue** studied philosophy in Australia, the United States and Germany in the 1970s and 1980s, and taught philosophy at the Australian National University in the mid-1980s. Subsequently, he worked in overseas aid, including on a project to design a new poverty measurement. His first novel, *German Lessons*, was published by Palaver in 2019.

**Stephen Duckett** is a health economist, currently health program director at the Grattan Institute. He has occupied leadership roles in health services in Australia and Canada, including as Secretary of the Commonwealth Department of Health and Ageing (Australia). He is Emeritus Professor of Health Policy at La Trobe University.

**Anne Elvey** is managing editor of *Plumwood Mountain: An Australian Journal of Ecopoetry and Ecopoetics,* and editor in chief with Melbourne Poets' Union. Anne was editor of *Colloquium: The Australian and New Zealand Theological Review* from 2012 to 2017. She holds honorary appointments at Monash University and the University of Divinity.

**Jane Fisher AO** is Finkel Professor of Global Health, Monash University and Director of Global and Women's Health. She is a clinical and health psychologist with longstanding interests in the social determinants of health, and healthcare participation.

**Philip Freier** is the Archbishop of Melbourne and served as the Anglican Primate of Australia between 2014 and 2020.

**John Funder AC** has held leading positions in medical research, including as Chair of the International Society for Endocrinology (1996–2000) and Director of the Baker Medical Research Institute (1990–2001). He is a Vice-Chancellor's Professorial Fellow at Monash University, and a Professorial Fellow at the Centre for Neuroscience at the University of Melbourne. He is an expert in mineralocorticoid receptors and aldosterone biology.

**Raimond Gaita** is Professorial Fellow in the Faculty of Arts and the Melbourne Law School, University of Melbourne and Emeritus Professor of Moral Philosophy, King's College London. He is a Fellow of the Australian Academy of the Humanities. His books include the award-winning *Romulus, My Father* (Text Publishing) and *A Common Humanity: Thinking about Love and Truth and Justice* (Routledge).

**Bill Gammage** is a historian at the Humanities Research Centre, Australian National University. His book, *The Biggest Estate on Earth. How Aborigines made Australia* (Allen & Unwin), describes how traditional Aboriginal society allied with fire to promote and protect Australia's plants and animals.

**Sally Gardner** is a former dancer. She was a Senior Lecturer in Art and Performance at Deakin University from 2004 to 2017 where she remains an Honorary Research Fellow. She co-edited the journal *Writings on Dance* from 1985 to 2012.

**Ross Garnaut AC** is Professorial Research Fellow in Economics at the University of Melbourne, previously distinguished Professor of Economics, Australian National University, Director of the ANU Asia Pacific School of Economics and Management. He is the author of a number of influential reports on climate change to the Australian Government.

**Ross Gittins** is the Economics Editor of *The Sydney Morning Herald* and an economics columnist with *The Age* newspaper, Melbourne. He is a winner of the Citibank Pan Asia award for excellence in financial journalism, has been a Nuffield Press fellow at Wolfson College, Cambridge, and a journalist-in-residence at the Department of Economics, University of Melbourne.

**Maithri Goonetilleke** is an Australian general practitioner and Associate Professor of Global Health at Monash University. He has worked extensively in Eswatini, Sub-Saharan Africa where he established the Indigenous-led, non-profit organisation, Possible Dreams International, which works at the interface between HIV, Indigenous Swazi culture and structural inequity.

**Tom Griffiths AO** is a historian whose books and essays have won prizes in literature, history, science, politics and journalism. His books include *Hunters and Collectors* (Cambridge University Press), *Forests of Ash: An Environmental History* (Cambridge University Press), and *Living with Fire* (co-author Christine Hansen, CSIRO Publishing). He is an Emeritus Professor of History at the Australian National University.

**Paul James** is a writer on globalization, sustainability, and social theory. He is co-author of *Globalization Matters: Engaging the Global in Unsettled Times* (Cambridge University Press), an editor of *Arena*, and Professor of Globalization and Cultural Diversity in the Institute for Culture and Society at Western Sydney University.

**Kate Judith** was part of the protest movement to protect the forests of South East NSW. Following that she lived on the edge of the forests of far East Gippsland. Now she is an Environmental Humanities scholar, currently writing with mangroves to consider what it is to be between.

**Rimona Kedem** is an Israeli-born, Melbourne-based artist whose work is held in public and private collections around the world. She trained at the Avni Art Academy in Tel Aviv and at the Art Academy of Mexico and has held numerous lecturing positions at schools and universities internationally. She exhibits regularly at Qdos Arts, Lorne, Victoria. (rimonakedem.com)

**Thomas Keneally** is an internationally distinguished, multi-award-winning writer. His books include, *The Chant of Jimmie Blacksmith*, *Schindler's List*, *The Crimes of the Father*; and non-fiction works, *The Great Shame*, and *The Commonwealth of Thieves*. He is a Fellow of the Australian Academy of the Humanities, the American Academy of Arts and Sciences, the Royal Society of Literature, and recipient of an Irish Presidential Distinguished Service Award for services to Irish culture. He is an Australian Living Treasure and lives in Manly, NSW.

**Ian Kerridge** is Professor of Bioethics and Medicine at the University of Sydney, Haematologist and Bone Marrow Transplant physician at Royal North Shore Hospital in Sydney and a Founding Director of PRAXIS Australia.

**Paul Komesaroff AM** is a physician, researcher and philosopher at Monash University, Melbourne, where he is Professor of Medicine and Executive Director of Global Reconciliation, an international collaboration that promotes communication and dialogue across cultural, racial, religious, political and other kinds of difference.

**Catherine Larkins OAM** is an East Gippsland artist and arts activist who works collaboratively with Aboriginal artists and the broader community: www.wurinbeena.org.au. A lecturer in Visual Arts for more than thirty years, she pioneered new ways to deliver tertiary arts education to isolated rural communities. Her arts practice addresses issues of cultural and geographical remoteness, racial and socio-economic tension and reconciliation.

**Greg Lehman**, a descendant of the Trawulwuy people of North East Tasmania, has worked in a range of Indigenous research roles over thirty years, investigating deaths in custody, return of land, management of World Heritage associative values, reconciliation, education, history and identity. He is a past director of the Riawunna Centre for Aboriginal Education.

**Will Mackey** is a Senior Associate at Grattan Institute. An economist and data scientist, he joined Grattan in 2017, and has worked in the higher education, household finances and health programs. Will holds a Bachelor of Finance and Economics from RMIT University and a Graduate Diploma in Economics from the University of Melbourne.

**Freya Mathews** is Adjunct Professor of Environmental Philosophy at Latrobe University. Her books include *The Ecological Self* (1991), *Ecology and Democracy* (editor) (1996), *For Love of Matter: a Contemporary Panpsychism* (2003), *Journey to the Source of the Merri* (2003), *Reinhabiting Reality: towards a Recovery of Culture* (2005). She manages a private biodiversity reserve in Central Victoria.

**Hugo Muecke** is an artist and nurse based in Sydney. He has worked as a graphic designer and illustrator and his art has appeared in solo and group shows as well as commercial publications. Hugo wishes to acknowledge the Sydney Local Health District/ Royal Prince Alfred Hospital, and all the health care workers and other services, including the mental health team at Murrumbidgee local health district, who responded to the bushfire crisis.

**Stephen Muecke** is Professor of Creative Writing at Flinders University, South Australia, and is a Fellow of the Australian Academy of the Humanities. Recent books are *Latour and the Humanities,* (Johns Hopkins University Press) and *The Children's Country: Creation of a Goolarabooloo Future in North-West Australia* (Rowman and Littlefield).

**Miranda Nation** is an award-winning writer and director for film and television. She studied at the Australian Film, TV and Radio School (AFTRS) and Jacques Lecoq École Internationale de Théâtre, Paris. Her debut feature film *Undertow* was released in cinemas in early 2020.

**Susan Norrie** is an Australian artist working primarily with found film and original video installations to explore political and environmental issues. Norrie sees her moving-image work as a combination of art, documentary and film. In 2007 she represented Australia at the 52nd Venice Biennale. In 2019 she won the Don Macfarlane Prize.

**Bruce Pascoe** is author of *Dark Emu* (Magabala Books), which develops evidence of pre-colonial cultivation and construction by Aboriginal peoples. He is a Country Fire Authority volunteer and battled the 2019–2020 bushfires near Mallacoota and in New South Wales. He is a professor at Jumbunna Institute for Indigenous Education and Research, University of Technology Sydney.

**Philipa Rothfield** is Honorary Professor of Dance and Philosophy of the Body at the University of Southern Denmark, and Honorary Faculty at La Trobe University. She is Creative Adviser at Dancehouse, Melbourne, and co-author of *Practising with Deleuze,* (Edinburgh University Press). Her book, *Dance and the Corporeal Uncanny* (Routledge) was published in 2020.

**Guy Rundle** is correspondent-at-large for *Crikey* (www.crikey.com.au). He is a former editor of *Arena Magazine* and contributes to a variety of publications in Australia and the United Kingdom.

**Lorraine Shannon** is a keen gardener and nature-writer living in Wentworth Falls, NSW. She has been a long-term environmental activist as a member of the Association for Literature and the Environment, and founding member of Kangaloon creative ecologies. She is also a member of Wild Mountain Collective.

**Will Steffen** was science adviser to the Australian Government Department of Climate Change, 2004–2011. He is currently a Climate Councillor with the Climate Council of Australia, and was a Climate Commissioner on the Australian Government's Climate Commission and Chair of the Antarctic Science Advisory Committee (2011–13). He was Inaugural Director of the ANU Climate Change Institute (2008–2012).

**Anika Stobart** is an Associate at the Grattan Institute, which she joined in January 2020 following three years working in policy at the Australian Government Department of Agriculture. Anika holds a Bachelor of Laws and a Bachelor of Science from Monash University.

**Helen Szoke AO** has had a career spanning community, health, education, regulation and international development. She was Chief Executive of Oxfam, 2013–2019, and Deputy Chair of the Australian Council for International Development. She has served as Australia's Federal Race Discrimination Commissioner and as the Victorian Equal Opportunity and Human Rights Commissioner.

**Paul Valent** is a psychiatrist and traumatologist. He co-founded the Australasian Society for Traumatic Stress Studies and was founding president of The Child Survivors of the Holocaust in Melbourne. He has written books on trauma and its treatment. His recently released book, *The Heart of Violence: Why People Harm Each Other* (2020), deals with perpetrators of trauma.

**Jessica Weir** is a Senior Research Fellow at the Institute for Culture and Society, Western Sydney University, and a Visiting Fellow at the Fenner School of Environment and Society at the Australian National University. For almost twenty years, Jessica's scholarship has been supported by research collaborations with Indigenous peoples on land and water issues.

**Bhiamie Williamson** is a Euahlayi man from north-west NSW and south-west QLD, with family ties to north-west Queensland. His fields include Indigenous land and water management, Indigenous youth, and Indigenous governance and data sovereignty. He is a member of the Mayi Kuwayu Data Governance Committee and the ACT Bushfire Council; and is a PhD candidate at the Australian National University investigating Indigenous Men and Masculinities.

**Alexis Wright** is a member of the Waanyi nation from the Gulf of Carpentaria and author of the novels *Carpentaria* (Giromondo) and *The Swan Book* (Giromondo). She is the only author to win both the Miles Franklin Award (for *Carpentaria*) and the Stella Prize (for *Tracker*). She is Boisbouvier Chair in Australian Literature, University of Melbourne.

**Arnold Zable** is an award-winning writer, storyteller, novelist, and human rights advocate. His books include *Jewels and Ashes*; *Cafe Scheherazade*; *The Fig Tree*; *Scraps of Heaven*; *Sea of Many Returns*; *Violin Lessons*; *The Fighter*, and *The Watermill*. He has conducted numerous workshops using writing as a means of self-understanding and healing.

www.ingramcontent.com/pod-product-compliance
Lightning Source LLC
Chambersburg PA
CBHW051537010526
44107CB00064B/2757